Story Craft
A Born Storytellers Theory and Teaching Manual

About the Born Storytellers

The Born Storytellers is a program of creative writing created by Kevin Price, teaching students the craft of story writing. It began in 2005 and has been a regular part of the curriculum in several Western Australian schools from junior primary classes through to upper high schools. Since its inception, the Born Storytellers has published more than 40 anthologies of students' work and edited and published over 500 young authors, many of whom have gone on to further literary studies.

More information can be found at www.bornstorytellers.net

Kevin Price

Kevin Price has been earning his living as a writer and creative consultant since 1988, starting as a magazine columnist and advertising copywriter. He developed an interest in story and the theories behind the craft of writing stories in the early 1990s and considers himself, apart from a writer of them, to be a long term student of story. He has been teaching the Born Storytellers program of story craft to Western Australian students, both children and adult learners in schools and writers centres since 2005. He is currently enrolled as a PhD candidate in Creative Writing at Murdoch University in Western Australia.

Story Craft

A Born Storytellers Theory and Teaching Manual

KEVIN PRICE

Crotchet Quaver

Published in 2014 by Crotchet Quaver
119 Ridgewood Loop Bullsbrook Western Australia 6084

© Kevin Price 2014

This publication is copyright. Subject to statutory exceptions and provisions of fair dealing under the Copyright Act 1968, no part of this work may be reproduced without the written permission of the publishers. The moral rights of the author have been asserted.

Reproduction for educational purposes

The Australian Copyright Act 1968 allows a maximum of one chapter or 10% of the pages of this work, whichever is the greater, to be reproduced or communicated by any educational instutution for its educational purposes provided that the institution (or the body that administers it) has given a remuneration notice to Copyright Agency Limited (CAL).

A CIP catalogue record for this book is available from the National Library of Australia.

All inquiries should be addressed to the publisher.
Crotchet Quaver
119 Ridgewood Loop Bullsbrook Western Australia 6084

ISBN: (paperback) 978-0-9875402-1-8

On Creativity and the Writer

The word 'creativity' is everywhere, all over the media; it's the buzz-word of the digital era. Business leaders are calling for it, educational theorists proclaim it, and self-help books teach it. Writers have always been using it; but what exactly is a creative writer as opposed to a mere writer without the qualifier? Great writers, like Philip Roth, often claim that creative writing cannot be really taught; that it really is innate genius, the divine *bardic* spark.

Another common view, especially in the academy, is that creative wring depends on great reading, the study of the Big Books. We learn, in other words, from models like Shakespeare or Dickens or, if you are postmodernist inclined, Pynchon. This is an entirely reasonable argument, but is reading widely all you need to be a good creative writer? The odd thing is that we do not expect a musician to learn simply by listening to great violinists or pianists; nor do we expect actors to learn from simply watching plays. Yet creative writing alone has had this mystical aura, where would-be writers are to become great simply through osmosis.

No — let us be honest — creative writing is a skill, and like any skill, it can be taught and perfected. Talent is vital, of course, but it is not the only ingredient.

How do we teach creative writing, however, without making it into a mechanical process? That is, without taking the really exciting, surprising, even eccentric — the creative 'it'— out of the whole activity. Kevin Price's book shows how the skills can be taught using a theoretical base that is neither reductive nor itself unimaginative. A teacher of the discipline of nine years' experience, Kevin has shown in his own praxis how, by engaging with the craft of storytelling, young people can learn the most inspiring ways to weave their own riveting, heart-breaking, moving and/or simply hilarious tales. Kevin brings out the creativity in the young writer.

Teachers will find that this book will make the process of teaching creative writing accessible and engaging; it is a course of work which is logical, organised and also enjoyable. Most importantly, it shows a way to teach creative writing that helps students find the stories from their own experiences, emotions, visions and wild imaginings. Teachers will find it inspires them to also want to tell their own great yarns.

Dr David Moody
Murdoch University

Introduction: The Born Storytellers Program and Your Writing Project 10

Part One | Theories and Readings

Chapter 1: The Narrative, the Episodes and the Transformation

Defining Story 10
How to Find Your Story 14
The anatomy of a Story Idea 18
Summary 23
A review of your story idea development 24

Chapter 2: The Reign of Homo Fictus

Character Design and Development 25
Character Creation 31
Character Change 42

Chapter 3: Who Else is in the Playground?

A Circuitry of Other Characters 46
The archetypes 47

Chapter 4: The Playground

Creating a Setting 61
Choosing and Creating Your Setting 64
How to put the reader in the picture 68

Chapter 5: Conflict and the Forces of Opposition

Narrowing the Space 70
The shape of story 73
How conflict lulls the reader into the Fictive Dream 80
Patterns of character conflict 84
Conflict and the Story-world 85
Summary 87

Chapter 6: Plot and Structure

Elements of Structure 88
From plot to plan 98
What makes a climax? 107

Chapter 7: Dialogue & Scenes: Let's talk about it

- The functions of dialogue 109
- Pacing the Narrative 128
- Where most failures occur in dialogue 131
- How to write dialogue that is specific to the action 132
- How to write dialogue that is Poetic 133
- How to write dialogue that is Sensual 134
- Dialogue Techniques 137
- Writing Scenes 147

Chapter 8: Voice and Point of View

- The Voice of the work 151
- Point of View 152
- The relationship of character to plot 154
- POV Decisions 159
- Conclusion 162

Part Two | Your Project Workbook

- A Story Planning Process 164
- Tackling your project 166
- Step One | Find and develop your ideas 167
- Step Two | Create your main character 180
- Step Three | Populate your story 199
- Step Four | Create your story world 206
- Step Five | The conflict 227
- Step Six | Develop Your Plot and Step Sheet 231
- Moving Ahead 243

Part Three | Additional Discussions and Exercises

- 1 Daily Writing Practices 250
- 2 Discovering what to write about 253
- 3 Discovering characters 255
- 4 Story World 260
- 5 Dialogue 263
- 6 Developing a scene 264
- 7 Exploring Voice and POV 266

Introduction: The Born Storytellers Program and Your Writing Project

The very idea that anyone could write a book about how to go about writing stories and consider it complete is absurd: the subject is far too vast, with far too many variables. Therefore, this book is incomplete. It is a gathering of ideas that have originated in thinkers and scholars the world over — from other writers who have made the journey — ideas I have borrowed and distorted, bent to my own usage (because writing is like that) and then combined with what I have learnt in the years I have spent teaching students how they can master the craft of writing stories. These ideas offer you a way to go about the task. But it is a way, not the only way.

It is incomplete in another sense, because it needs you to complete it. Of course one of the curious things about stories is that writing them is only part of their completion anyway. Completion comes from the reading. The project section that makes up Part Two of this book will help you develop your story: guide you on a path of things you need to know in order to become a writer of stories. But it is also incomplete because the path continues well beyond this course, well into the rest of your life.

Part One is a series of chapters discussing a theory of story. It begins with a discussion on what is story. But it is a cursory discussion at best because it limits the idea of story to the action the storyteller takes in order to appear the magician. Story is that curious thing that turns people's ideas around so they think about the world differently. Use the theoretical discussions to inform your thinking, to trigger ideas and develop habits of writing practice. Don't use them to dictate the way you should or should not approach your writing. Your job is to complete the work I have left unfinished.

You will find that character features dominantly throughout the theory, because character is the only reason story exists — not only the characters in the story, but the character of human endeavour, of human capacity, of the human condition. Characters in stories may not be real, but they are drawn from the humanity we know and see before us. We tell stories because we want to understand that humanity and the changes it undergoes, the changes it faces. That's why telling stories is of such importance.

Part Two is your project. By reading some of each chapter from Part One along with your project, you will develop an understanding of how story works. It will help develop your critical thinking as much as your creative practice. Part Three contains additional exercises and discussion topics that you can use to further your understanding and practice. They are not mandatory to completing the project, but can help you better understand the concepts presented here.

Finally, there is a bibliography of books and writers on whose knowledge and experience I have unashamedly called. If you are serious about creative writing, you would do well to read some of these. This book, without doubt, contains its errors and you are encouraged to bring them to my attention. I hope, in any event, that you find the book useful. I look forward to seeing your name in print.

Kevin Price 2014

Part One
Theories and Readings

Chapter 1
The Narrative, the Episodes and the Transformation

Defining Story

This program is about the craft of dramatic story writing, therefore a logical starting point is a definition of story itself. When we understand what we are striving to achieve and how we intend to affect readers, we are better placed to ensure that what we design meets those requirements. The following discusses a way to define a story and provide a model against which the final story can be tested.

What is a Story?

In the Western World, Aristotle, who lived between 384 BCE and 322 BCE, is considered to be the first to express what we might think of as a 'theory of story'. While people who write stories today are known as authors (although they may also be playwrights and scriptwriters in various disciplines), in Aristotle's day they were known more as 'Poets.' It was these poets who were responsible for forms of entertainment known as the *epic*, the *tragedy* and the *comedy* — forms that reached audiences through plays and recitals. In *The Poetics*, Aristotle says: 'As for the story, whether the poet takes it ready-made or constructs it for himself, he should first sketch its general outline, and then fill in the episodes and amplify in detail.' At that time, 'story' represented a historical account of some particular happenings that were told or dramatically related to an audience, thus it comprised of episodes that were told to the audience through their specific details.

The Oxford English Dictionary tells us that 'story' came into the English language some time in the early thirteenth century to give an 'account of some happening'. Back then it was defined as a 'narrative, true or presumed to be true, relating to important events and celebrated persons of a more or less remote past; a historical relation or anecdote.' This definition closely resembles what Aristotle refers to when he says a poet takes the story 'ready-made or constructs it for himself'. There is an assumption that the story is a historical fact accounting for something that happened, the details of which could be embellished by the teller.

Today we understand the idea of story much more as 'a narrative of real or, more usually, fictitious events, designed for the entertainment of the hearer or reader; a series of traditional or imaginary incidents forming the matter of such a narrative.' So, if we combine Aristotle's instruction with the OED's more recent definition, we begin with the idea that:

A story is a narrative made up of either real or imaginary episodes, the details of which are designed to entertain the hearer or reader.

More Than a Narrative of Events

A narrative is defined as 'a spoken or written account of connected events'. But if I simply recounted to you the events of my getting out of bed this morning, having breakfast, starting my daily work on this book, breaking for a cup of coffee, taking my lunch, going for a walk around the block, eating my dinner, watching tv and going to bed at the end of the day, you wouldn't say that I'd told you a story — even though I have just given you an 'account of connected events'.

In short, you would say, 'Nothing happened!' Indeed, nothing happened *that was of interest to you*, therefore I did not entertain you with my little anecdote. This then is clearly not a story.

So what is it that makes a series of incidents entertaining to the reader or hearer? According to the Oxford Dictionary, entertainment is 'the action of providing or being provided with amusement or enjoyment'. That is, it is an *experience of pleasure*. So, for a 'story' to take place, the narrative must produce an experience of pleasure for the hearer or reader. Of course, pleasure comes from many things — we find pleasure in horror, in fantasy, in comedy, in tragedy, in romance, in adventure, in crime ... and this pleasure comes from the knowledge that the events being told to us, in the end, have some meaning.

So let's embellish my account of this morning some.

> *I got up this morning on the wrong side of the bed ... when I poured the milk onto the last of the cereal I had in the house, it came out all lumpy. It looked gross, like vomit. Smelled like it too. I gave it to the dog, who simply turned his nose up at it and walked away. I hate to start work on an empty stomach, so I decided to go down to the local coffee shop for breakfast. But when I went to pay, my bank rejected my eftpos card. Cannot pay, it said. I'd already eaten the food and had no other money. I offered to wash dishes to pay for it, but the cafe had a dishwasher. The owner, a fierce, foreign-sounding woman, about half my size, wanted to call the cops and have me arrested. I offered her my watch. She said she didn't need another watch. I offered her my phone. She told me she didn't need a phone, and to sit and wait for the cops. At that point, I felt that I had no choice but to pull the gun I carried in my waist band....*

By now I'm reasonably certain that you're interested, that you're finding this situation somewhat entertaining. You are quite likely wondering what happened next, or what happened in the end. All of a sudden these events of my day are of interest to you, offering you some entertainment because they leave you wondering what will happen to the character in the story. There's the promise of pleasure to come.

What all this means is that a story must offer you a *narrative of episodes*, in which the details cause you to wonder what will happen in the end because there are *consequences* in each of the actions the character takes. What do I mean by consequences? Consequences are those things that follow *as an effect* of another occurrence — like a row of dominos falling because you push the first.

How would the consequences change if I hadn't got up on the wrong side of the bed? Or if I had other food in the house? Or if the milk wasn't off? What if my bank hadn't rejected my eftpos card?… Any change in these situations would change the outcome, they affect the consequences.

What you can see here is that *one thing leads to another thing* — that there is a direct relationship between events and each action that results in worsening the situation. So if I pull that gun, there's a good risk that things are going to get a whole lot worse. Right? Let's see what happens….

> *I pleaded for the cafe owner to put the phone down before she called the cops, and talk to me privately in the corner of the shop. We went to the far end of the counter and, not wanting to alarm other customers, I lowered my voice to a whisper.*
>
> *'Do you have problems with customers not paying you?' I asked, and quickly added, 'Apart from me, that is.'*
>
> *'Yes,' she said. 'Every day we get young louts come in here and make racist jokes and steal cookies. The cops never catch them.'*
>
> *'If I can help you out, will you let me pay you for my breakfast tomorrow?'*
>
> *'How can you help me out? You can't pay. You're just another one of those louts.'*
>
> *'No,' I assured her. 'I'm not. It's just that I got out of bed on the wrong side today …' — as though that were explanation enough — 'But I've got something that will guarantee those louts will never steal from you again.'*
>
> *'Do I look like a piece of bread that needs buttering? You wait for the cops.'*
>
> *'No, no!' I said. 'I'm not … look, I've got something I'm sure will help. Look …' Slowly, very slowly, appearing as placid as possible, I took the gun from my waist band and held my breath as I slipped it into the owner's hands.*
>
> *'Show them the pointy end of this,' I said. 'They won't bother you ever again.'*
>
> *The owner smiled at me and, with her back to the customers, tried the pistol for size in her hand. Then she slipped it into the pocket of her apron.*
>
> *'You can have breakfast here again tomorrow,' she said, 'on the house.'*
>
> *I left the cafe and walked back home, pretty darn pleased with myself. It's amazing what you can do with a toy gun.*

It is the promise of the consequences that result from a character's actions that maintains the interest of the audience. But that's not all there is to it. The other vital issue is that a story is always about a *human character who is worthy of our interest.* In other words, you become interested in what happens to the character *because* they are human and because their situation promises some entertainment.

There's a good chance that you could relate to pouring milk that was off onto the last of the cereal; and to the eftpos card being rejected due to lack of funds. But, I can hear you say, what if the character is a lion or a train? Well, *Simba*, the Lion King, and *Thomas* the Tank Engine are interesting not because they are a lion and a train, but because they are *human characters in odd shapes*. They do human things.

What Makes Us Human?...

To be human is simply this: humans have the unique ability to look forward to the future. They have the ability to consider the future consequences of today's actions. They can call upon the experience of the past to understand the possibilities of the future. They can call upon the knowledge of the past to shape future consequences. This is more than simply memory, it is *experience and judgement.*

And much more importantly, it is the fundamental reason why we tell stories. We tell stories to help others understand changes in the world and in their human condition.

At one point in *The Lion King* (Mecchi & Roberts, 1993), Simba is confused about how to face the future because that means he has to face his past, something he's been running from for so long. Rafiki bashes Simba over the head with his staff.

> *Simba: Ow! What was that for?*
>
> *Rafiki: It doesn't matter it's in the past. (laughs)*
>
> *Simba (massaging his head): Yeah but it still hurts.*
>
> *Rafiki: Oh yes, the past can hurt ... but the way I see it, you can either run from it or ... learn from it.*
>
> *Rafiki swings his staff again. Simba ducks.*
>
> *Rafiki: Ah! You see ... so what are you going to do?*

This is what it means to be human: using the experiences of the past to predict the future. Storytelling is exactly the same thing.

A story is made up not only from consequential episodes, but those with details that involve human characters who the reader or hearer cares about. Readers want to know how a character is going to get out of the trouble they are in, or whether love will last. They want someone they can love. Someone they can hate. Someone to cry over. Someone to laugh with. The trouble the character is in may or may not be of their own making, but what is obvious to the reader is that if this character *does not change something, and change it quickly*, they will not get out of the danger, or win the love of their perfect match. Only when that change happens do we realise the story is complete.

A story, then, is a realisation that something fundamental has changed when we are told of what happens to a worthy human character when they do something to get what they want. It is made up of consequential episodes narrated in details that are designed to entertain because they promise an experience of pleasure.

Key concepts

- **Something fundamental changes…**
- **Worthy human character wants something and acts to get it …**
- **Narrative of consequential episodes …**
- **Designed to entertain …**

How to Find Your Story

Now that we know what makes a story, we can set about coming up with an idea and developing it. A useful way of getting started is to develop some ideas of what you want to write about, convert an idea to action and create a premise and a snapshot statement of the idea.

Discovering What You Want to Write About

One of the greatest challenges is to figure out what you want to write about. Writing a story is, at first, a process of making decisions. You have to decide *what* it's about, *who's* in it, *where* and *when* it takes place, *what* happens, *why* and *how* … and every decision you make affects every other decision in what seems to be an endless process. But it is important to bear in mind that you can always change a decision.

Some things are easier to write about than others. For example, it's easier to write about something that happens if it has already happened to you; it's easier to write about a place you can see every day; it's easier to write about people who you actually know … you get the idea, I'm sure.

What you choose to write about will always be far more important than any decision you make on how to write it. Which means that the key to powerful writing is to make a decision to write about something that is important to you personally. If it's important to you, then it's quite likely to be important to others.

You may be aware of the expression, 'Write what you know.' This can be both good advice and poor advice. If we limit ourselves to writing only what we know now, how do we grow beyond that? Writing must also be a process of discovery. My view is that there are different levels to this idea of 'what you know'. There are things you know because you've experienced them. There are things you know because you've read about them. But there are also things you know because your imagination can dream them, and your heart can feel them.

Therefore, the critical first step is to become familiar with what you know.

Premise

A premise is simply a proposition from which a conclusion is drawn. We take a character and subject them to episodes that complicate their life, which then results in change. Making this sort of argument is the premise; an argument involving the character and particular circumstances that lead to a conclusion in which that character experiences some turning point — some transformation.

Say, for example, I want to write a story about someone who falls in love and dies. It could prove the argument that 'great love leads to death'. From that argument I would know that my story involves a great love between two characters, and I would know that, in the end, one — if not both — of the lovers will meet their end. How that end comes about, whether the great love is ever fulfilled, what keeps the lovers apart ... are all aspects that are not important to the premise. Those details, the episodes of the narrative, could be told in many different ways.

Romeo and Juliet, for instance, could be argued to be a story with the premise: 'Great love defies even death' — that is, the love lives on even after the death of the lovers. The tragedy of the story unfolds when Juliet feigns death with a powerful sleeping draught. Romeo thinks she is dead, so he drinks poison and dies next to her. When Juliet awakens, she discovers Romeo has died and unhesitatingly drinks the same poison and they are united in death. Death occurs to both of them because they were willing to defy family tradition and discard life for perpetual love. Love transcends the death because its consequences are felt beyond the deaths.

The Lion King could be said to have the premise: 'Exile leads to freedom'. Of course this is also the premise for Hamlet. Simba is wrongly blamed for the death of his father and hides in exile. When he is visited by the ghost of his father he is called to set things right and on discovering the truth, disposes of the tyrant, Scar, and in claiming the kingdom, sets his mind free of guilt and the pride free of tyranny. The premise works to keep the episodes of the narrative directed towards its inevitable conclusion, not the other way round. In essence, your premise guides all the action of the story into proving the argument. It allows you to question any episode you propose for your story by asking how it contributes to the concluding argument of the premise.

The paradox of premise is that it is both strangely simple, yet devilishly complex. But, because it is a statement of the dramatic transformation of a dramatic character through a dramatic struggle, as a way of thinking through what it is that you really want to write about, it can be very useful.

How to Find Your Premise

Our definition of a story tells us that it hinges on a character transformed through actions they take to get what they want. The premise, therefore, is a short-hand statement of the outcome of that drive: a thumbnail statement that suggests character through conflict leads to conclusion. You cannot have a great love or a truth without character; a path that 'leads' somewhere is not likely to be completely free of obstacles, therefore the character can expect some conflict on the way to the conclusion. This conflict will be the forces that are ultimately responsible for the fundamental change that takes place.

It is important to bear in mind that a premise is true only within the story, it is not a universal truth. A premise sets out to validate the simple fact that in 'story', something strange that is true to human nature happens — the storyteller enables the audience to see things in a new way. But, while involved in it, it's strange. Which means that I could quite easily write a story that 'electricity leads to precious metals' because it could be true in the fictional world I create to prove it, although it may not be very interesting. Or that J.K. Rowling could write a story that proves magic leads to liberation.

EXAMPLE:

> Let's say we are going to write a story about a chicken crossing the road to reach the other side. The premise: crossing the road leads to the other side. Crossing the road suggests character; leads to suggests conflict; the other side suggests conclusion (character through conflict leads to conclusion). This premise is something I can believe in, I can argue it with conviction; it may be a metaphor for learning to have a balanced view.
>
> But the events unfolding in the chicken's journey may make crossing the road extremely perilous. It could be a four-lane highway; the pedestrian bridge could be guarded by a fox; there may be a KFC on the other side.... What happens as the events unfold are the obstacles to proving the premise; they come in the form: 'But crossing the road is not possible …' However, the truth remains that the only way for the chicken to get to the other side, is to cross the road. This is a truth that applies only to this story and, come hell or high water, I will prove it.

In other words, only events that will act as obstacles to the fulfilment of this premise belong in the story. The chicken heading off to circumnavigate the world and thereby arrive at the other side of the road by circling the globe does not belong in the story because this story is about crossing the road, not about getting to the other side — getting to the other side is simply the conclusion of the journey — the same as Romeo and Juliet is about a great love, not about death. The premise dictates that crossing the road is the only permissible journey. This has the effect of amplifying the drama and I will invent many obstacles to the journey that will test the character of the chicken: it has to prove it is a worthy character — otherwise no story, right?

The premise governs the story by identifying that a dramatic struggle takes place in order to effect a dramatic transformation. Such a struggle requires two equally powerful arguments to be present — that is, the opposing argument is inherent in the struggle. The struggle is the conflict between crossing the road leading to the other side, and crossing the road not leading to the other side — it may, instead, lead to death, or a dinner box. A change takes place to a character because one side of the argument prevails through the struggle, but during the course of the action, there are convincing counter-arguments that cause the potential of the outcome to see-saw.

This leads us to that other vital aspect about premise: it must be something you are able to write about with conviction, something you personally believe in. A story is far more powerful when the author has something important to say, when you write about things that mean something to you at a personal level, something that if you convince the world is true, would make it a better place. It may be preposterous to others, but not to you.

Finding your premise is not easy, but it is an important part of the planning. It will help you keep the drama of the story tied to a single-minded idea, ensure you know what the story is about, what outcome your character is striving for, help identify the characters involved in the struggle and the type of struggle going on, and concentrate the story in its genre. It takes considerable effort and can be frustrating because it is, at least at first, counter to the normal process of thinking about story.

> **We rarely start with a Premise and go looking for a Story Idea. More often you have an idea for a story first. You then need to go back and forth between story idea and premise several times, shaping and moulding, testing and exploring, until it gels. You must be prepared to spend considerable time on this process if you want a strong idea you can exploit with conviction.**

The Anatomy of a Story Idea

Story ideas are everywhere. But identifying a good story idea for you can be challenging and daunting unless you know where and how to look. Note, I said for you. Not everyone sees the same idea the same way, which is what makes stories so fascinating. The following discussion will introduce you to some good writing practices to help you develop a sense of looking for, recording and evaluating potential story ideas.

You might have a very clear idea of what's important to you, but the story idea that's going to help you prove it remains elusive. It is often difficult to pin down. We need to work our way into an idea that might begin as a spark of intuition, something that holds the potential of the story, something to which we might say, 'there's something there,' even though we may not know what that something is. So what is the creative act surrounding the idea? how is it formed? how do we draw upon that genesis … that spark? to form something that will hold the weight of a story? How do we work our way in?…

Our usual process is that we think of an idea that inspires the writing of the story and say to ourselves: 'That would make a good story.' We then make the assumption that the idea we thought of is at the beginning, and then proceed to think about what happens next. This is often not helpful. The truth is, the idea we thought of is usually much closer to the crisis/climax of the story — the ending — than the beginning because it is usually the moment of transformation that we see as the good idea, the moment when opposing forces produce something new — a sort of collision of imagination.

What we need to do, therefore, is think about what happened before that moment, work backwards through the episodes that lead to the climactic point. Knowing what happens at the end of the story makes it far easier to work out a premise, and that gives you a goal to write towards.

Finding the Spark

Finding the *spark* is tough because no-one can tell you where it is, what it is, or when you will sense it. It is something that will strike when you're least expecting it — in the shower, while you're jogging, during maths … anytime except the moment you really need it — and if you're not looking at it the right way, it might pass you by completely. James N Frey in *The Key* calls it 'the germinal idea'; I call it the 'spark' because it's what lights the fuse; it is the idea that originates the story process. It can be inspired by anything: a feeling, an image, a vague recollection of an experience, a person you met, someone you saw on a bus, an uncle who drank too much, someone who did something bad …

You may have seen it on a news story, heard about it in a snippet of conversation, recalled it from a family anecdote, observed it in passing, seen it in the pages of someone else's book … these are all ways writers come by ideas. The important thing is to get into the habit of spotting them and recording them when they occur.

A term I like to use to describe these fleeting ideas is *arrival*, because often an idea is something that happens unannounced. An 'arrival' is an odd thing; it sort of hits you in the guts, gives you a little twist down low that makes you feel slightly unsettled. Why? Because it's new, because it hasn't been seen before; even if it's derived from a story or a fact that already exists, what makes it different, unique to you, is your point of view, your perspective, your take on the 'spark'. And that is why you should follow it.

The following six basic tenets are to help guide you in the discovery process. Then you need to develop a habit of looking, testing, filtering and recording. These tenets are flexible principles that you can apply to your daily practice.

1. Keep an Idea Bank or 'Think' Book

A small notebook (or several in series) in which you record all 'arrivals' and subsequent jottings about these arrivals. This notebook becomes your idea bank to which you turn for germinal ideas (sparks), climactic ideas (explosions), medial ideas (fires) and pivotal ideas (flare-ups). There may be no order to your notebook or it may be well ordered and indexed, it doesn't matter — what matters is that this is where you store your 'arrivals', and where you explore them.

2. Play

All creativity is derived from 'play'. You may think I'm joking, but I'm not. Think back to your own playing as a small child, to some of the things you had to invent in order to 'realise the moment'. You were being creative when you adapted plastic buckets for drums, when you floated pieces of paper in the running streams, when you forced a friend to answer a riddle. Think about the things you used to make your inventions, even if they were entirely 'make-believe' or virtual.

Develop a sense of 'play' even when you're being serious. What do you play with? Anything that comes to mind. Play with words. Play with colours. Play with shapes. Play with objects. Build things. Tear them down. Put two opposites together and see what it produces. Create buildings and structures in your mind that solve impossible problems.

Make 'play' a natural part of conversations. Create a habit out of play. Change the way you tackle a piece of music, change its timing, its tempo, its chord structure…. Change the order of things you've written — reverse sentences; read whole passages in reverse (both those you've written and those written by others) and record strange word combinations that appear. Play with the way people appear to you — change their features, change their walk, their voice, their society….

You get the idea: do a lot of playing.

3. Dream

This is bit like playing, only you are giving up your conscious self to your unconscious self and letting your mind run free. When we dream in sleep, our unconscious self is actively informing our conscious self of things that surround us but are out of sight to us. It's an odd sort of madness. It's important to try and capture this sensation and use it to your advantage.

Record vivid dream moments you may have had during sleep in your 'arrivals' notebook when you wake up. It doesn't have to make sense, but if you were involved in some dream-world adventure, try to capture the moment and the feelings it produced. Set about dreaming (or day-dreaming) when you get a chance and record the experience afterwards in a short jotting.

4. Review

Spend time roaming through your jottings to try and see things that you've written in a different way and rewrite them. Reshape the shapes, recolour the colours, change genders, change orders, change roles of the players, combine ideas, divide them ... constantly reflect on and review your ideas, they will help you recognise new 'arrivals' when they occur, and they will help you build a deeper pool of ideas from which to draw when you need them.

5. Read

This cannot be understated. Read a wide variety — that is, read stories in different formats (books, comics, scripts) and read different types of stories (try genres you may not normally visit). Read biographies. Watch films and (good) television with a critical eye to the story. Go to the theatre. Take particular note of potential ideas that authors leave lying on the page. Think about other people's stories from different points of view — told from the eyes of another character, for example — or even how that story might be if the main character were only a minor character. Reshape the story into a different genre (turn fantasy into adventure, romance into science fiction ...) change the genders of the characters. Consider what might have happened in one of these character's lives before this story took place ... after this story took place ... if it took place in another land.... Jot your thoughts in your ideas bank.

6. Observe

Be alert to seeing things that are of interest to you, and seeing into the detail of them. This is a little more complex than it seems, for you must be free to capture the observations and write about them without censoring your thoughts and emotions. It may lead you to believe that it is all utter nonsense, but that's perfectly okay ... in fact, the more silly things seem, the more useful they can sometimes be, which of course leads you back to Tenet 2 (play).

When you write your observations, try to capture the essential aspect that makes it of personal interest to you and write in terms of the senses — what you see, what you hear, smell, taste and touch. Watch people in public places and make up occupations for them, relationships for them ... eavesdrop on their conversations and write what you hear. Study the way they pick their nose, scratch their ear, shift in their seat ... Capture anything that assails your senses and jot it down. You never know when a rotting odour emanating from behind a restaurant leads you into a murder investigation, or the start of a romantic liaison. It all depends on how you look at it. The key is to describe everything you can about that moment of observation.

Fleshing out the Story Idea

A story idea needs to have at least one of the following components, but the more it has, the stronger it is.

Intrigue — an idea with intrigue is an idea with something about it that begs to be explained. This may be an element of human nature, of behaviour, natural phenomena; scientific discovery, or development of fantastic origins ... it has to offer the potential for suspense.

Unique twist — a turning point in the story (or several of them) causes the characters to experience some reversal(s) of fortune, this surprises the reader/listener and leads them to feel an 'aha' moment. Try for a unique twist in the end, as well as one or two throughout the narrative.

Colourful character — the last thing anyone wants to read about is an uninteresting character. An idea which has a character at the centre of the action who is different, behaves differently, is the product of unusual social circumstance, or physical manipulation makes for more interesting reading than the bland guy next door. Consider an unusual occupation as a powerful key to a colourful character, in particular an occupation that is out of kilter with the usual expectations in that genre. It helps to break stereotypes.

Unusual item, object or moment — when something within the story is something that every character wants, wants to be part of, or wants to avoid, there is potential for great dramatic action. Alfred Hitchcock called it the McGuffin.

Once you have your idea, you need to develop a story 'snapshot statement' — the story idea expressed in the form: 'This story is about [a character] who did [something] to get [what they want].' The snapshot statement contains the over-arching or 'high concept' idea, the basic drives of character and conflict that hold the story together and make it work, as well as the ending.

Perhaps the following example will help.

EXAMPLE

The Spark:

A bank robber gets caught when he interrupts an amateur's robbery attempt.

With a little bit of brainstorming on the idea, I decide the story is about the amateur bank robber, not the professional. Research into some bank robberies gives me some clues about how I can twist the facts of a real story into my fictional one; this gives it a sense of what is known as 'verisimilitude' — that it could have actually happened. The professional bank robber, we'll call him 'The Belmont Bandit' because he works the Eastern side of the river, had already stolen $6 million from local banks over a period of about two years. That's a lot of loot and a reward of $150,000 for information leading to his arrest has been offered.

The 'spark' on this leaves open a lot of possibilities. And because I want to focus on the amateur, the main question that comes to mind in my brainstorming is, 'Why was he attempting to rob a bank?' The obvious answer is that he needed money. So, in terms of a premise, I can suggest that he ends up with what he wants: money. The unique twist is that he doesn't get it the way he originally intended, which was to rob a bank, but instead he gets it from the reward.

A bank robbery is of course an unusual item in the life of an ordinary citizen, not too many people — especially people who are generally not crooks — want to rob banks. The intrigue of the idea, though, needs to come from his motivations. Why does he need money so desperately? What event triggered this need for money: was it inability to work, the loss of his girlfriend, his overly generous nature?...

Keeping in mind that I want my character to be colourful — someone who is a little different — the circumstances of his need for money should be in keeping with this quirky nature. I decided to name my character Joe. He had a girlfriend, Sally, whom he loved very much, but he lost her to a far wealthier individual. He was convinced that the only real difference was the money, and if he had the money, he could buy her a diamond ring and he would win her back. Bingo! An idea is born.

So the *snapshot statement* for this story is:

This is a story about a guy who loses his girlfriend and decides to rob a bank to win her back. When his robbery attempt is interrupted by another robber, he unmasks the robber and claims a reward for his arrest.

I like this because it adds intrigue to the idea, there is a certain oddness that the very idea of robbing a bank could win back a lost love, and it still has a unique twist in the tail. As a story idea, it is strong with the promise of dramatic transformation and entertainment.

So, what's the premise?

Only a guy with a 'great love' for a girl would go to the lengths of robbing a bank to win her back. In the end he is rewarded for his struggles. Therefore the premise of this story is, *Loss of great love leads to happiness.*

The above example demonstrates that the premise is not the 'story idea'. The story idea answers the question: 'What is the story about?' and it is directed to what the character does in order to get what they want. The key to discovering the conflict the character has to pass through, is to backtrack from the end using the question *Why?* and the answer, *Because ...*

Why did he end up rewarded? *Because* he unmasked a serial bank robber. *Why* did he unmask a serial bank robber? *Because* the bank robber interrupted his own bank robbery attempt. *Why* was he attempting to rob the bank? *Because* he needed the money? *Why* did he need the money? *Because* he wanted to buy his ex-girlfriend a diamond ring. *Why* did he want to buy her a diamond ring? *Because* he was convinced it would bring her back to him. *Why* did he need her to come back to him? *Because* he loves her greatly.

Therefore: *Loss of a great love leads to happiness.*

> ## Summary
>
> A story is the realisation that something fundamental has changed when we are told of what happens to a worthy human character when they do something to get what they want. It is made up of consequential episodes narrated in details that are designed to entertain because they promise an experience of pleasure.
>
> Story is the key to what it is to be human because it illustrates change and how we can deal with it. Story is a pleasure experience that happens in the mind of the reader or hearer. It comes from being told a narrative of consequential episodes that result in a worthy human character being transformed in some way. When we set out to write a story, this is the experience we want to create for the reader or hearer.
>
> Prominent guiding principles in the design of creating a story include a premise, which is a short-hand statement of the story idea summed up through its conclusion. It is expressing what you want to write about in a statement of character through conflict leads to conclusion. Two other guiding principles include a spark or germinal idea which is the idea that inspires the story, and a snapshot story statement that expresses the story idea as what action the character takes in order to get what they want.
>
> Gathering, filtering and developing story ideas takes regular practice, just the same as learning the scales on piano takes practice. You need to get into the habit of gathering, recording and working with your ideas.

A Review of Your Story Idea Development

The following lists a number of things you might like to think about in developing your ideas. A story idea needs to carry substantial weight if it is to make it through to the end. This and the discussion points and exercises on this chapter will help you design your story. Remember, it is a process that goes back and forth quite a bit. Even though, in the end, you need to settle on one idea, you should continue collecting and developing ideas. Be prepared to spend a fair amount of time on this.

1. Write something that may change your life. The fact is: if a story is important to you, it is very likely to be important to others who are like you.

2. Look for what's possible within the story. This is a moment where you suspend disbelief and limitations, and consider what is *possible*. Possibilities can alter from genre to genre, for example your story idea might offer certain possibilities in a science fiction mode, but entirely different ones in a fantasy mode. Try to consider all possibilities and list them down.

3. Identify the story problem and challenges. All stories centre on a problem of some sort, and this problem then presents different challenges that have to be addressed and dealt with. Try to find the central problem of the story idea, and then list all challenges associated with it. If you identify a different problem, list the challenges associated with that one as well.

4. Find the internal logic of the story. The logic organises your story into its organic unity, connecting the beginning, through the middle to the end. Consider the main character's 'journey' through the story as the key to your logic.

5. Define the 'best' character in the story idea. The best character is the character who the story is ultimately about. Your original idea may have arisen from a situation in which a character is placed, but once you begin the discovery process, that character may not necessarily be the 'best' character about whom to tell the story. Search for the character who is the most fascinating, complex and challenging in the idea.

6. Identify the central conflict. This is a simple question of 'What is being fought over, by whom? And Why?'

7. Discover the cause-and-effect pathway. We are interested in the connected consequential episodes that take the main character through the conflict and see him or her emerge out the other end. Try to identify the path in which A leads to B, which leads to C, to D and so on....

8. What is the main character's possible character change? The story needs to place the Hero character within a dramatic situation that causes him or her to change. What is the change that takes place? (HINT: Begin with the way the Hero is at the end, and then create a weakness the Hero has at the beginning.) Weakness multiplied by the Action of the conflict, equals Change in the character.

9. Does your Hero have a moral choice? Try to ensure your Hero has to choose one of two possible outcomes that determine a way for life to continue. Dilemmas drive story and when your character has to choose one direction over another, it forces your reader to develop sympathy for the character's circumstances.

Chapter Two
The Reign of Homo Fictus

Character Design and Development

A story is about who does what, when, where, to whom and why. It is about fictional characters and the opposition that exists between them. This section will discuss some of the key principles that lie behind character design and introduce you to techniques for creating and developing interesting and strong characters.

Homo Fictus is No Ordinary Person

James N Frey, in *How to Write a Damn Good Novel* says:

> 'Fictional characters — *Homo Fictus* — are not ... identical to flesh-and-blood human beings — *homo sapiens*.... Readers demand that *Homo Fictus* be more handsome or ugly, ruthless or noble, vengeful or forgiving, brave or cowardly, and so on, than real people are. *Homo Fictus* has hotter passions and colder anger; he travels more, fights more, loves more, changes more, has more sex. Lots more sex. Homo Fictus has more of everything. Even if he is plain, dull, and boring, he'll be more extraordinary in his plainness, dullness, and boringness than his real-life counterparts. *Homo Fictus* is not the same as an ordinary person, *Homo Fictus* is more.'

Homo Fictus offers the reader a glimpse into humanity by representing all of those things we need humanity to be. In order to do that, they must be larger than life, which means they are both more exceptional and more mundane: more powerful, more villainous, more handsome, uglier, braver, more scared, nobler, more vengeful, more forgiving ... they possess every emotion and every capacity ordinary people possess, only on a grander scale.

The most important thing to bear in mind when creating characters is to create contrast between them and contradictions within them. Contrast creates not only conflict, but also interest for the reader. You can easily imagine such conflicts coming from differences in religious or political attitudes, social status or upbringing, but conflict can be driven by any of the dimensions of character. David and Goliath stories (such as Jack and the Beanstalk) derive some of their greatest interest from the obvious differences between the characters. The physically smaller Hero has to learn and use a different kind of strength in order to vanquish the giant villain.

As you will see in the following pages, there is a range of different dimensions to character in which you can create dynamic differences that will help lock characters into the story, pit them against each other, pitch them together in ways that cannot be unbound, ensuring they cannot escape until the end. Create your characters so that their dimensions fall on opposites sides of 'average' and you will be well on your way to building interesting characters.

It's not only important to find contrasts between characters, but also between the abilities of a character, and the action you want them to perform. For example, a Hero might be called upon to exert stupendous physical strength when a wall collapses around him, but if he is small and without the required stature, you have created opportunity for growth and inner conflict.

It is also important to develop contradictions within a character. Such contradictions often arise from simple oppositions within different dimensions of character. For example, imagine a character who was raised in a very religious family. Outwardly they appear pious, but inwardly reject religion altogether. Imagine the internal struggles of a young gay person living in a homophobic family. A character with contradictions enables you to develop powerful connections with your reader.

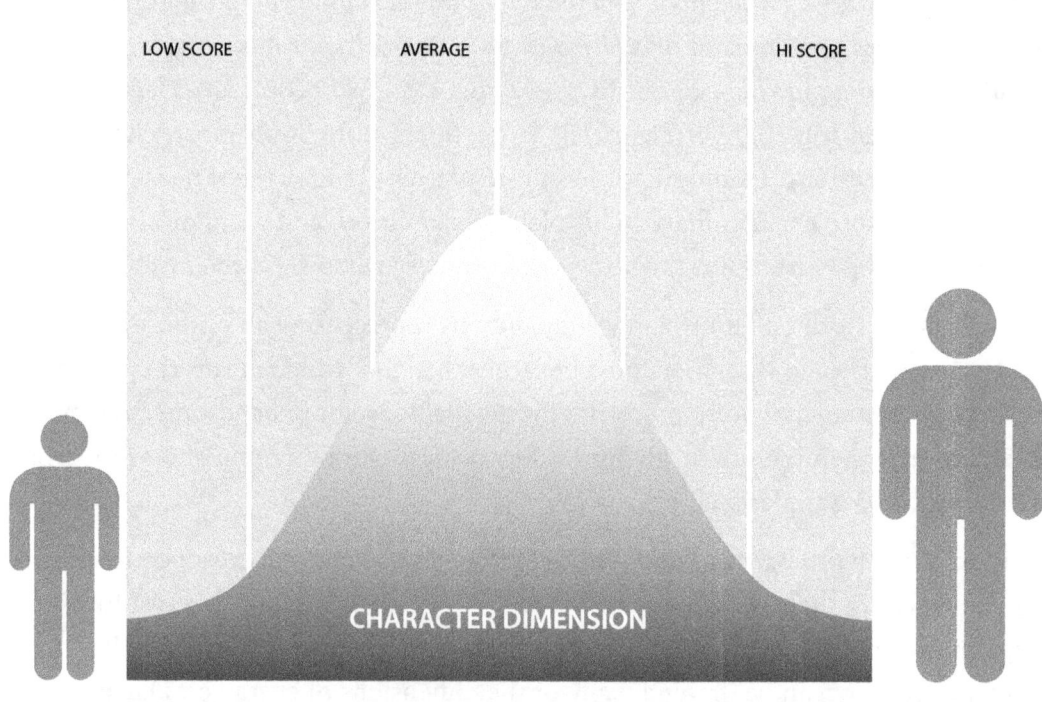

Opposites in character dimensions create contrast in characters

More than One Character

Let's talk terminology for a moment. The character who is at the centre of the story (you remember the one who *wants* something and *does* something to get it; the one the story is *about*; the one who *changes*?) goes by several names. By and large, the most important character, the *central* or *main* character is also the *Hero* and *Protagonist*. We know, of course, that stories inevitably involve more than one character.

What is important here is that you must realise that every other character in the story is connected in some way to the *Hero/Protagonist*, either in opposition or alliance or both. A character with no relation to the Hero has no impact on the core conflict of the story, and therefore has no role to play in it.

The other equally important character is the *Villain* or *Antagonist* of the story. This is the character representing the main obstacle to the Hero getting what they want. The next section in this book will discuss many other characters we frequently find in a story's *circuitry or cast of characters* and how you go about establishing and developing their relationships to the main character.

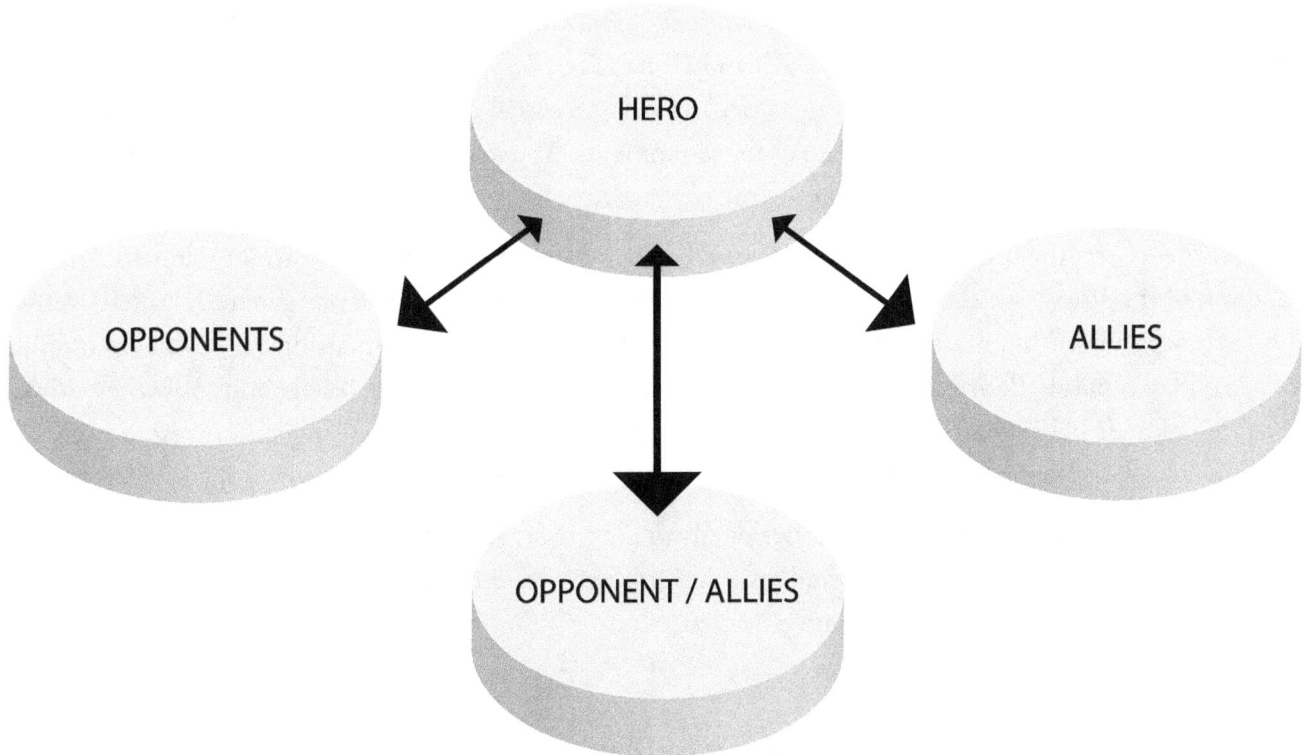

All other characters have a relationship of opposition or alliance or both with the Hero.

While other characters are in opponent-ally relationships with the main character, among them there are mainly two *types* of characters: *Bit Players* and *Full Characters*. In *Section Three* we will discuss different functions of characters, but for the moment it is important to understand the simple difference between them.

Bit Players ... are not very complex, rather a bit flat, one-dimensional. They are not very deep. They are used to add environment and atmosphere to the scene in which the main players are acting. They are on the outer; readers don't take a lot of notice of them. They may be used to make us laugh, transport a main character, introduce characters to each other ... they have no real power on their own to hold the reader's attention. Their roles are important in keeping a story glued together or helping it unravel, but they are not the *who* of the story; consequently we have no interest in them outside of 'the moment' they carry out their function. In the end, they require no resolution.

In a story like *Shrek 2*, for example, there is the Ugly Sister who runs the bar and introduces King Harold to Puss-in-Boots; the two men the transformed Shrek and Donkey take the clothes from; the rescue team who break Shrek and Donkey out of gaol. These characters are used to move the story along, to help transition from one moment to another, but they are not used to tell the story. Scuttle in *The Little Mermaid*, the three Vultures in *Jungle Book*, Zazu in The *Lion King*, The Weasly twins in *Harry Potter* ... they all provide comic relief, they cause the story to turn and signal reversals of fortune, but you don't really know them other than what they do at those moments. You know nothing of their inner thoughts, their secrets, their passions. They have no depth.

Full Characters ...on the other hand (including the Hero and other characters who are instrumental in the action of the story), are those who are used to tell the story. They are what are generally called 'well-rounded' characters. They are complete in the sense that they have multi-dimensions. They have complex motives and conflicting desires and are alive with passions and ambitions. We learn about how they think, we can judge their behaviour. They have committed great sins and borne agonising sufferings; they are full of worries, woes and unresolved grievances. In the end, they must be resolved.

For characters to be well-rounded, the reader needs to get the sense that these characters existed long before the story began: that they have lived long and full lives. These are characters, whether they are good guys or bad guys, who are worth knowing.

The Crucible and the Unity of Opposites

In order for a conflict between characters to rise to a climax, it is necessary that the characters in the story have a *unity of opposites* between them so entrenched that no compromise between their points of view can be reached. They will be so bound to each other that it will be a fight to the finish; so opposed that one must destroy the other in order to live. The *unity* is one where opposites are joined to destroy each other.

In order for Jack (Jack and the Beanstalk) to survive, the giant must be destroyed — there is no compromise. The same is true of the Pirates and Davy Jones, of Simba and Scar, of Harry Potter and Voldemort. The crucible in which the characters are placed must be one that bonds them in such a way that neither can simply quit half way through — it is a conflict to the bitter end.

A crucible bonds the story's premise to the character because of compelling reasons why the character can't simply get up and leave.

From working through your story design principles — developing a story idea, premise and story snapshot statement — you will have a pretty good idea of the following key elements:

- **Central character**
- **Core conflict**
- **Change that takes place**

The core conflict of the story illustrates the difference between what the central character wants, what they are striving for, and the forces of antagonism working to prevent them achieving their goal. It's what keeps the character in the story, what binds them to its action and the outcome. They cannot escape the story until the outcome is realised.

This sets up an important element of the story. The core conflict is a representation of the character's *desires*, but what the character often fails to realise is what they *need*. Need and desire are separate: a character knows their desires, but usually not what is is they actually need in order to fulfil those desires — the character's need is the internal representation of the conflict, invisible to the character and preventing them arriving at the goal.

The conflict driven by desire keeps characters in the crucible of the story; the hidden need of the character keeps the conflict alive. Quite often it's the difference between the character's desires and their hidden need that creates dilemmas the character must resolve in order to progress. As soon as the character no longer requires their hidden need, the conflict is at risk of dissolving. If the conflict is at risk of dissolving then the character might as well just walk away, which would make the story meaningless because there would be no transformation. The stakes must be high enough to prevent that from happening, and always be the focus of the action.

EXAMPLE:

> *Let's say there's a teacher. He's at a dreadful school, lousy headmaster, too many kids, learning is secondary to attendance and discipline ... he hates the school and the job, and it's easy to see why. The reader quickly gains sympathy for the situation.*
>
> *Why doesn't he just leave?*
>
> *His wife left him a few months ago for another man and this is the school his kids go to. It's the only chance he gets to see them. He took the job after the wife left. She tried to have him removed but was unsuccessful. She'll try again. If he can stick it out for another four years, he will be part of his children's lives for that time. For him, that's worth fighting for.*
>
> *But he needs to get over the idea that he's a victim. Being a victim gives him cause to hate the school and the environment; he walks around with a chip on his shoulder; it pushes people away from him. If he could overcome his victimhood he would realise that the world is not such a bad place and he could manage other ways of being with his kids.*
>
> *Being a victim is what keeps him in the crucible, and in conflict with his wife. We (the reader) see this going on and we want him to get over it, but he's steadfast in his beliefs, he's locked into his behaviour and he's not going to change without a real shake up, which will come at the end of the story. This is his psychological need.*
>
> *Perhaps he also lied to get the job, which presents a moral dilemma for the character. If he told the truth he puts his relationship with his kids at risk.*

Find the connections that keep your character bonded with other characters and the circumstances in the story that maintain the pressure on the core conflict. Make sure the only way out is to go all the way *through* the story, block all other escape routes with insurmountable obstacles.

The core conflict is the secret to character. It emerges from the combination of the main character's desires and hidden needs, but it is also that to which the character must respond, which means it also helps shape the character. Your character design must match the needs of the conflict, and the conflict must grow out of the character. If the character does not match those needs, then the story will fail.

Character Creation

In the process of creating characters, you have to act like God. You are developing a representation of a particular 'human condition' from the bare bones. In the *Art of Dramatic Writing*, Lajos Egri says, 'Character is the fundamental material we are forced to work with so we must know character as thoroughly as possible.' It means forming the vessels into which you can pour your ideas and aspirations; to which your readers can add their own. In creating characters you have to be original in devising the personality and relationships, you need to delve into mysterious backgrounds, create probable futures; imagine impossible births and deaths. You have to be daring. Be promiscuous. Nasty. Vicious. Clever. Formidable. Characters must be an extension of your own imagination if they are to be believable and yours.

The following discussions offer a wide range of tools you can use in creating and developing the 'lives' of your characters.

Principles of Identity

Identity is that by which we know a person, character or thing. It is formed from the actions that produce or register notability (deeds), a location from which those deeds emanate (place), what is said about that notability (word) and the culture, conventions or traditions (behaviour) associated with it.

For example, when you present yourself at an international border, you are required to produce a passport, a particular type of identity document, along with a form you have completed to obtain a visa — permission to enter or leave that country. Your identity document will show others what you look like, tell them your age, where you've come from, what other places you've been granted entry to. Your visa application will identify your occupation, where your journey commenced, where it will end, the means of your transportation. Some people are denied entry because of their reputations — reports recorded against their past — or behaviour that class them as 'undesirables'.

Identity can be reduced to four particular 'character pillars'. These 'four pillars' are present in every identity, but one will usually dominate and even, during the course of a story, change. It's a good idea to think of your character in these terms to begin with because it helps shape up who they are and what 'human condition' they represent.

1. *Deed* — What a character 'does' and how they perform in the sphere of those deeds is often the most significant identity factor in how a reader and other characters perceive them. Identity is often determined by a character's occupation, and skill or proficiency level. The reader gets to 'see' the character through this functional element. Often a name is drawn to identify such an attribute. Sometimes the name comes with a title that identifies the seminal 'deed' of the character.

2. *Place* — Where a character performs their deeds is crucial to presenting the idea of the character to other characters and the reader. Identity can also be determined by the origins of a character, where they come from. This can be a physical location (other country/state/territory) or a social location (upper class/working class) or a psychological location (intelligence/intellectual impairment). Characters can be known and named by their origins, or place of practice.

3. *Word* — How the character explains their deeds, or how it is explained by others on their behalf. Characters can be identified by what others hear about their exploits without ever meeting them. This is often the case of 'celebrity' characters. You can use many different physical attributes to communicate the idea of the character, such as clothing, posture, voice, and so on — both to other characters and the reader.

4. *Behaviour* — Characters can be identified by the way they behave, their mores or cultural responses to situations. This form of identity emerges in face-to-face situations with other characters and the reader, reflected through reactions and responses.

Determining the dominant factor of the character's identity helps establish how the character will fit into the narrative environment, as well as create opportunities of contrast and conflict with other characters.

Imagine, for example, four politicians in a dinner-table debate, each with an identity based on a different dominant pillar. One is known for her deeds, she's a doctor and has healed many people of a diabolical illness, but she is not known outside of her town. Her name could be Dr Valiant Healy. Another is known for the place she comes from, a wealthy place, where the streets are paved with gold. Perhaps she is Arial Goldstreet. A third is known for what people say about him, a soldier whose fame is widespread, hard and demanding, with fixed ideas on how things should work. Call him General Steele. And a fourth behaves as though he has not a care in the world. He can be Freeman Manners. Place these people in a debate over government sponsored health care and watch the sparks fly.

Focussing on these factors can help create completely different personalities, that can be specific to the issues that are at the core of your story.

Name

The name is the principal symbol and the foundation of identity. David Lodge in *The Art of Fiction* says, 'The naming of characters is always an important part of creating them, involving many considerations and hesitations ...' The writer uses the name of a character as a way of symbolising what that character may represent to the wider world of the story, and to the wider world of the reader and their experience. In many cases they are used as comic or satirical devices (Donkey, for example), others to broadcast the nature that lies at the heart of their character (Scar, another example).

Names in the hands of the writer, as Lodge says, are never neutral: they always offer the reader a signal about the character, even if it is ordinariness. Once the right name is found, the character grows into it and takes actions that suit it, create their own 'story' around it, often responding to it. Names can carry a lot of weight in the story, their meanings frequently symbolising historical, religious and social aspects beyond the story itself.

A name should not be considered lightly because a name in fiction has to do a lot of work, and characters who stick in our minds tend to have names that conjure meaning to us — and that meaning is extended throughout the story and often beyond. Spend enough time with your characters and their identity will emerge. Identity, of course, is more than simply name; it is name within the context of the pillars of identity discussed above.

Rebus, for example, is a word describing an enigmatic representation of a word or phrase by symbols or pictures. It is the name Ian Rankin chose for his (now) famous detective, described in the Chambers *Dictionary of Literary Characters* as 'a natural outsider, having been brought up in a Fife mining town but now working in smart-but-sordid Edinburgh.' He is clearly enigmatic, a symbol of law and order who is frequently at odds with his superiors — 'whom he sees as dishonest or self-serving' — and has a string of failed relationships with women. The name suggests that this character belongs in the story because he doesn't belong in his environment, yet carries a valuable moral dimension.

The key is to conjure names that cause a sensation of curiosity in the reader, which can be driven by some degree of 'rub' between the character and the environment. Mythological names can offer excellent choices too. *Salander*, Steig Larssen's character from the *Millenium* trilogy has a connection with *Sala*, a Babylonian war goddess.

Harry Potter offers a certain combination of regal bearing and ordinariness. 'Harry' most likely derives from a knight of the round table (Harry le Fise du lake) which suggests fealty and loyalty. He is described the Chambers *Dictionary of Literary Characters* as ' "the boy who lived", having survived a lethal curse by Lord Voldemort … he grows up knowing nothing of his past, but at … Hogwarts he must confront his celebrity.' Potter is a classic Hero, his identity emerging from what is said about his existence (word). As the story evolves, he grows into his identity, wrestling with self-doubt to prove himself on his own terms (deeds), bright and resourceful and fiercely loyal to those around him (behaviour) and combating the evil of Voldemort within the wizard world (place). The name Harry is synonymous with loyalty and valour, and a Potter is an artisan who solves practical problems with artistic abilities.

When you are thinking about your characters' names, think about who they are in terms of their identity: What are their deeds, where are they from and where are they located now, what do others say about them, how do they behave? How can you catch their essential nature in a single word? How can you play with those words in order to express something interesting about your character? Be simple, don't create a name no-one can pronounce, or that does not resonate with the world of the story.

Important considerations when naming characters:

- The right name can provide symbolic expression of character through attitude, personality, social position, character defect ...

- Inventive, allegorical, comic, cynical, dark, ordinary, familial ...

- Contrast in names between characters, or even between surname and first name helps to build character complexity ...

- Readers want to 'know' the character and the name is the first point of 'contact'...

- Two-syllable strength, poetic constructions, natural inflection ...

- Attributes of the masculine (strength, order) and the feminine (feelings, understanding) can create conflict within characters ...

- Sexuality is often identified and questioned through name ...

- The name as story device, creating signs and symbols that connect to other devices through the narrative, exploring plot and intertextuality ...

- Don't create names that are too hard to pronounce. There is a tendency in fantasy and science fiction works to create names with awkward juxtapositions of letters that make them difficult to pronounce. It's easy to forget that reading is a verbal act, and even when reading silently, the sounding of the word is important.

- Don't create names that risk the production of a stereotype. One of the biggest challenges is breaking stereotypes, and quite often a name conjures up 'type' before it reveals the character. Often the simplest of names work best.

- To avoid stereotyping try to create a name that holds some surprise element about the character.

- Remain open about the name — it may pay for you to get to know the character reasonably well before settling on a final name (but the name may also come first and open up new possibilities for identity).

- Avoid clumsy combinations of syllables, make sure it's easily pronounced, poetic in sense, and sounds the way the character behaves.

- Have the name reveal an aspect of character (for example, Scar in The Lion King — it suggests a deep wound, it has a dark sound and therefore suggests a dark character, it is illustrated with an actual scar).

- Be poetic, find a rhythm in the syllables that works not just for the character, but for you and the story.

- Choose names (especially for key characters) that have some deeper meaning for you personally (it will help you write more convincingly about them).

Try to find names that add extra dimensions to characters and avoid names that are hard to sound out. A character's name should build on the character's central idea and project an image of the idea of that character, including the character's ambitions and strengths to the reader.

Creating Three-dimensional Characters

Lajos Egri in *The Art of Dramatic Writing* talks about the character's 'bone structure' and lists many attributes of character in physical, social and psychological dimensions. (This list is reproduced in Part Two of this book: *StepTwo, Create your characters* to help you develop the details of your character's make-up.) Working through this list helps you to make decisions about the character that create contrast and conflict.

To understand the action of any character, you need to look closely at what motivates him or her to act in the way they do. Egri's three dimensions help form a character background and influence motivation. A character's background will mould the behaviour and attitudes of that character in action, which determines how the character will respond to other characters around them and the circumstances in which they find themselves.

The first of the three dimensions is the *Physical*, the fundamentals of appearance, size and space. Egri says, 'Our physical make-up colours our outlook on life'. Short people and tall people do not have the same perspective on the world around them; thin people and fat people are talked about differently; different skin colours have long determined people's positions in many societies; people with different disabilities — blindness, deafness, plegia; people with illnesses ... all engage with the world differently. Physical attributes affect mental development.

The second dimension is the *Sociology*. A boy in Muckinbudin, for example, grows up quite differently from a kid in Fremantle, and even more differently from one who's grown up in another country. This means that under certain social circumstances, he will behave differently — near water, for example, or around animals. The relationship a character has with others often depends on social circumstance. But the actual differences between these characters can only be known after some investigation has been carried out *into each of them*. Who were the parents? Were they healthy? Wealthy? Do they have lots of friends, or few? What are the friends like? What influences did they have? What kind of schools did/do they attend? What do they like to eat, wear, talk about? What do they think about, like or dislike?

Third is *Psychology*. Your main characters need to be alive with great passions and strong emotions: they want things very badly; envy, greed, ambitions, hate, malice. They need to be emotional firestorms. Therefore you need to let them have thoughts that are their own. These thoughts might put them in conflict with other characters — their parents for example. Here we find a character's phobias and manias (Ron Weasly's fear of spiders, Hemione's obsession with perfection, Arial's passion for her prince ...), complexes, fears, inhibitions, feelings of guilt and longing, fantasies and dreams. You may include such things as how intelligent the character is, things they are good at doing, special abilities, habits, irritability, sensibility, talents and so on.

In many respects, the *psychological* dimension is the product of the *physical* and the *sociological*; it is how the character comes to think about ambition and often the reason there are frustrations and complex personality issues that stand in the way. At the heart of your central character lies a psychological need that impedes the character's progress towards their goal. This is a critical aspect of your Protagonist or Hero character, and one that the reader should grow quickly aware of, but remain elusive to the character themself. It is this hidden need that most often gets in the way.

Shrek, for example, wants to get his swamp back. But Farquad imposes a quest on Shrek, demanding he rescue Fiona and return her in exchange for the swamp. Fiona sees Shrek as her knight in shining armour, her rescuer, and falls in love with him. We also see Shrek falling in love with Fiona, but psychologically he is not prepared for it, his physical make-up has ensured that he has been alone too long, preferring solitude to the company of others; he has no experience of his emotions, he is unaware of Fiona's true physicality and sees her only for the beautiful princess she represents. As the story progresses, we watch Shrek push Fiona further away, and we feel for him, urging him to lighten-up a bit, to recognise his feelings — and her feelings — to put aside his selfish ego ... Shrek's *psychology* is the product of his *physicality* and *sociology*.

The Fourth Dimension: Sources of Power

One of the key differences between real life and the story world is that, in real life, we are born into an environment over which we have no control, and our growing up is a matter of fitting in, and coming to terms with it. In life, we don't know what's in store for us in the next minute, the next day, week, year ... we move into the unknown every single minute of the day. Part of the art of being a storyteller is to give the reader a sense that the future is safe, that you do know what's in store, that you possess great magic in being able to predict the transformations of life as they happen before our very eyes — and to understand them. You have power beyond the ordinary to control the fates of men, heal, inflict pain and punishments, and settle differences.

You are God.

Homo Fictus's situation is a little different from a real person's because you create your character from little bits of life you have observed and you design aspects of your character to fit the world you want them to inhabit. You do this at the same time as you design aspects of your world to accommodate the curiosities of the characters who will inhabit it. Knowing your characters by 'profile' is to understand the history you have given them, and to reckon on the way they will react under particular circumstances in which they find themselves, and to the prodding they get from other characters. Not only that, you also know exactly who your character will interact with because there are no characters who do not have a connection to the main character. Therefore you are creating a closed system (which we call a *crucible*) that gives off the impression that it could just as easily be real (which we call *verisimilitude*). But to do that, you need more than Egri's tridimensional model and the timeline, articles, interviews and journals discussed in the project and exercise sections of this book. You need the mechanism that fabricates a reality in the imagination of the reader. You need the connections.

To a great extent, Homo Fictus only exists in your reader's mind (consider the reader to also be the moviegoer, theatre-goer and game-player). Your job as a writer is to trigger a reader's imaginative engagement in which they will become involved in the character's trials and triumphs, often making comparisons between the character's circumstances and their own, all the while unravelling and solving problems in order to see the story world with increasing clarity.

The reader, however, has a unique perspective that is not available to you, the writer. Unlike you, they can observe a problem that you present from a disinterested point of view while *simultaneously* experiencing what it feels like to have the same problem the character has. The reader's perspective is made possible because of their relationship as observer to the story's goal, viewpoint and plot — which you provide through your main character and their relationships with others characters.

This dual sense of 'seeing whole' and simultaneously 'experiencing the struggle' produces the phenomena we know as 'story', which really only occurs within the reader's mind — what Christopher Huntley and Melanie Philips, the authors of *Dramatica*, termed the 'story mind'.

Character Balance and Drives

Stories both expose and employ characters in the telling by using them to represent the motivations of the reader, often working at cross-purposes and thereby giving rise to the conflicts that create the moral argument of the story's problem. These conflicts play out between the main character and the circuitry of other characters, conditioned by the circumstances which brings them together. This creates what we know as a 'story problem'.

A story's problem is represented by an imbalance that becomes evident because we see the central character striving for something against difficult obstacles. The external view of the obstacles is usually represented by the expression of conflicting desires of other characters or the obstruction of natural or artificial barriers. However, there is also an internal view at the heart of the problem and this is manifested through an imbalance of four key elements that are identified as having either masculine or feminine values.

According to Christopher Booker in *The Seven Basic Plots*, the division of feminine-masculine lies in the polar opposition of egocentricity and blindness to seeing whole on the one hand (Masculine), and selfless feeling and vision of wholeness (Feminine) on the other.

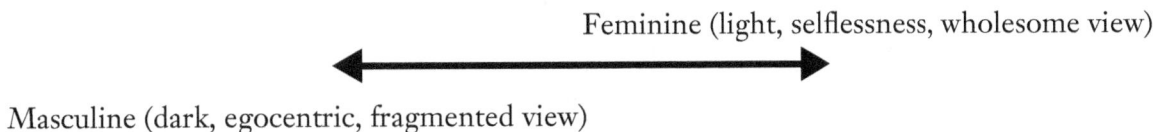

Feminine (light, selflessness, wholesome view)

Masculine (dark, egocentric, fragmented view)

The point of a story is to show, in some sense, that a character can only be fully reconciled when there is a balance of the feminine and the masculine present, thus in the happy ending, 'the prince rises out of the darkness to claim the keys to the kingdom and fulfil the dreams of the princess lover'. In so doing, the prince, while battling a powerful nemesis, also overcomes the dark stranglehold of his ego and accepts a more balanced view, which is provided by the princess lover. In this sense, the only way a Hero can really develop is by fully realising his masculinity in a positive way in perfect balance with his inner feminine. The same (but opposite) view applies to the heroine, in which she must fully develop her femininity in a positive way in perfect balance with her inner masculinity. This is the realisation of *transformation* we discussed in the first chapter in our definition of story. It is the goal of the story.

Masculine characteristics are those of *strength* and *order*, while *feelings* and *understanding* are Feminine values. (Naturally enough, these are better viewed as lines representing degrees rather than fixed values.) Part of your character design can take into account to what degree a character exhibits each of these attributes, and to what degree those attributes will change in the story's transformation.

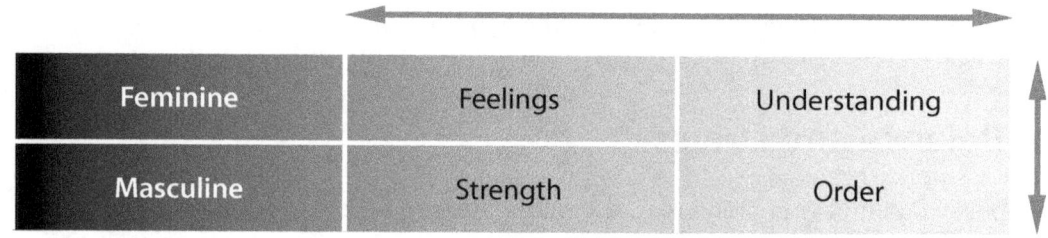

For example, we may want to tell a story where our premise is, *great love defies even death*. Our main character begins the story with hardened feelings from previous experience. His attitude maintains a rigid order about his life, unforgiving, unrelenting and resisting anyone getting too close to him. He is egocentric; he puts his overabundance of strength and order attributes to use to protect his ego, not to serve others. His view of life is fixed into fragments created by prior experience and limited imagination.

He meets someone who challenges his fixed beliefs. She is free and flirtatious. She plies him with tenderness and sympathy after he's been involved in a dangerous battle, tending his wounds. They are opposites, and are attracted to each other, but they quickly discover that their circumstances prevent them from being together.

As they grow it becomes clear to us — although not necessarily to him (these are lessons he has to learn the hard way) — that in order for him to love again he has to grow in feelings and understanding and reduce his hardness of attitude and heart. She has to grow in strength so she can weather the storms ahead. His completeness arrives when he is so full of understanding at her death, and wracked by the terrible feelings of loss, that the only thing left is for him to take his own life so that they can be together forever.

He is complete and therefore resolved, but their great love lives on in myth and legend.

A story becomes 'realised' when the reader experiences the *inner* transformation of the main character who has spent most of the story repressed by a combination of an overshadowing dark force and an inherent egotism that disables action in the way that would satisfy the moral argument. Therefore, in the character's timeline at the point the story begins, the character needs to be shown as having some characteristic that manifests itself as a psychological flaw, an egocentric weakness. It is worth spending time generating (or uncovering) believable wounds that are likely to generate such a flaw. The flipside of the psychological flaw is a need for the character to correct this defect. The reader will see it, but the character will not — not until it has been fully tested.

> **Your main character needs to have been deeply wounded in some way in the past. The wound should be severe enough to cause a psychological flaw to manifest itself in the present. This wound can be physical or sociological, but something severe enough to create a deep and lasting psychological effect. When the wound generates the flaw, the behaviour becomes more believable.**

Actions and Decisions

Another aspect of the external and internal nature of the character lies in the distinction between *actions* and *decisions*. As Egri points out, a character must grow from pole to pole, shaped and conditioned by the conflicts they encounter. You engage a main character to prove a point about a given human condition, and that character can only prove the point as a consequence of the transformation that takes place. Every step along the way consists of an external *action* and an internal *decision*. These are immutably tied to one another: your character will act because of a decision, and will make a decision because of an action. Actions and decisions are in constant flux and directed to certain outcomes, depending on the role of the character. Moreover, actions and decisions are tied to four dynamic elements that create the *story presence* of the character.

Story Presence

Observe a character walking into a scene for the first time. Unconsciously, you are prompted to ask, 'Why? — Why is that character in the scene?'

Hard on its heels, a second question emerges: 'What is this character seeking? — What are they looking for?'

These two questions make two opposing poles of the four dimensions that determine presence. The first, questions the character's *Motivation* — Why are they here? In other words, what background has driven that character to be there?

The second questions the character's *Purpose* — What is their desire? What do they want?

Taken together these two elements are the bookends of presence: *Why are you here? What do you want?* Each of these elements has an *action* (external) and an *decision* (internal) value. Your main character will be here *to pursue* the goal, and *realise* its existence — make it happen. These actions will give rise to — or be derived from — decisions characterised by urging *consideration* from others to pursue the same goal in the *knowledge* that its value exists. In other words, *the knowledge of the goal as something that could happen* is the complete image of that character's purpose in the story, who is motivated by *consideration of its pursuit*.

But two dimensions don't deliver a full picture to the reader's story mind. We need to add to those first two questions a question of the *Method*, and of *Evaluation*:

- How will they go about it?
- How do they measure progress?

Staying with your Protagonist — who is motivated to *pursue* the goal because someone has put it to them to *consider* its worth — your character's method will be to *stimulate* the pursuit (get it going) supported by a decision of *certainty* (either certain it exists, or certain it's attainable, or certain that its attainment will yield the desired effect) and will measure it by the *influence* of the action (what happens to others and the circumstances) through *truth or reality* of progress.

These dimensions give the reader a precise picture of the nature of the character in terms of their presence in the story.

Therefore, our fully rounded character must exhibit a style of *Action* and *Decision*, and be *Motivated to action*, leading through a chosen *Method of acting*, a means of *Measurement* to an ultimate *Purpose*.

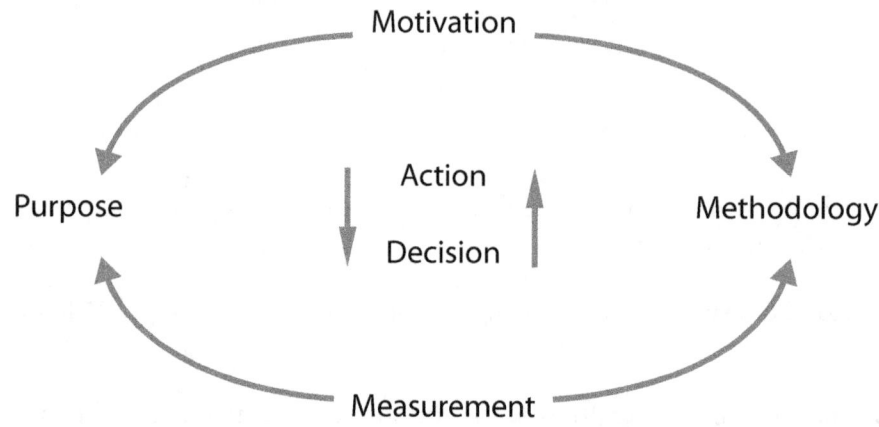

A typical Protagonist's profile

	Action	Decision
Motivation	Pursue the goal or solution to the problem	Encourage consideration of the pursuit
Method	Stimulate the drive to pursue	Hold a degree of certainty about the goal
Evaluation	Determined by the influence on the situation	The truth or reality of the action towards the goal
Purpose	The goal actually happening	Knowing it's benefits and outcome

AN EXAMPLE:

Joe, a young and talented artist, wants to marry Sally, a somewhat conservative and methodical banking executive. In their short relationship, she has proven to be his muse and he suffers when they are not together, even though influential friends, and particularly her family, believe they are incompatible. So he is motivated by a degree of self-preservation and self-awareness, but he knows that having Sally close grounds him in his work and that is a benefit for all who are affected by it. Therefore he takes the attitude that all will benefit from this marriage. He initiates the action by calling her for a lunch date, at which he intends to pop the question. He is certain she feels the same way and is strong enough to resist the naysaying of her family and friends. He believes that when she accepts the ring, it will then be a truth upon which he can plan the rest of his life. Of course Sally's 'yes' is the happening he is banking on and the knowledge will become fact.

But he has to get through the lunch, yet ...

A story can unfold on Joe's profile, but Joe may perhaps be unaware of other events that could upset his purpose.

> *When he loses Sally to another man, Joe's resolve remains steadfast and he continues to stimulate progress towards his goal, remaining certain that it is the right thing. His loss of Sally results in lost commissions, poor gallery sales and poor studio performance, which confirms the truth that without her, he is lost and unless he initiates a drive to recover her love, his influence as an artist is doomed. It is only the actual occurrence of her acceptance of his love that will satisfy his desire; this knowledge to Joe is the truth, the reality.*

Of course we all know that life isn't that simple. But no matter what obstacles we place in front of Joe, he will always respond as a man motivated to consider his 'truth' and take action to pursue what he believes at that time he needs.

Character Change

Characters are not static. They are in a constant state of change. One of the main functions of story is to show the changes taking place to characters. This is the change in a particular 'human condition' that is under examination. These changes come about from environmental influences — the economy changes, a man's health changes, the society changes, technology changes.

A character, therefore, is the sum total of his 'tridimensional' make-up and the influences of the environment in which he or she is placed at that particular time.

EXAMPLE:

> *A young man meets a young woman under the right circumstances and he is drawn to her by their common interests in music and entertainment. Soon enough, the common interest grows into fondness and sympathy, which grows and before long becomes attachment, and then infatuation. They spend more time with each other and the infatuation grows into devotion, then rapture, then adoration … and love. If nothing has upset the harmony of this relationship, they marry and live happily ever after.*
>
> *But suppose that, just as the couple reach the stage of love, a malignant gossiper informs the young man that the girl was previously the girlfriend of a man with whom he has had problems in the past, someone with more power and influence than he, and that she was seen in his company. This new information may make the young man shy away from the girl, in which case the mood will change from attachment to coolness, then to malice and to antipathy. If the girl is defiant and not sorry for her behaviour, antipathy might become bitterness, and bitterness might develop into detestation and hate. (Adapted from Egri.)*

Such a simple love affair is subject to any number of variations. Its course can be altered by money (too much or too little), health or sickness, financial or social status, heredity — in fact any of the 'tridimensional' elements can be part of the environmental influence on the relationship. Environmental influences may be used to correct the path of a character, to force the character back to the right way, or to split them asunder.

Constant change is the essence of existence. The *I Ching*, translated by Richard Wilhelm, teaches us that everything has the tendency to pass into its opposite — an increase must eventually become a decrease, and vice versa. The opposite is contained within. A man has the capacity to love, yet hate the very thing he loves. Friends become enemies; enemies become friends. Heroes turn coward; cowards become heroes. It's often said there is a fine line between a genius and a fool. These contradictions and their innate forces are the things that create change.

A character driven by desire pushes in one direction. An opposite force (another character, environment, attitude …) pushes back in the opposite direction; the result is the character's growth. Because all conflict arises from the character's tridimensional and environmental background, there are inherent contradictions that can cause conflict, and therefore growth.

Character Growth and Finding the Ruling Passion

You must know your characters thoroughly — not only as they are today, but as they were earlier in life, and as they will be tomorrow or years from now. A man who was brave ten years ago may be a coward now, and for any number of reasons — age, physical deterioration, health, financial status etc.

Character is revealed through conflict — the cycle of wins and losses the character experiences in the game of life. This cycle begins with a decision or an action that a character makes, a decision or an action arising directly from the premise of the story. This sets in motion decisions and actions from the opposing force, which leads yet again to another decision, and so forth. These decisions and actions — one resulting from another — propel the story to its ultimate destination, thereby proving the premise. Egri called this development 'pole-to-pole growth' because it shows how a character grows by incremental movement from progress and setbacks towards their resolved state at the end of the story. A character grows through making the correct move as well as the incorrect one — but grow they must, in order to be a real character.

A character grows by shifting attitudes, behaviours, emotions and opinions from one pole to another, often oscillating from a negative to a positive, back towards negative and again towards positive … until a final destination is reached. This growth occurs in small steps. A character will often only tentatively make the change and not fully commit to the change by moving towards change and then retracting to the previous position before attempting change again. It is not possible for a character to change from *hate* to *love* in one step — the character must go through a number of small steps, some forwards, some backwards, even those off to the side, in order to reach the final destination.

Polarity in a story creates tension in the story, movement in the characters and a stirring of emotion in readers. It is essential, because it provides readers with an opportunity to associate with the drama being played out and the turmoil going on within the characters. Characters are often at odds with other characters and the world in which they are playing. This is the function of polarity.

In How to Write a Damn Good Novel, James N Frey talks about characters acting at 'maximum capacity', and the need to know a character's ruling passion: 'the central motivating force … the sum total of all the forces and drives within.' The ruling passion is at the heart of what makes a character tick, it includes and involves inner strength, perseverance, compassion, a win or die attitude, relentless determination to succeed, wilfulness…. For your Hero, life is simply incomplete if these motives are not satisfied. As we discussed in *the crucible*, a Protagonist cannot just give up and cave in, they must see it through to the end. They must strive to live. Or die.

Harry Potter will not stop until he knows the truth about his parents and the threat that Voldemort poses to the world is vanquished. Simba will not rest until he takes his place in the great circle of life. Arial will not give up until she has satisfied her desire for her human prince.

The ruling passions cause a character to face obstacles the author places in their path by their circumstances, other characters and forces that might prevent them from satisfying their motives. Strong characters will do anything — face any hurdle — to overcome the obstacles, acting at 'maximum capacity' at all times. 'Maximum capacity', according to Frey, means characters 'will use any and all means available within their particular capacity to achieve their ends.' They will handle all problems you throw at them cleverly and efficiently, without wasting energy on fumbled speech or action that would lead them into a situation that would paralyse them.

For any situation your character is in, you must know what the possible outcomes are. You cannot give your character powers that allow them to escape a situation if those powers are outside the boundaries of their capacity. If, for example, your heroine has no capacity for magic, then she wouldn't cast a spell. If she can't fly, then you wouldn't have her fly out through the window. If there's no phone, she can't call for emergency services. You need to test your character's maximum capacity by asking, 'Would they really do this?' And then, ask: 'What else could they do that is more ingenious, surprising, or funny?' always keeping within the capacity of the character.

It is maximum capacity performance that enables your character to grow and develop and your reader to buy into your story. It is maximum capacity that tests your character's ability to contest the final outcome, to overcome weaknesses … to recognise weaknesses in the first place.

What this means, of course, is that you must identify your character's *talents*. Talent is something they can do better than anyone else and it arises from *aptitude* and *inclination*. Something in their DNA at birth and in their nurtured environment, and a connection to their naturalness as a child, triggers an association with a practice towards which they become inclined. Initially the talent may be undeveloped. Early in life they will have practiced that which was at first difficult until it becomes easy; then, as they grow, that which is easy becomes simple. What is simple is easy to do.

Aptitude derives from a capacity to do; a capacity from available mental and physical space. Inclination arises when something grows to be of interest. We get interested in something; we find the time and space to practice it, often under the guidance of a gifted teacher or Mentor.

You must also identify your character's weaknesses. A character's weaknesses, especially in the face of their ambitions and the forces of antagonism that impede their progress towards their goal is where much of the drama arises in a story. Find the talent; exploit the weaknesses and you will grow interesting and committed characters.

Chapter Three
Who Else is in the Playground?

A Circuitry of Other Characters

Once you have some understanding of your story, its premise and who the character is at the centre of it, the next step is to populate the story's playground with other characters.

To some extent, your story premise will dictate who the necessary characters in your story are, and you need to test the validity of a character against your premise. If the character has no effect on the premise, or is not affected by the argument of the premise, then that character has no part to play in the story, and you should question any desired presence. On the other hand, if a colourful character suggests itself to you because of circumstances that have developed, or because of a new relationship that adds to the dramatic value of the story, then you must consider that character's role.

Most important of all, any character in your story must have a relationship with the main character. This relationship may be direct or indirect, but unless a character's presence affects the main character, either by their 'gadding' against the circumstances, or by a relationship with the main character, then they have no part to play.

A triangle of story dynamics:

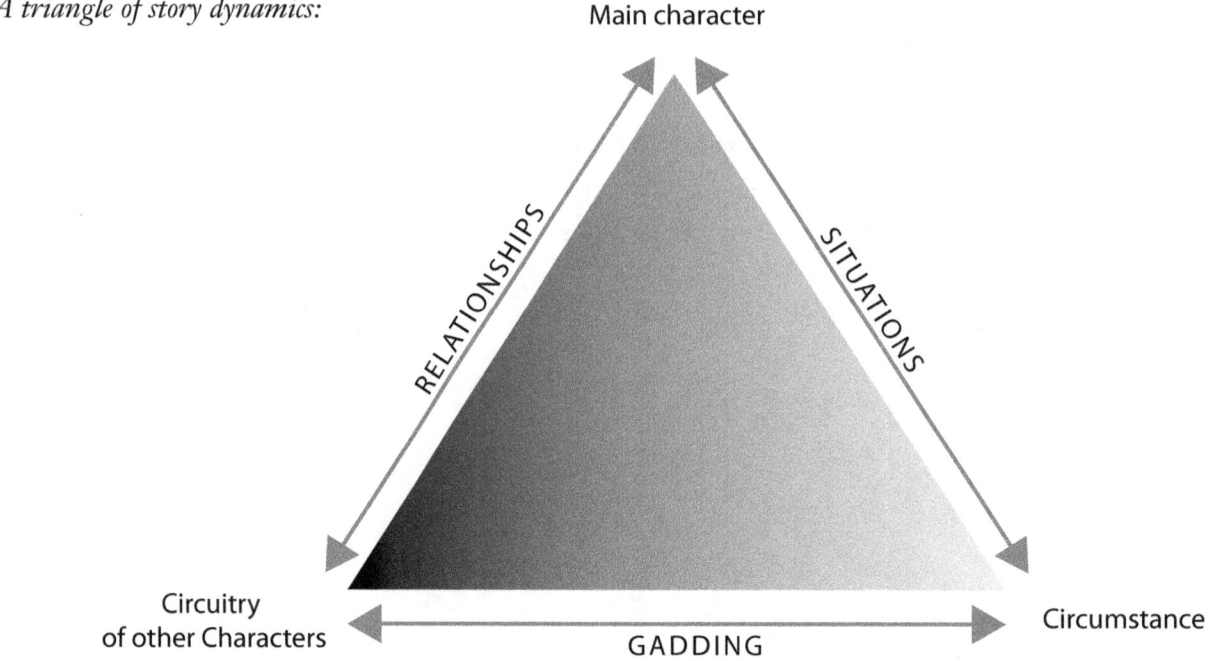

Dynamics Created by Circuitry of Others

A story needs a main character, a circuitry of other characters and the circumstances (the environment) in which they find themselves. These are the dynamic elements — those that change. But what we are actually interested in is what lies between these dynamics.

Every character in the story *must* have a relationship with the main character (even though that relationship at times might be through a third party); every circumstance the main character is involved in *results* in a situation (location or position with reference to the circumstances); every other character has a *gadding* effect (either positive or negative movement) on the circumstances to which the main character is central.

> *Gadding* **is the combined effect of 'goading for a reaction' and 'moving idly in search of experience' within the frame of activity. Thus any character can alter the circumstances by occupying or vacating space, bringing and removing experience, or by goading a reaction for movement from other characters.**

A story moves along as a result of the dynamic system at play; actions are caused by gadding, and circumstances are altered, which in turn gives rise to changing situations, affecting the relationships between the main character and the others.

To orchestrate characters effectively, you need characters who are capable of forming relationships with the main character and each other, which are then tested, broken and reinforced.

Literary theorists have been known to suggest that characters are merely functions within the 'text' but we are going to show that, from the writer's perspective, they are far more than merely functions: they are living breathing hotbeds of emotions with the power to involve a reader in their passions and desires.

The Archetypes

According to Christopher Booker in *The Seven Basic Plots*, Carl Jung, who developed the theories of archetypes, described them as 'the ancient river beds along which our psychic current naturally flows.' Such is the human mind that no storyteller can escape from the archetypes: they are the basic coding of the human psyche, and therefore the building blocks around which stories are told.

We view dramatic action of the reader's story mind through eight archetypal patterns. These patterns function as 'types' and contain groupings of particular attributes of 'character presence' that we looked at in the previous chapter — they are characteristics that can be seen as *masks* or *patterns of behaviour*.

All characters are at the same time individuals and types: some designed to drive the story, others to influence those who drive. It is in the dynamic relationships between them that the fireworks happen, and knowing where differences lie is not only knowing characters, but knowing people. Once you understand and map the interactions between the core character archetypes, your story will begin to take on form.

The Archetypal Pattern of the Main Character

The reader seeks a resolved situation. At the beginning of a story, the reader senses that the world is out of kilter in some way. They want to know what happens to fix this situation. The conclusion may not resolve all of the moral issues — it might only narrow its focus on a single issue within the moral argument. The character under the microscope is the *main character*, otherwise known as the *Protagonist* or *Hero*, and they are either being tested for moral rigour, are testing the morals of another character, or the circumstances in which they find themselves.

1. We are usually introduced to the Hero in an initial phase showing us that they feel, in some way, constricted. This sets up a tension the reader expects to be resolved and leads directly into the action of the story. This phase is often outside the main events of the story, used specifically to illustrate aspects of the character's nature that will be tested or required in the contest of the crisis to come.

2. This is followed by a phase which Christopher Booker in *The Seven Basic Plots* calls, 'opening out'. The Hero senses that they are on the road to some new state or some far-off point of resolution. The reader is subsequently drawn into the world of the story, lulled into some sense of anticipation; a threat is looming although it is still some way off, perhaps not fully formed, its presence is felt and its importance increasingly evident.

3. The Hero then enters into a more severe phase of constriction where both the strength of the Villain's dark power and the Hero's weakness become more obvious. The reader grows more anxious towards the outcome, and questions the actions and decisions of the Hero against the morality of the circumstances. The Hero comes up against powers well beyond their capacity, forcing them to turn back on themselves.

4. This leads to a phase where, although the Villain's dark hold is still dominant, the Hero is preparing for a final confrontation and their talents come to the fore. This eventually works up to the nightmare crisis/climax, when opposition between light and dark is at its most extreme and the pressure on everyone involved is at its greatest.

5. Finally, it culminates in the moment of reversal and liberation, when the Villain's grip of darkness is fully broken and the story ends on the sense of a final opening out into life anew, with everything at last resolved. The Hero claims the prize.

Eight Core Archetypes

The following discussion provides a sound foundation for developing a cast of characters for your story.

These 'core archetypes' are inspired by a story model suggested by Christopher Huntley and Melanie Anne Philips in *Dramatica, A new theory of story*; four are the characters whose decisions and actions *drive* the story — those who are actively involved in the core conflict of the story and working for the 'goal' of the story or against it. The second group of four are supporters or influencers of the first four, their actions and decisions do not drive the story; rather they react to the decisions and actions of the driver characters and interact to influence them. They are the *passengers*.

Definitions

Drivers — **those characters whose interactions determine the thrust of the story's effort to solve the problem.**

1. *Protagonist* —the principal driver of the story; the one who is faced with a problem to solve; the one whom the story is about; the one seeking the goal and who takes the lead in the cause. Usually 'light' in nature, but with serious defects in character that are subject to transformation, often the result of some deep wound which itself is resistant to transformation or repair; courageous, clever, resourceful with a special talent that emerges due to the pressures of the story; lives by own rules, idealistic, loyal, stoical, cynical, frequently arrogant; born of a special birth and headed for a special destiny and 'marked' in some way.

2. *Antagonist* — opposes and undermines the Protagonist's pursuit and attainment of their goal; the one who loses if the Protagonist is successful in solving the problem. 'Dark' in nature, highly egocentric, narcissistic and cruel, driven by a belief in their own infallibility and self-serving desires; motivated by greed, lust, ego, vanity; unforgiving and self-righteous. Completely lacking in empathy and ideology.

3. *Guardian or Mentor* — functions as a teacher or sage representing the conscience and moral perspective of the Protagonist's pursuit of the story's goal. A 'light' protective character, often in the form of a wise old man, young unavailable woman or anima; eliminates obstacles and illuminates the path ahead; appearing at critical moments to offer advice; intervening when things are going wrong. Their chief concern is that the goal of the Protagonist is reached. Also a crucial 'impact' character who stands in the way of the Protagonist, usually to redirect the Protagonist in a different direction, as well as holder of magic tricks, knowledge and special tools. The Guardian character is often 'sacrificed' to make way for the Protagonist to grow and take responsibility for their own success.

4. *Contagonist or Threshold Guardian* — functions in opposition to the Guardian, placing obstacles to hinder the Protagonist's pursuit of the story's goal, and particularly deflect them from it. A 'Dark' figure, often in the form of an unrelenting parent or carer, thus the person 'guarding the threshold' which the Protagonist must cross in order to move forward. This character often appears as a Trickster or Tempter, representing temptation, aiming to draw the Protagonist away from their goal. Sometimes this character appears in the form of the Antagonist's ego, acting as a henchman, using power in a treacHerous manner and blinding the Protagonist, restricting conscience.

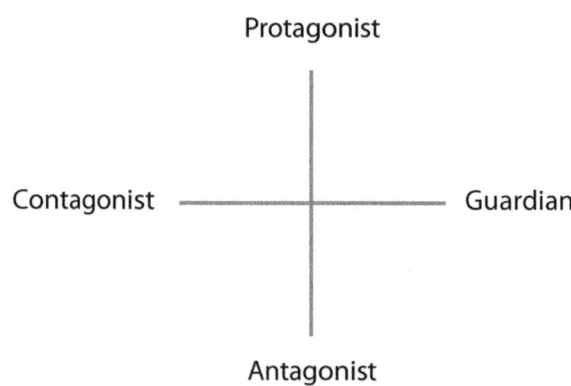

Passengers — **those characters whose interactions influence the outcomes and behaviour of the Driver characters**

5. *Sidekick* – one of the most important and influential characters in the cast, a Sidekick is a faithful supporter of whatever goal the main character is pursuing. Sidekicks are unquestioningly loyal and serve the purpose of revealing the true character of the Protagonist by providing the audience view of the special world. Often seen as the only character who can question the Protagonist's motives at the most personal level and get away with it, the Sidekick is the closest of all characters to the Protagonist. Quite often it is the Sidekick who provides the required level of 'feelings and understanding' to the Protagonist's 'strength and order' (or vice versa) throughout the course of the narrative up until the moment of transformation and the Hero acquires them himself, or through the consummation of the interest in the 'lover' character, at which point the Sidekick bows out gracefully.

6. *Sceptic* — playing directly opposite the Sidekick and to balance that character's total confidence in the Protagonist, the Sceptic represents doubt in the Protagonist's ability to achieve the goal. The Sceptic raises the voice of the indicators that portend failure, often dramatising the potential of failure through conflicting interactions with the Sidekick and complementary interactions with either the Antagonist or the Contagonist.

7. *Reason* — occupied with rational explanations and logic, the Reason character is calm, collected, aloof, cold, argumentative and intellectual. The Reason character often lacks 'empathy' and is used to point out logical flaws to the proposed solution, making grandiose plans that often fail because the personal concerns of others have not been taken into account. The Reason character exhibits the most 'masculine' characteristics of strength and order and is resistant to change, except under highly rational explanation.

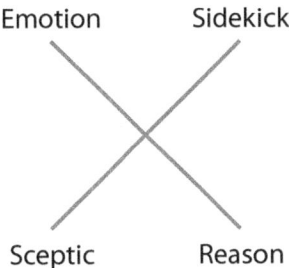

8. *Emotion* — in the same way that the Antagonist opposes the Protagonist, so does the Emotion character oppose the Reason character. The Emotion character is quick to anger, and quick to empathise; is frenetic and disorganised and passionately pursues its goals. Often it finds that its advancement is frustrated due to wasted energy from thoughtless pursuit of unfulfilling enterprises. If there is a 'love interest' in the story and it is not a classic romance structure, it is usually to be found in the Emotion character. The Emotion character is the ultimate Feminine character with abundant feelings and understanding, and is often misdirected or coveted by the Contagonist character in that character's objective of deflecting the Protagonist from their goal.

The archetypes provide a basic map of characters at play in a story. It is important to remember that the archetypes represent 'masks' that players wear. Some stories do not have all eight archetypes, some stories have a character wearing more than one archetypal mask at different times through the story. Even a story in which there is only a single character, that single character can at times be seen to wear the mask of a different archetypal character.

When we combine all eight archetypes in the story into their oppositions, we can see at a glance the relationships between them. This is helpful in developing the way your characters interact. It is also helpful in developing the 'type' of character you may need in order to produce the required response in the Protagonist.

For example, your Protagonist may have struck a particularly difficult moment in the story, a moment where you need another character to redirect the Protagonist and steer them in the right direction. You have a choice of two characters who can do this: the Guardian character, who can reach into a bag of magic tricks and produce the right tools, education or magic to change the Protagonist's path, or you can use a Contagonist character who acts as a Threshold Guardian, momentarily deflecting the Protagonist from the goal. You can have the Guardian and Contagonist characters enter into a direct confrontation, the outcome of which will change the Protagonist's direction.

Knowing how the archetypes function is an important way to create dynamic and interesting characters. Quite often archetypes can 'borrow' from other masks, even appear as their opposites at times, which helps create super-complexity in your characters. The critical thing about using this type of technique is to make sure that only one version of that mask is in the action at a time. Many stories have two Sidekick characters, for example, (Harry Potter, The Lion King) … when both are present, it's helpful to have one take a different mask momentarily.

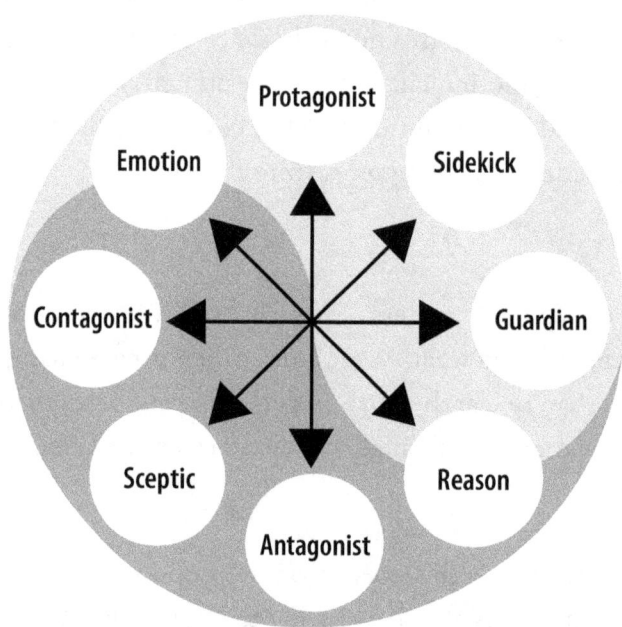

Masculine/Feminine Light/Dark Principles

The progress of a story usually marks out the journey of one character. In the beginning, we are shown the main character in some situation or conflict that demonstrates a weakness or flaw in the character. In order to be a 'whole' person, a character (a Hero in particular) requires a balance of four characteristics: Strength, Order, Feelings, and Understanding. Strength and order are considered 'masculine' characteristics; feelings and understanding, 'feminine'.

> A complete happy ending depends on reconciliation between masculine and feminine principles. The principal characters in the story wend their way toward some ultimate goal that makes them complete; makes them whole because they have found the things they have been searching for. But in the end, the resolution of the Hero affects far more than that one character. It affects others in the realm too.
>
> If a Hero is to bring balance to their own character, they must also bring balance to the world around them. This may be a 'light' Hero who spends most of the story under the shadow of a dark power and learns through the story what 'psychological need' is required to bring balance; or a 'dark' Hero who finds redemption in the light giving forces of others.
>
> In the end, the story finds a balance of the masculine and feminine, and the Hero is transformed by bringing those missing elements, which manifest as a 'psychological need', into their character and world. The complete happy ending is achieved when the shadow of the dark power has been thrown off, things that have remained hidden have been exposed, a just authority has been re-established over the new world of the everyday, and harmony and love prevail over the land.

If a Hero has been struggling against a dark power to save a Heroine or claim the 'treasure', the Hero must be shown to be fully masculine. In the beginning he may be inflexible and egocentric, or weak and ineffectual. But as the story unfolds and the constrictions of the dark power tighten, he will be forced to open up in ways that connect him positively with others, with all that is beyond him, with the flow of life. In the mythic story, this is usually forced upon the Hero by the Guardian or Mentor character who stands as an obstacle in the path of the Hero. Eventually, the Hero will take on both masculine and feminine qualities, thus bringing the story to a wholesome close.

The balance of masculine and feminine also represents the balance of light and dark, hard and soft, the positive and negative, upper and lower, inner and outer — all of which can be used in the identification of character roles within the story mind.

In most stories the wholeness of the ending is centred on the union of the Hero with the Heroine, or the masculine with the feminine. The action of the story is eventually reduced to what may be seen to be a three-way struggle: the battle between the light force of the Hero and the dark force that has come between him and the Heroine. Sometimes the malevolent dark force is within the Hero himself, sometimes within the Heroine. But, regardless of how it is viewed, the dark power that stands between the union has to be overcome, and all that matters is whether the right balance of qualities can be brought to bear to achieve the goal.

From whichever perspective we view the story, the essence of what is happening remains the same. The reader sees a world polarised between an upper 'dark' realm in which, for most of the story, the dark power holds sway with its egocentricity, heartlessness and blindness — and an inferior 'light' realm containing the potential for balance and wholeness. Eventually the scales tip and the centre of light in the story emerges from the shadows, ends the division and brings everything into perfect balance and harmony.

Extending the Archetypes

Each archetypal character we have discussed so far serves the story by way of their *dramatic function* — what they do and how they relate to each other and the reader. We often find that the Protagonist and the Antagonist borrow some of their values from the other characters, which is what makes for truly complex characters. There are additional archetypes that help extend the functions of our core archetypal characters.

The Hero

The Hero is generally accepted as another name for the Protagonist. But in some unique situations the two may be separated — in a similar way a bipolar personality works. The Hero represents the search for identity and wholeness. The Hero's decisions take them towards a balanced male/female character. The Hero is the central action figure and all actions are focussed on pursuing the objective. The Hero should perform *all of the decisive* action of the story — especially at the critical moments. Part of the story's resolution is the Hero's self-discovery of identity; therefore all decisions are focussed on self-discovery.

The Shadow (or Nemesis)

The Shadow is an extension of the Antagonist, represented by the dark side. Whether it's an inner dark side, someone simply led astray or an enemy hell-bent on death and destruction, the Shadow does not agree with the direction taken by the Hero, and will work to gain sympathy for their point of view. As the drama deepens, and the Hero's ambition gains momentum, the Shadow will keep pace, and give the reader a reason to doubt the Hero's purpose, and/or ability to reach the goal.

The Shadow's main function is to challenge the Hero and provide a worthy adversary in the struggle, creating conflict and revealing the true nature of the Hero's character by putting them in life threatening situations.

A Shadow character need not be pure evil. It is often far more effective if they are shown to be human, with some admirable qualities. In a similar way to a Hero character, they need to be vulnerable, with character flaws. Defeating a Shadow character should raise a moral question in the reader, as Shadow figures do not consider themselves to be Villains. Rather, a Villain is likely to be the Hero of their own myth, and their enemy is the reader's Hero.

Shadow characters can come as external forces, or as an inner force within a Hero's own personality. How the story deals with different kinds of Shadow often has to do with the type of story that is being told. A Shadow can be anything that has been suppressed, neglected or forgotten within a personality. While anger can be a positive and healthy force, for example, repressed anger can be dangerous. A Shadow is motivated by a purpose that is opposite to that of the Hero's.

The Mentor

The Mentor character is an extension of the Guardian and is usually embodied in a wise old man, wise old woman or some anima form (Aslan for example), which may also be an animorphical character, or a young (but sexually unattainable) woman. The function of the Mentor is to teach and give gifts. The Mentor's decisions are based on 'seeking the right road' and are often given as images of what the Hero may become if they follow the path; they can be parental in nature. As such, the Mentor (as Guardian) is a classic *Obstacle* character in the action of the story: standing in the way of the Hero in order to force them to take a different path.

The Mentor has two fundamental actions that are designed to assist the Hero: Teaching (and reciprocal learning from the student), and Gift-giving in the form of a magical weapon, key, important clue, nourishment, medicine or life-saving advice. However, the gift should not come automatically — it is something earned through sacrifice, achievement, learning or commitment. In teaching, it is important that the Mentor does not seek out the student, but that the student seeks out the Mentor.

Special Mentor Functions:

Sometimes the Hero is a reluctant participant in the adventure and needs an extra push to get involved, such a push often comes from the Mentor. The Mentor may also show the Hero something to motivate them into action, overcome fear, and thereby commit to the adventure.

The Mentor is also frequently used to 'plant' information, ideas or devices that will become useful later in the story. This 'planting' is often delivered early in the story and immediately overshadowed by action causing the reader to forget it. Then, later in the story, that information or device becomes central to the action.

Threshold Guardian

An extension to the Contagonist, the Threshold Guardian guards certain paths the Hero may want to travel with the purpose of distracting the Hero from his real purpose. Such characters stand guard to the entry to special places and the mythological woods, preventing the unworthy entering.

Threshold Guardians represent the Hero's inner demons — neuroses, emotional scars, dependencies and self-limitations that curtail development. In order for a Hero to survive their quest and overcome the Shadow, they must overcome or deal with Threshold Guardians on the way; these are the tests that let the reader know the Hero is making progress. They test the Hero's resolve that they are determined to accept the challenge and see it all the way through.

Testing the Hero is the primary dramatic function of the Threshold Guardian. Heroes can deal with these apparent obstacles in a number of ways. They can turn and run; attack head on; use craft, deceit or lie; bribe or turn the obstacle character into an Ally. In this way, the Threshold Guardian acts as an obstacle to change. Whenever the Hero moves towards change, they often come up against a character resisting that change. This will be mainly because the character benefits from the status quo, and any change may threaten them.

Threshold Guardians also provide signals to the Hero that things are changing. Attacks from Threshold Guardians force the Hero to take a new direction, which may ultimately help them in their fight against the Antagonist. Heroes can learn from Threshold Guardians in similar ways they learn from Mentors — although usually in adversity rather than as student-teacher. In such a situation a Threshold Guardian can become a *pseudo-ally* as a Hero recognises resistance as a source of strength.

The Ally

Allies can be seen as an extension of the *Sidekick* or as additional, *pseudo*-sidekicks. The Hero usually needs someone to stand by them, stand up for them and stand with them against greater adversaries. As such, Allies can serve a variety of functions for the Hero, including: companion, sparring partner, conscience (although this is frequently the function of the Guardian character), comic relief, messenger, scout or driver.

Allies perform many mundane tasks, but their main function is to bring out the humanness of the Hero character, adding extra dimension and challenging them to be more open. Both Mentor and Threshold Guardian characters can act as Allies from time to time; and Allies can assume the masks of other archetypes from time to time. (See the discussion on archetypes as masks, below.)

In Many Hero's Journey stories, the Ally character is responsible for introducing the reader to the special world (or mythological woods) — a Threshold Guardian may stand as an obstacle to its entrance, and a Mentor may kick the Hero into it, but it is frequently the Ally who provides the reader's view of the special world.

Allies can take on different forms, such as guardian angels, imaginary friends, animals, spirits, robots and helpful servants. Allies can also represent powerful internal character forces that can come to the Hero's aid in a spiritual crisis, and can be used to suggest alternate paths for solving problems and provide personality extension for the Hero, allowing expression of fear, humour, or ignorance that may not be appropriate for the Hero.

The Trickster

In our core archetypes, the role of Trickster is frequently given to the Contagonist. However, the Trickster is an archetype that can also be used to extend the Sceptic character, and the mask of the Trickster may sometimes be worn by an Antagonist or a Guardian.

Tricksters bring Heroes and audiences down to earth by provoking the Hero and their chosen direction. A Trickster character has little faith in the Hero, pointing out folly and hypocrisy in the Hero's actions. This action is a powerful catalyst for change because it can draw attention to a situation that isn't going anywhere, especially where characters are taking themselves too seriously. Tricksters are often needed to inject a little humour into the situation so the reader can see where the Hero is making mistakes. This allows the reader to hope the Hero corrects their ways, knowing the consequences of what might happen if they do not.

We can often see the Trickster changing sides — they may be servants or Allies working for either the Hero or the Shadow and may be attracted by one side or the other, primarily by the *rejection* of what they see as the status quo. Tricksters will employ many forms of trickery in order to draw attention to the weakness of a situation; they are adept at deceit and sarcasm, exceptionally cunning and resourceful. Their main function is to undermine the status quo of any situation.

The Herald

Herald characters issue challenges and announce the coming of significant change. They can be seen as an extension of the Reason character (sometimes interchanged with the Emotion character), acting as keepers of records, responsible for planning and providing the reader with identification of other characters in their roles.

Most stories begin with a Hero in some sort of repressed state, but one in which they have managed to 'get by' one way or another. Then, all of a sudden, a new energy enters the situation, one which makes it impossible for the Hero to continue as they were. The new energy is that of the Herald.

The Herald announces the *need* for change in the status quo, drawing the reader's attention to why it is needed. While often a person, it may also be some force such as an earth tremor, meteor or hurricane. Sometimes it's internal, like a voice, a feeling or a sickness. Sometimes the Herald is simply a method of getting the news of impending change to the Hero, something that alerts them to the need to take action.

While it is usually embodied within a Reason type character, it could be a temporary mask worn by any of the other characters and of either a positive or negative force in respect of the Hero's position.

The Shapeshifter

Heroes often encounter a Shapeshifter in the form of the opposite sex, which can be seen as an extension of the Emotion character. In stories where there is a love interest (but not classically a romance), the Emotion character is usually the primary focus of this interest, and in the turbulent development of a love affair with this character will change from one form to another, often in violent and dramatic turns from the Hero's point of view.

Shapeshifters change appearance or mood, usually at pivotal moments in the story, and are difficult for the Hero to pin down. The Shapeshifter serves to provide the necessary balance in allowing the Hero to become 'whole' but can also frequently throw things completely out of whack by being too much too quickly. Sometimes this character functions as a teacher or a member of a family who is close to the Hero but 'unavailable' in terms of close relationships.

The Shapeshifter character can often appear when the Hero has an internal vision of the qualities of their 'perfect match', and then projecting those qualities on the person they see as the best fit. But in reality that person does not have those qualities, and the difference may appear to the Hero as a Shapeshifter. Like the Herald, the Shapeshifter can be a catalyst for Heroic change, and force the Hero to rethink their position, and thereby move closer to becoming whole.

The Shapeshifter often couples with the Trickster and introduces doubt and suspense into the story. The Trickster may draw attention to the *possibility* of doubt, but the doubt will usually be aimed at a Shapeshifter character. This enables suspense to be brought into the story, in a 'will she/won't she?' manner. Betrayal is the tool of the Shapeshifter, and is often used as a means of getting the Hero to act in the way they need to. The Shapeshifter is also often at the mercy of the Shadow character — sometimes they are one and the same (Jekyll and Hyde), at other times, the Shapeshifter character is the means through which the Shadow character reaches the Hero and puts them under pressure.

Archetypes as Masks

Complex characters are made up of different aspects of multiple characteristics. Building complex characters means you can use different functions of the different archetypes with different characters as your story requires them. A character may enter a story as Herald and develop into a Trickster character, and finally resolve as the Contagonist. The archetypes can serve as particular aspects that characters don, like a mask, in order to provide a story function at a particular moment. The important thing is to maintain contrast and tension, and ensure that the use of archetypes always serves the story and the growth of its main characters, not the other way round.

At the centre of these archetypes is the fact that they are always relative to the Hero — everyone has a relationship of either opposition or alliance or both with the Hero. This relationship can change in the course of the story, in many cases it is such a relationship that is the actual change that produces the story (how a romance works, for example). Using archetypes is a particularly helpful way to maintain conflict through the story (and therefore reader interest) and you should experiment with fitting archetypal masks to different characters at different times.

There is only one real caveat to bear in mind and it's in relation to staging a particular piece of business or scene. It can be confusing to the reader to try too many 'masks' at once, or have a character wear multiple masks at the same time. Be sure to have only one 'type' functioning in that particular mask at a time. Even when Weasley and Grainger are together in a scene with Potter, one of them maintains the Sidekick function while the other dons a different type of mask, or remains a more distant ally. If they were to complete for the Sidekick mask at the same moment, the reader would end up confused. This was given voice when in *Shrek 2*, Donkey, in no uncertain terms, ejected Puss-In-Boots from the Sidekick position. As it turned out, Puss, after starting in a Contagonist function, ended up the Guardian character, an interesting and highly plausible change of sides and moral values.

Circuitry and Orchestration

A great deal of advice on characters implores us, as writers, to ensure that our characters are 'fully realised' and 'well rounded', but there is an importance in 'flat' characters that should not be understated, and how that plays into the power that is derived from a unity of opposites and their struggles in pole-to-pole growth. All characters strive to fulfil their destinies and become 'whole' as Homo Fictus derived people, driven and limited by their relationships with others and the circumstances in which they find themselves, but there are certain genres in which 'flat' characters often remain the spectators who provide the catalyst for change and growth. Developing your circuitry of characters begins with positioning characters to work for the story.

What the discussion on archetypes above shows, is that every character has a specific role or function that serves the purpose of the story.

Key points

1. The Protagonist is the most important character and all other characters represent an opposition, an alliance or some combination of the two, perhaps in alternation. (See-saw). Even a love interest character (Emotion character) will be in opposition to the Protagonist, their coming together must result from breaking down a barrier that is keeping them apart. It's important to keep in mind that a love interest may not be the main concern of the story, but a subplot acting to show the main character's position within the circumstances.

2. The Protagonist creates all other characters. There are two complexities of character: bit parts and full characters. Bit parts are intentionally flat; they are usually single-function characters in the story only to carry out a specific action, walking on and off only when they are called, usually in response to circumstances or reacting to the gadding of other characters. Full characters on the other hand are drivers of the actions and decisions of the story, overshadowing and undermining the Protagonist at each call; they have deep level relationships with the Protagonist and other players.

3. Good orchestration depends entirely on being in conflict at different levels. This means creating the means of conflict at physical, social, psychological levels, as well as within the spheres of motivation, methodology, judgement and purpose. Actions and decisions taken by characters (gadding) throughout the story will serve to affect the relationships at these levels because they will change the situations.

4. Make the choice of archetype specific and individual to the character as demanded by the circumstances of the story. This means making the connections between characters specific to who they are and where they are. For example, a Mentor's powers need to be unique and specific to the circumstances of the story, and limited by specific weaknesses of the character. Be germane.

5. Allow archetypal characters to wear other archetypal masks from time to time. This increases their level of complexity and provides the story mind with a way of viewing alternate storylines using interesting character dynamics such as inner conflicts. Be careful not to have 'twins on stage' though, a Guardian temporarily wearing a Contagonist mask should not appear on stage together with the Contagonist … make sure the imposter has left the stage before bringing the real character back.

6. The Sidekick is one of the most important characters because they illustrate the role and importance of the Protagonist. A Sidekick is fully a passenger character, having no part in making decisions or driving the action of the story, but that doesn't mean a Sidekick does not play as an obstacle character from time to time.

7. Characters need to have attraction between them, even between Protagonist and Antagonist, there is often some common element that brings them together (they often want the same thing); but there must be conflict that threatens to pull them apart. In many attributes they are opposites — the short and tall — the oppositions creating conflicts and strengthening them; and those oppositions highlight the potential in one character to transform the other through their actions and decisions.

8. Every character has a view towards, and a relationship with the moral problem identified in your premise. This means they have a way of acting according to their position in opposition to the views and relationships of other characters.

Chapter 4
The Playground

Creating a Setting

In Chapter One, we established a working definition for story:

> **A story is the realisation that something fundamental has changed when we are told of what happens to a worthy human character when they do something to get what they want. It is made up of consequential episodes narrated in details that are designed to entertain because they promise an experience of pleasure.**

This suggests that we are mostly interested in what happens to at least one character worth taking notice of, and observing the change that takes place in that character as a consequence of the episodes laid out in the narrative. In other words, our focus is on characters — who they are, what happens to them, why, when and how.

But an equally important aspect is *where* — we are talking about the location of the story, in the sense of both place and time. So our above definition needs to be bracketed by its setting. The storyteller's job, therefore, is to do more than imagine the narrative of consequential episodes as described above, it is also to:

> **Imagine a complete and credible world and inhabit it with passionate characters who contest the conclusion of a central conflict, reaching a point in which the outcome tilts in favour of one against the other and all small matters resolve to make it worthwhile.**

Does this alter our definition of a story? No. It adds a required depth to it.

Let's look at a few examples:

Harry Potter's stories show the growth of a young pre-teenage boy into adulthood through a series of events in which obstacles are placed before him that cause him to alter his behaviour and outlook on life as he battles to discover the truth about his parents. As the stories progress, and as he grows, the obstacles become seemingly more difficult to overcome, the truth more mired, and Harry becomes increasingly aggressive in dealing with his nemesis until there is a final showdown, and the outcome tilts in his favour.

The story takes place in two major settings — or story worlds: the world of the wizards and the world of the muggles; and Harry is by necessity required to pass between these two worlds. The obstacles he faces in the muggle world are initially of the very ordinary human kind, but as things develop, this world is encroached upon by increasingly dangerous events originating in the wizard world.

Within each of these worlds, the story is set in quite particular environments. In the beginning we are made familiar with the fairly ordinary London suburb in which Privet Drive and the Dursley's home is located. It is repeatedly pointed out in the opening pages that Privet Drive is not a place where unusual things are expected to happen. The Dursley's house is reported as being somewhat nondescript …

> *'… but Privet Drive had hardly changed at all. The sun rose on the same tidy front gardens and lit up the brass number four on the Dursley's front door; it crept into their living room, which was almost exactly the same as it had been on the night that Mr Dursley had seen that fateful news report about the owls. Only the photographs on the mantelpiece really showed how much time had passed.'*
> (J.K. Rowling.)

The main setting for the Harry Potter stories, however, is Hogwarts: a school with features that parallel any fairly ordinary but old English boarding school. But the reality of the environment ends at its apparent physical similarity. The environment is uniquely set out to accommodate the magical world of Harry Potter's schooldays as a wizard-in-training. The familiarity of a school environment enables readers to push aside any disbelief about the place and its magic.

Harry's first sighting of Hogwarts occurs after using a magical portal at the train station, which he has to master in order to pass into the wizard world, and a journey by train during which he is introduced to the characters who will become his lifelong companions, eventually arriving at a small dark platform where they disembarked.

> *'The narrow path had opened suddenly on to the edge of a great black lake. Perched atop a high mountain on the other side, its windows sparkling in the starry sky, was a vast castle with many turrets and towers.'*

Although our first sightings of the settings of Harry Potter's stories are visual, the impacts are far more than simply a coloured backdrop against which the action of the story takes place. They very quickly become part of the action of the story. The forces of the two worlds impact upon the characters, providing a necessary crucible that helps bond them together.

No attempt is made to provide an overall description; rather particular details are used to create moods that affect emotions both for characters and readers. The settings provide obstacles that must be overcome; they influence the character's behaviour and provide useful framing for portraying a character's attitudes about the world around them.

As readers, we know that Harry Potter's worlds don't actually exist, but because we are given enough clues that enable us to identify with the behaviour and attitudes of the characters who inhabit those worlds, we go there quite willingly. What's more, we willingly suspend disbelief about the world as it is portrayed just so that we can find out what happens to the characters. In other words, the fundamental change that takes place in a story is wholly dependent upon its setting for credibility.

The complete and credible world required to carry a story provides the physical and cultural landscape, the environment and atmosphere that a reader needs in order to accept the premise being offered by the characters and the conflict that lies before them. Imagine for a moment how the Harry Potter stories would work if the wizard world was set in a modern city landscape among skyscrapers; if the school was more like 'Sky High'? Or 'East High' from High School Musical? Which characters would no longer be able to inhabit the world? How would the main characters have to change in appearance, language, belief and behaviour in order for the narrative to work? What in its series of consequential episodes would have to be eliminated? What new events would have to replace them?

A setting takes part in the story in the same way a character does. It can be considered another character, exhibiting similar traits to Homo Fictus. Settings can change over time, they can grow old and decay; they can be renewed or replaced. They can act benignly or take on more sinister roles. The setting is an integral part of the character's actions, where the clever author causes drama through the careful selection and omission of details. Using a particular character's point of view can enhance the drama of a setting. The Kings Park lookout, for instance, will have a different meaning for a young lover than for a man focussed on murder.

Margaret Lucke in *Schaum's Quick Guide to Writing Great Short Stories*, (1999) says:

> The story world can be modelled on a real place or it can be wholly imagined. It can be restrictive or expansive, small or large; a room, a building, a neighbourhood, a city, a region, a planet. Settings are frequently layered, with smaller ones contained within larger ones — we are in this room in this house in this neighbourhood in this region, like a set of wooden dolls that nest one inside the other. Each layer contributes to the richness of the fictional environment.

A story takes place in the setting it's given because it can't happen anyplace else. When description is called for, try to weave it into the character of the story itself eliciting mood, atmosphere and character using the full scope of a physical place, as well as its social and psychological dimensions to aid the reader in the suspension of disbelief about the events.

Stories make use of multiple and different settings as they progress, but, as we have seen in the Harry Potter stories, the different settings remain within the bounds of the world imagined for the story. Setting shapes characters and characters shape setting — the two work together to provide the engine of the story. By disclosing the details, the setting gives the reader part of the intrigue, part of the romance, part of the mystery, allowing them to become emotionally involved. In many cases the details enable familiarisation, tugging on a reader's conscious knowledge of the place or the time. In other cases, they are part of the reader's *de-familiarisation*, prompting the reader to break with the familiar world. In either case, the colourful background is integral to the shaping of events, establishing mood and bringing readers into the story.

Choosing and Creating Your Setting

Famous novelist, Dean Koontz in *Writing Popular Fiction*, says that genre or category fiction needs five powerful ingredients, and *the dimensions of each change according to the genre of the story*. They are:

1. A powerful plot

2. A hero or heroine

3. Clear, believable motivation

4. A great deal of action

5. A colourful background.

In Section One, we discussed the development of your story idea, and you have been encouraged to develop a story snapshot statement and establish a premise. We also discussed the importance of thinking about genre, and that one of the early decisions you need to make is what genre of story you are writing. In many ways, a decision on genre is your first decision on setting, because the genre itself affects the *where* and *when* of the story.

As you can imagine, a science fiction story will have a different setting to a romance, as it will to a frontier/western, a spy thriller, a detective story, a fantasy or a magical realism story. That is not to say that a science fiction story can't have romance, or that a detective story can't have fantasy. After all, Harry Potter has many elements of a detective story, but it is a fantasy. Anthony Horrowitz's Alex Rider adventure story, *Point Blanc* is a spy thriller, but it involves some fantastic science as part of its plot. Knowing what type of story you are writing is the first step to understanding its setting.

Building Relationships Between People and Place

We said earlier that setting shapes characters and characters shape setting — each affects the other according to the type of story you are telling and the nature of the plot you are pursuing. These are the dynamite of the mining venture: you mix them together and … *kaboom!* — a story evolves from the rubble. The following three dimensions offer sound ways to build dynamic settings.

The Character's Reaction to the Place

Is the character a visitor, a newcomer, or a long-time resident? Natives and strangers notice and respond to different things. Long-time residents have greater knowledge about a place, but they frequently take for granted sights, sounds, and quirks of culture that an outsider finds novel or colourful or strange. To depict a setting more vividly, Lucke suggests making at least one character a stranger. The eye of the immigrant is unique and such a character can draw the reader's attention to details that a local would ignore.

A character's emotional response to a place is equally as important as any familiarity or strangeness. Are they comfortable here or out of their element? Are they insiders or outsiders? A person's attitude towards a place often reflects little on the amount of time they've spent there —we can fall in love with a locale at first sight, or dislike a place where we've lived for years. Thinking about characters gives you some insight into the way they live and the conditions of their place, from their rooms, homes, streets, suburbs, towns, cities, countries. Spend some time describing part of a character's setting in specific details, details that you couldn't see unless you were there.

The Reaction of the Place to the Character

Your Protagonist must deal with reactions other characters have to them — their level of knowledge, their attitude, and their degree of affinity to the kind of person the Protagonist is. The circuitry that other characters create, which we talked about in Chapter Three, are part of the setting. These characters, both collectively and as individuals, will hold certain beliefs and exercise cultures that arise from their place; they will act on those beliefs and cultures in response to your Protagonist's actions.

Residents in different locales are also likely to differ in their upbringing, lifestyles, and behaviour and will act according to those environmental factors in the face of your Protagonist's actions. Residents of a big city will create different complications for your Protagonist than would residents of a small town. Big city residents are more likely to be less individual, whereas those of a small town are more likely to have highly individualised small details that could affect the outcome. How the people of a place react to your Protagonist is instrumental in the nature of the core conflict your Protagonist faces.

Environmental Circumstances to Which the Character Must Respond

Place has a significant influence on the behaviour of its occupants. Action is constrained by the weather, the terrain, the nearness of neighbours, the distances between important points, and the objects that are or are not at hand. In the opening scenes of *Point Blanc*, by Anthony Horowitz, Alex Rider makes use of a construction site and the crane within to take action against drug dealers operating a lab on a river barge.

The clothes our characters wear to their means of transportation are all determined by the setting. A character who is out of place, wearing the wrong clothes, using the wrong tools, reading the wrong instructions, unable to understand the language ... will be ill equipped for the journey ahead. The setting is where writer and characters both discover resources and challenges. You should think about how your settings make life difficult for your characters.

Fictionalising a Real Setting

There are advantages to using a real place upon which to model your story's setting. To some extent, any city, any country town, any forest, any mountainside ... has elements that can be distorted and extrapolated to form the setting of an imaginary place. A gritty background can be found in practically any city where urban decay has been allowed to fester unchecked. Buildings can be made taller, smaller, older, newer; transport systems retrograde, futuristic, cluttered, uncluttered — in fact whatever you find around your own everyday locations can be used to create a dynamic setting for your story, regardless of whether you are writing historical romance, science fiction, detective fiction, politico-thrillers, fantasy or magical realism.

So irrespective of where your story is ultimately set, the starting place for your research can be your own backyard — where streets intersect with highways, rail lines dissect communities, native vegetation grows, or is swamped by foreign imports, house numbers run according to how far they are from the nearest street corner, streets are named to commemorate past citizenry, bird life flourishes, or it suffers from feral cat problems, drains clog with garbage ... Look around you and notice what names appear on the gateposts of the houses in the streets, what other messages are left for passersby to see. Your own backyard has examples of the types of cars the common man drives, how they are parked, how much security homeowners employ — in fact the minutiae of the neighbourhood is the juice of the story.

The knowledge you are seeking is *intimate* knowledge: it matters to you and, because it matters to you, it will matter to your readers. Details of the setting can become instrumental in the central conflict. Things around you have to be labelled, named, measured, quantified, identified — so they can be put to work in the narrative and give your reader a sense of belonging and understanding.

Inventing the Setting

If you are writing science fiction or fantasy, you will most likely be inclined to want to invent your own setting. In such a case, you will need to make your imaginary world complete in all its details. If you are invoking mythical realms in a fantasy world, you will need to research such myths as handed down from the traditions they came from. Myths abound in all cultures throughout the world: from Australia to Africa, from South America to Scandinavia. It is important for the verisimilitude of your story that your mythic world meets not only the needs of your characters but the expectations of your readers. If you are using history in your story, either as part of science fiction or fantasy, you need to research the period enough to understand the landscape of the time.

The science aspect of science fiction is also an important part of developing a setting. You need to make clear-cut decisions about the science that is involved in the story — space travel, time travel, medical science, biological science, other worlds, inner worlds … and how the science impacts upon the setting itself. Superman comes from a planet with a red sun, the effect of which, here under earth's yellow sun, gives rise to his super-human powers. These powers are then manifested in different ways, and challenged through other scientific developments by his enemies. The science itself will form an integral connection between the characters in the story and the world in which they exist, and how they manage to survive there.

Similar arguments can be made about fantasy, and the incorporation of magic, the demonic, the presence of evil, or supernatural … how these aspects are drawn into the story will have a profound effect on the choices made for setting and character.

Some commentators suggest that if you are writing about an imagined setting then you do not need to be accurate. I contend this is a mistake. You need to be at least as accurate as a real setting, but in different ways. Yes you can create the geography, the landscape, the architecture, the manners and so forth … but you need to ensure that whatever aspects you make up accord with the needs of the story and are explained in great and minute detail. After all, you still need to convince the reader that the place exists.

How to Put the Reader in the Picture

1. Make the sense of time and place central to the beginning of your story and every new scene. This doesn't need to be heavy description, but use enough *particular* details for the reader to create a mental image of *when* and *where*. Once the main setting is established, this is best achieved through the action of the characters.

   EXAMPLE: Alex Rider's arrival at *Point Blanc* (Anthony Horowitz)

   The academy at Point Blanc had been built by a lunatic. For a time it had been used as an asylum. Alex remembered what Alan Blunt had told him as the helicopter began its final descent, the red and white helipad looming up to receive it. The photograph in the brochure had been artfully taken. Now that he could see the building for himself, he could only describe it as … mad.

2. Particular and specific details embedded in the action create the 'you are there' feeling for readers. Start with rising action and describe as you go along, picking out the 'telling' details and leave the generic details out. 'Telling' details are details that characterise a person or place specifically, but 'clincher' detail is the detail that needs you to 'be there' to witness.

   EXAMPLE: The opening paragraph of *There are Some Days* (Frederick Forsyth)

   The St Kilian roll-on roll-off ferry from Le Havre buried her nose in another oncoming sea and pushed her blunt bulk a few yards nearer to Ireland. From somewhere on A deck driver Liam Clarke leaned over the rail and stared forward to make out the low hills of County Wexford coming closer.

3. Be sensual. A place only comes alive when we can sense it in full depth. Seeing is largely a two-dimensional experience. Although we see with perspective, it is not until we bring the sense of touch to bear on what we are seeing that we realise true depth. We may see something before us, but our understanding comes alive when we explore how we 'feel' about it. Our senses are linked. A perfectly barbecued piece of steak (for non-vegetarians) looks appetising, smells delicious, tastes yummy, melts in the mouth and sizzles on the plate.

4. Employ the details that give you the best access to the mood of the work. The detail of a gritty urban landscape sets the mood perfectly for a mugging. If the action springs from the setting all the better.

5. Let the action tell the story by revealing how your characters respond to the setting. Showing emotional responses reveals far more about a situation than merely telling. Avoid describing what happens. Let the action follow the mood and the characters will show the reader the place in all its gritty detail — without you having to describe much at all.

EXAMPLE: *The Client* (John Grisham)

Mark took a deep breath and knocked on the door. He could hear chairs move inside. 'Come in,' someone said, and the voice was not friendly. He opened the door slowly, stepped inside, and closed it behind him. The room was narrow and long just like the table in the centre of it. No windows. No smiles from the two men who stood on each side of the table near the end. They could pass for twins — white button-down shirts, red-and-blue ties, dark pants, short hair.

Chapter 5
Conflict and the Forces of Opposition
Narrowing the Space

The literature folk like to speak of *tension*. Tension is a reader's emotional response to the conflict a character is involved in within a particular situation. Tension is the desired outcome for the writer of dramatic works.

Readers experience tension in a story when they sense characters undergoing some form of strain, that they are being stretched in their relationships with other characters or the world around them; that their experiences have removed them from their zone of comfort. As a result, the reader will experience some form of emotional strain.

In the *Poetics of Space*, Gaston Bachelard looks at Henri Bosco's *Malicroix*, in which a humble house appears at first to lack resistance in the face of a great storm, yet through its dramatic struggle it demonstrates great fortitude. Bachelard says the author takes time to 'show the narrowing of the space at the centre of which the house is to live like an anguished heart.' The 'narrowing of the space' has the effect of increasing the tension from the moment of silence to the moment the first signs of the storm striking — the anticipation period. Tension, Bachelard argues, must grow from something humble into a symbol of strength, and be composed of a point of aggression and a point of resistance. The focus on both the aggression and the resistance can be dramatically increased by the 'narrowing of the space'.

In *The Seven Basic Plots*, Christopher Booker speaks about 'constriction and release' — that whenever we identify with the hero or heroine, we share their experience in terms of constriction and release as the story unfolds. As characters face ordeals or come under threat we feel tense and apprehensive, and then as the threat is lifted, we can relax. The effect of the growing conflict doubles itself as the audience mirrors the experience of constriction and release.

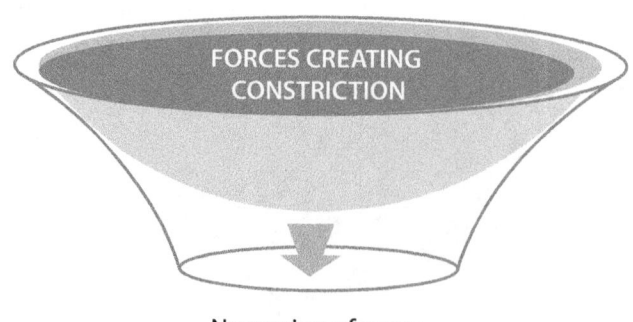

Narrowing of space

In a story which is well constructed, Booker says, 'these phases of constriction and release alternate in a kind of systole-diastole rhythm which provides one of the greatest pleasures we get from stories.'

As a story proceeds, the swings from one pole to the other increase in intensity and may become more extreme until usually the most violent of all comes with the story's climax. 'This is the point where the pressure of the dark power is at its greatest and most threatening, followed by the miraculous reversal and release of the ending.'

Booker sums up by saying that the inmost rhythm of our experience with story is of an initial sense of constriction, followed by a phase of relative enlargement, followed by a more serious constriction. At the climax the threatening pressure on the Hero is at its greatest, which is released in a final, much deeper act of liberation, 'coupled with the sense that something of inestimable and lasting value has been won from the darkness.'

Tension Arises from Conflict

In order to produce tension for your reader, you must generate and manipulate conflict between characters with whom the reader has formed some bond, creating anxiety, suspense and excitement. The reader must have some emotional investment in the characters involved. Usually this relationship is expressed in terms of *sympathy*, *identification* and *empathy*. Conflict is the tool that generates the relationship and therefore tension.

So how do we, as writers, go about ensuring we get the investment? I suggest it lies in four critical aspects of story design, three of which we have covered in some depth, the fourth to be explored in Chapter Six — Premise, Character, Story world and Plot.

The job of the storyteller is to take a human condition and subject it to an experimental process and document the results. The microscope under which the storyteller puts the human condition is conflict, or perhaps more scientifically, *antagonism*, which is defined in the Macquarie Dictionary as 'the activity or the relation of contending parties or conflicting forces.'

The root word of *Protagonist* and *Antagonist* is *Agon*, a Greek word meaning 'the assembly for a contest'. *Agoneus* was a name given to the God, Hermes, one of the Olympians, in recognition of his patronage for athletics. Thus *Protagonist* and *Antagonist* are the names given to those who assemble in a story for a contest.

A story involves episodes that are interesting because of the contest, because there are high stakes, because there is pole-to-pole growth, because a cause-and-effect relationship between episodes magnifies the potential outcomes. The product of the conflict in human terms is change. And change is what a story seeks to engage with.

The more challenging the relationship between the character under examination and the forces of antagonism they are facing, the more interested the reader becomes in the outcome. And as Booker's comment on tension indicated, we are interested most in how a character overcomes those forces, particularly when those forces are shown to be on a far greater scale than the obvious capacity of the character. In other words, the stakes are high and the challenge more or less insurmountable. Moreover, we are most interested in a character if there is some way of identifying with the situation in which they are placed. It is how a character responds to forces of antagonism that drives story.

As we said in Section One, defining your premise allows you to express the idea that inspires the story, and the controlling or structural idea that sums up the story's meaning through its climax. We also discussed how the premise expresses an argument in the form, *character through conflict leads to conclusion*. This means that in order to develop the story's full spine, you need at some point to make a statement of the conflict that's at the heart of the story; the conflict that causes change.

Let's return for a minute to my drama of Joe and Sally that I first introduced in Chapter One, *Fleshing out the Story Idea*.

> *I've decided I want to write about a young artist, Joe, who meets Sally, a girl who's the polar opposite of him. He's unkempt, unorganised, irresponsible, but wholly charming. Sally, on the other hand, a bank manager, is shy, prim, beautifully groomed, well organised and places very high regard in being responsible. Success to Joe has little to do with wealth, it is more to do with his art being seen. To Sally, though, wealth features fairly high on the success measure.*
>
> *I have them meet at an exhibition — literally bumping into each other — his elbow is bumped by someone passing and, as a result, he spills red wine on her white blouse. He attempts to immediately remedy the situation — she's embarrassed by both his clumsiness and the fact that he's groping her breasts in public. It's not a good start. I can have a lot of fun with this simple situation, but if I want to develop it into a story, I need to have some idea of where I want it to go.*
>
> *So, as a consequence of this meeting, and Joe's determination to redeem himself, they develop a relationship. It's tentative at first, but eventually it blossoms, with one small contentious point — she becomes increasingly frustrated by his irresponsibility.*
>
> *Joe has reached a point where he has decided to ask Sally to marry him. However, before he can pop the question his irresponsibility gets in the way yet again. This time it leads to Sally dumping him and taking up with a guy with obvious wealth — someone we might have thought is more suited to her disposition anyway.*
>
> *Joe reacts badly to losing her. He becomes depressed and convinced that the only attraction about this other guy is his money, which leads Joe to start making desperate moves to show Sally he's in the race.*

In the end, he decides the best way to get the money he needs is to rob a bank and, after a great deal of planning, he makes his move.

Not by design, he finds the first person he sees upon entering the bank is Sally. He can't go through with the deed and is about to run, when another would-be robber bursts in and points a gun at Sally. This is too much for Joe, and in an act of heroism, he goes to Sally's defence and unmasks the robber, getting shot in the process. In the end, Joe's heroism teaches him how to correct his slide, and wins Sally back.

The central conflict of this story lies in Joe's desire to win back the girl he lost. Her heart is the 'object of desire', in the word of Alfred Hitchcock, The Mcguffin

The Shape of Story

Determining the argument the story will explore provides a controlling idea, or a crucible in which the conflict at the core can be cooked. The three controlling elements are the *Protagonist*, the *circuitry of other characters* and the *circumstance* in which they are all brought together. It is the circumstances where the conflict erupts, but it is brought about by the tension in relationships between the Protagonist and the other characters and the situations the Protagonist is in.

Having spent considerable time designing characters and placing them with others, it is time to turn their special features into oppositions.

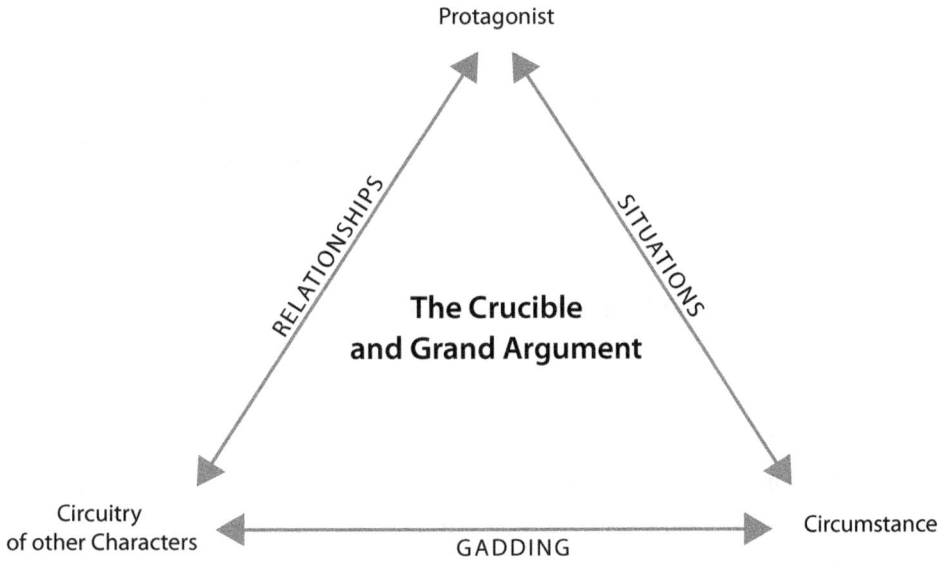

Characterisation is a term the literature folks like to use when discussing how well motivated a character is; how easily we understand their goals, how complex they are in terms of their behaviours, how closely they resemble our understanding of type. It's important to understand that *characterisation* is something applied after the character has been created (*-isation* is a verb suffix that describes action following some line of action, practice, policy etc; or acting towards or upon, treating or affecting in some way). Primarily it is how character is revealed in the act of reading. While important, it is vastly different to the act of creating the character and developing their roles and functions in the story, and getting them to act according to their desires and maximum capacity.

To present a *well-rounded* character, you need to consider the many design issues discussed in Chapter Two plus the causes of the conflict that lie at the heart of the story's premise. We discussed earlier, the principles of the multi-dimensional character, the three groups of attributes: physical, social and psychological, which enable us to know *Who is this person? What does he look like? What does he do? Why does he do it?* But it is the *contradictions* that are contained within this design structure that give you the power for conflict.

You must have a Protagonist capable and willing to go the full distance demanded by the story's core conflict regardless of the consequences, and an Antagonist presenting a most diabolical alternative future. The Protagonist must face forces of antagonism that appear, in all respects, to be insurmountable. Therefore your character design must include complex multi-layered attributes, many of which are hidden from readers and other characters, and are contradictory in order to promote conflict. Conditions that a character wants to keep secret are powerful fuel for conflict.

> *A character may have an illness that he does not want others to know about, which may be an important surprise in the climax; he may have a family member who committed murder, a secret that could shatter everything were it known; he may have a penchant for sexual deviancy, but fights every day to keep it under control.*
>
> *Or, she may be a charming thief, or have deep anxiety attached to her personal ambition.*
>
> *Contradictions arise from complexities of character make-up crossed with the need to keep aspects hidden from others.*

Character layers and presence in conflict

A character's innermost self — their identity, or 'centre' — is composed of different values of feelings and understanding (emotions), and strength and order (logic). A character becomes 'whole' when feelings, understanding, strength and order have achieved a certain balance. Part of the story process is to show that balance coming into being and the challenges involved in striving for that balance — this is the character transformation experienced in the story.

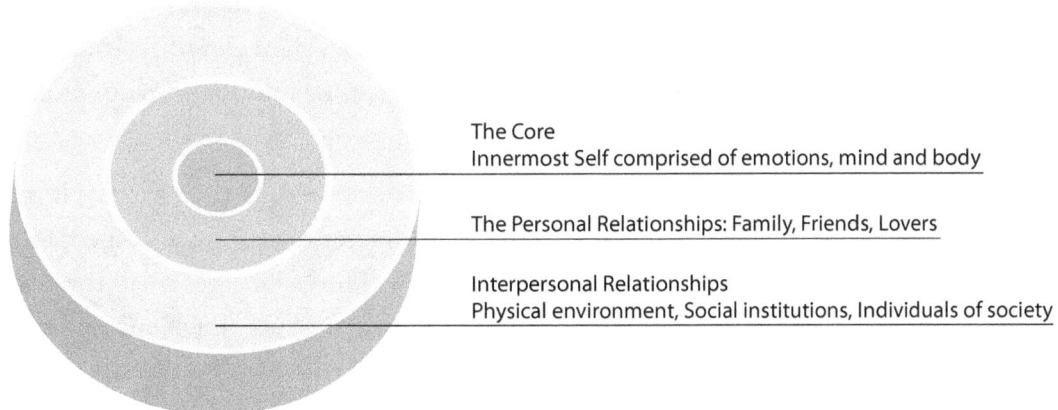

Each of these values (feelings, understanding, strength and order) is capable of containing contradictions. The innermost self is composed of emotions, mind and body. Any deficiencies must be strongly guarded from external knowledge and attack. A character will act to keep them hidden from others and they become accessible to others after only extreme levels of antagonism, and represent *inner conflicts*.

> *For example, a character's body may not respond the way he imagines it should: it may lack strength or deftness, or size and agility for a particular task, or it may succumb to illness or injury. His ability to maintain order may be compromised by poor direction. His emotions may betray his feelings, and his responses may be out of kilter with his self-image of character. He may lack the capacity to understand a certain situation, and react in a way to it that takes him away from his needs, or contradictory to his expressed desires. The character will act to keep these weaknesses secret from others, both allies and enemies.*

Moving outward from the the innermost self, a character interacts with a personal structure of the world around them. This personal structure takes the form of *family, friends* and *lovers* — the Personal Relationships — all of whom have an interest in helping the character find balance of emotion and logic, whether the character in question wants it or not. These 'do-gooders' are often at odds with the direction in which the character wants to move, but they constantly chip away at the outer shell searching for an opening that will let them into the core of the character. Sometimes they get by a fallen guard, sometimes they find a blocked pathway, sometimes they are deflected elsewhere. Frequently these players fail to react to circumstances in the way the character expects them to, which of course means they are the cause of the next level of conflict.

Further out from the centre, we find another structure at play — the Interpersonal Relationships made up of the environment of the character's world containing the *physical environment, social institutions* and *individuals of the society*, all of which have an influence on the progress a character is making towards balance of logic and emotion. These extra-personal forces push their way into a character's life, each seeking a way into the core. As a character moves to defend access by these forces, they find their reactions are often at odds with their desires.

A conflict works like acid, it etches away at the surface of a character revealing the next raw layer beneath. Conflict comes at a character from all three levels causing the character to change in respect to emotions and logic. As the character moves towards their goals, resistance will force changes in all three levels of interaction, the slowest and hardest changes coming from the character's core. Each encounter should work to peel back layers in an attempt to expose the character's inner core.

What drives the story is not conflict itself, but the conflict that is generated through resistance to the main character's desire. In order to examine this, character design needs to take into consideration the goals of the Protagonist, and the four dimensions we discussed in *Chapter Two* under *Character Presence*. These are:

- *Motivation* — provides the character with the force to move
- *Evaluation* — provides the character the standards by which progress is measured
- *Methodology* — provides the character the ways and means they use to achieve the goal
- *Purpose* — provides the character with the direction in which to move

It stands to reason, that spearheading this is the character's *desire* — goal or purpose — what it is they *want*. This want should have a direct bearing on the central conflict of the story.

> *In the case of Joe and Sally, Joe wants Sally to marry him.*

Within your character's three-dimensional design, from the details of their physical, social and psychological make-up, you should be able to pinpoint the following aspects of your character:

- *Weakness* — from the beginning, the character has one or more weaknesses that are holding them back from fulfilling their dream.

  > *Joe lacks the motivation to push himself to produce more than the bare minimum. He quickly and easily succumbs to his impulsive urges. Perhaps he is also a coward.*

- *Hidden Need* — this is a psychological dimension that exposes a moral dilemma in the character which, in order to attain balance of logic and emotion, the character must correct or resolve. The problem, of course, is that the character is not consciously aware of this need at the beginning of the story, and this awareness grows only as a result of the conflicts of the story's emerging situations.

Joe needs to control his irresponsibility that is hurting Sally and others in his character circuitry. But he also needs to become self-sufficient, and not be a leach to others.

Conflict can arise from any of, or any mix of, the four dimensions of Character presence:

- Joe and Sally can be motivated by the same desire

   To not end up lonely

- Their purposes can be identical

   To marry someone they love

- Their methodologies can be identical

   To test the other's love by forced absences

- But they could differ in their evaluations

   She might believe he indicates his love to her by giving gifts and calling late at night to tell her she's missed; he might believe she indicates her love by leaving him alone to work long and late and go drinking with his mates.

It is easy to see where things might go awry.

Harmony and Discord in the Playground

No Protagonist acts alone. Even in a single-character situation — in a story of a solo yachtsman circumnavigating the world, for example, the Protagonist carries a raft of other 'voices' who serve as other characters in the world of the story. As we discussed earlier, you need to ensure that your character design includes differences between characters that lead to and promote conflict. As we know, no marriage is easy all the time; no family relationship is easy all the time; no relationship with bosses is easy all the time. The reason is simply the differences in personality and world view.

Examine the circuitry of characters involved in your story and how they relate to the core conflict, and then in terms of their relationship to the Protagonist. Create oppositions between characters in their three-dimensional attributes that have a bearing on the conflict. Remember, the other characters are in the story only because of the core conflict and the Protagonist's need to contest it. Consequently, our interest lies in the *relationships* between the Protagonist and each of the other characters. The Protagonist's contradictions can only come to light in the interactions with the circuitry of other characters, and these produce *smaller conflicts* that play into the main conflict.

Orchestrating your characters not only requires differences and oppositions in character design, but also in the way they go about their business in the story.

While we have discussed many character archetypes, typically there are eight in most stories, each identified by the 'function' they serve in the story. These functions play an important role in how conflict is understood by the reader and the different conflicts that are being contested within other relationships.

The core conflict is contested by the Protagonist and the Antagonist. This is what the story is about — how the conflict is contested, how it is resolved, how far it pushes the characters in the human experience and what changes it brings about. The Protagonist is the character pursuing the goal; the Antagonist is the character trying to stop the Protagonist.

> *Joe is in conflict with Sally over her heart. He wants her to give it to him; she doesn't trust him with it. This is the core conflict. Sally is the Antagonist who resists Joe's attempts to win her love at every turn because he has demonstrated to her in the past that he cannot be trusted with it, on her terms. Joe is a committed Protagonist and is prepared to go to any lengths to succeed.*

Helping the Protagonist reach his goal, providing wisdom, special powers, tools and knowledge, is the Guardian, (also known as the Mentor). A Guardian character often acts as an obstacle character and stands in the way of the Protagonist, forcing them to choose a different path, usually for their own good. Opposing the Guardian in this effort is the Contagonist taking a contrary view of the Protagonist's objective, seeking to deflect the Protagonist and fulfil an agenda of their own. These two characters contest the moral conflict — conscience vs. temptation. The moral conflict illustrates to the reader what the Protagonist needs in order to fulfil their desire. This contest often results in sacrifice on the part of the Guardian, and sometimes a change of allegiance on the part of the Contagonist.

> *Joe's moral need is to be self-sufficient, to be grown-up, and not to leach on others. The story needs a character who is willing to help Joe win Sally's heart, but not at the expense of hurting others. There is also a need for a character who opposes this view, that winning at all costs is okay, so long as you win. Joe has a friend, Brian, who lures him away and into trouble. Joe's landlord, Luigi, is owed a good deal of money in back rent on his studio; he puts a lot of faith in Joe.*

The Sidekick, who is fiercely loyal, and the Sceptic who is unfalteringly doubtful represent the contest of trust — an opposition fired by confidence and doubt.

> *Sally has a friend, Joanne, in whom she confides. Joanne is fiercely opposed to Sally having anything to do with Joe. This character works to undermine everything Joe attempts.*

In order for the story to seem complete, a fourth conflict is contested by a Reason character and an Emotion character illustrating the opposition between intellect and heart: a conflict of rationality.

> *Sally's new boyfriend, Larry, is cold and calculating and has a very definite idea of what the proper course of action should be for her. He is in conflict with Joe's irrational and emotional responses to his situation, planning his every step to ensure that Sally is out of reach to Joe.*

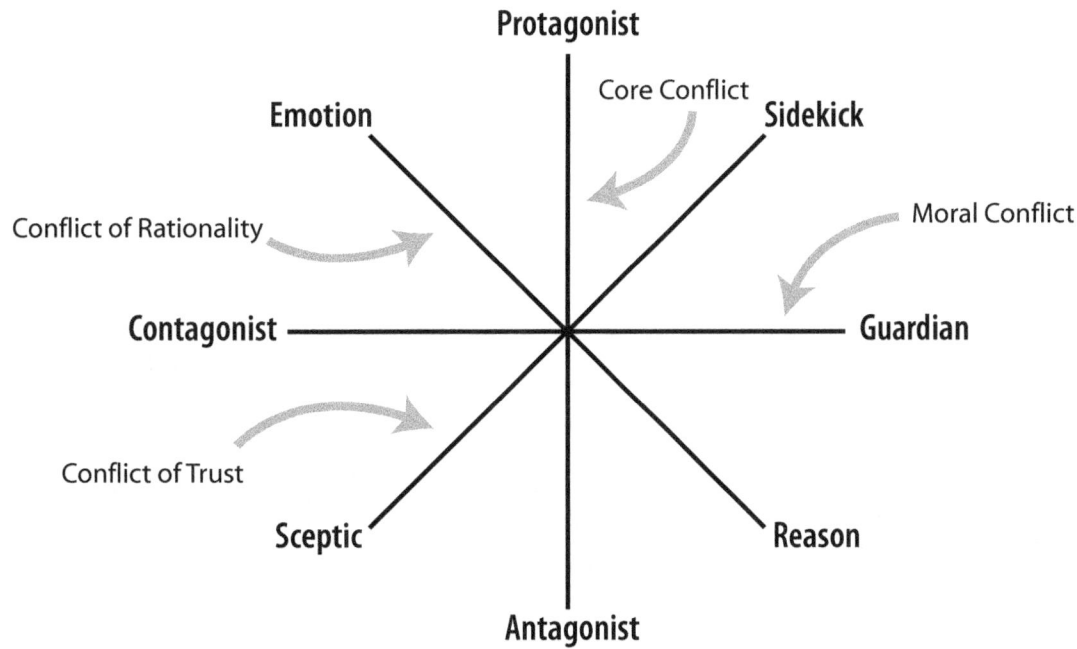

Note here that the Joe currently lacks both a discrete Sidekick and an Emotion character. While the story feels the need for both of these functions, it is possible that Joe himself fulfils the Emotion character role, and both Brian and Luigi at times could wear the Sidekick mask.

How conflict lulls the reader into the Fictive Dream

We have determined that the central driving force of the story is a character's desire for something (*character does something to get what they want*, right?) which is what the core conflict between Protagonist and Antagonist develops over. When the character expresses that desire in some way, forces of antagonism arising from inner, personal and interpersonal levels, together with the influence of the character's hidden need, create a difference between what the character expects to be the outcome and what really happens. This is a gap that we might refer to as the 'tension gap'. It increases the potential charge of the story because it forces the character to a decision: a dilemma, the outcome of which will either widen or narrow the gap, or create a new gap.

- A. The Protagonist seeks their desire with an expectation it will be fulfilled, taking action and making decisions based on that expectation.

- B. The opposition arising both from the multiple levels of conflict and their hidden need cause a gap to appear/widen between the desire and the expectation, creating tension.

- C. The gap produces a new reality forcing the Protagonist to take new actions and decisions towards their desire, or

- D. The new reality leads to an altered desire.

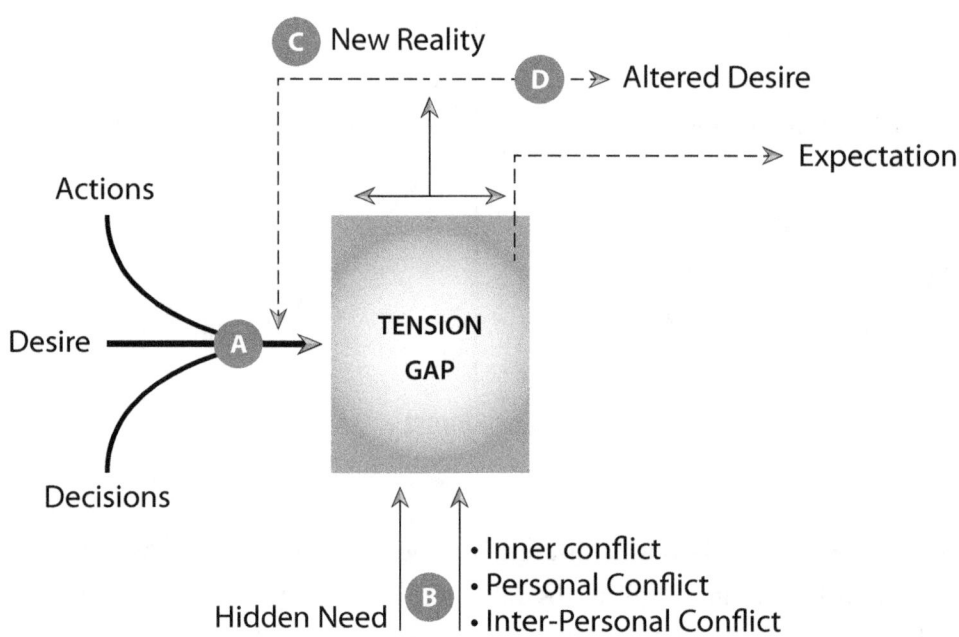

Joe has decided that tomorrow he will ask Sally to marry him (a decision that expresses his desire to claim her heart). But that night he goes out on a bender with Brian and ends up in hospital, which means he is unable to contact Sally and explain. Sally has been stood up. But it's not the first time! (This illustrates Joe's hidden need to be less irresponsible.) Because Joe stood her up, Sally chooses to go out with Larry, a rich and seemingly responsible man.

Joe's reality has changed, the gap has widened due to the pressures of his hidden need and action from both interpersonal and personal conflict levels.

His desire for Sally to marry him has a new reality; its satisfactory resolution has moved further away and now he faces greater opposition. He has to pursue the goal with extra vigour, either try a different tack with an altered desire, or give up.

This causes a new gap to open up and Joe has to pursue his dream along a different pathway, a decision that leads him to eventually attempt a bank robbery.

Every scene should seek out and exploit the tension gap between the character's desire, the direct opposition to that desire, and the forces of antagonism that result from the hidden need. It is through manipulating the tension gap that you bring the reader into the moral, rationality and trust dimensions of the Protagonist's goal. The gap widens in the reader's story mind when the conflict is testing a moral ambiguity to which the reader has developed a passionate response. It closes when that moral ambiguity looks like it might be satisfactorily resolved. The same is true when issues of trust and rationality are contested.

Artful use of conflict is to manipulate a tension gap between the Protagonist and the other characters, the circumstances of the story, and the Protagonist's inability to recognise their hidden need. This is done by making sure the character is always, as James N Frey says in *How to Write a Damn Good Novel*, on the 'horns of a dilemma' — forced to decide between two equally unattractive propositions.

The reader wants to see the gap closed and the character reconciled, and wonders if that will happen on the next page … and the next … and the next … (etc.) When the reader recognises the impossibility of the character's position, and feels that, in the same circumstances, they too would not know which way to go, the reader is said to be in sympathy with the character; that is, sympathetic to the character's position. This is the beginning of the Fictive Dream.

According to Frey, the Fictive Dream comes from a three stage process. In *How to Write a Damn Good Novel II*, he says the reader passes through three stages before reaching the dreamstate:

Sympathy ➤ *Identification* ➤ *Empathy* ➤ *Dreamstate*

Sympathy

Sympathy doesn't mean the reader has to *like* the character or find them *admirable*. Sympathy means the reader *feels sorry* for the character, and the *situation* they are in. This is achieved by showing the reader that the character is in terrible trouble — circumstances that bring physical, mental or spiritual suffering to the character, usually at the hands of another whose actions are demonstrated to be patently unfair, and made worse by the character's inability to resolve the problems caused by a hidden need. The first step, of course, is to place the Protagonist in terrible trouble.

> *After we've been introduced to Sally and learn that she's a woman with high and seemingly impossible standards, we meet Joe as he gets led astray by Brian. When, much later, when he's lying on the floor in a pool of blood, at risk of bleeding to death, the reader will feel sorry for him. While we may understand Sally's subsequent reaction to being stood up, it will seem a little harsh because she is not aware of the full circumstances and the impossibility of Joe being able to explain himself. And while we know that, at least to some extent, Joe brought it on himself, sympathy will remain with Joe.*

Identification

A reader identifies with a character when the sympathy they feel for them extends into support for their goals and aspirations, and the reader feels a strong desire for the character to achieve those goals.

> *Joe declares his love for Sally by letting the reader know that tomorrow he intends asking her to marry him. Things go awry and he is unable to ask that question at the time he planned to, and he is denied asking it henceforth. After the reader learns of Joe's slide into depression, they want him to succeed in winning her back — even though the reader may disapprove of Joe's chosen method, and feel that the risk is not worth it.*

Empathy

A sense of empathy develops in the reader when they are drawn into the situation through the use of sensuous and emotion-provoking details that explore the antagonism the character is experiencing from the story world, which in turn generates an emotional bond between character and reader. When you use emotional language and detail sights, sounds, pains, smells, touch, tastes … of the environment, you are using the power of suggestion to show the reader how the character is oppressed, how the story world has contracted and the space has narrowed, amplifying the point of aggression against which the character must respond.

When Joe's landlord comes upon him lying unconscious in a pool of blood, he notes the details of the situation — the broken glass that has severed an artery in his foot, his desperate attempts to reach a telephone, pools of blood indicating bleeding so severe that only a few minutes more and Joe would be dead. The reader will be in complete empathy in his desperate bid to save Joe's life. Once the medical issues have been explained to Joe and he's shown how close he came to death, the reader will be feeling with him all the way.

Dreamstate

The dreamstate, or total absorption in the narrative, can only occur when the reader experiences the character's pangs of remorse, feels their guilt, experiences their doubts and misgivings and takes sides in the decisions they are forced to make. Such decisions are of a moral nature and have serious consequences for the character in which their self-worth and honour will be challenged and questioned.

The reader can only participate when the character is facing an inner conflict. The reader will 'pull' for the character to make one decision over another, or take one direction in preference to another. Inner conflict is the expression of the conflict of rationality — intellect vs. the heart. The character will reason that one course of action is correct, but feel a different one is necessary. This is the nature of the dilemma.

After his recovery, Joe reasons that he has to face the imposter, Larry, in order to declare his love to Sally, but he feels that it will reflect badly in Sally's eyes because she will see him for the coward that he knows he is. The reader can see that it's a bad idea, but Joe persists in his belief. It occurs to him that she will see the Hero he wants her see, but his conscience is in turmoil because he knows he's a coward.

The character allows the story world to present two equally viable, but opposing courses of action, which follows its own pattern of contraction and expansion through the story. Find the dilemmas and milk them for all they're worth.

When you go into a character's head, there are conflicts in the past that have an emotional impact on the present and can be exploited.

Patterns of Character Conflict

Story centres on a contested object which creates the major dramatic question of the work, what we have thus far referred to as the *core conflict*. The object is a symbol of greater desires — *power, influence, wealth, sex, love, life and death, destruction*. Broader themes such as *war, love, colonisation, revolution, sport* … etc., are based on the same principles as singular actions.

Therefore the Protagonist is actively seeking the object in one of three phases:

- *Acquisition* — trying to obtain (or regain) the object
- *Maintaining* — trying to prevent loss of the object
- *Dispossession* — trying to remove or replace the object

And the prominent obstacle is the Protagonist's major weakness.

All conflict begins humbly, reaches a crisis and dissolves — at which point, a new conflict has to emerge or all interest is lost. This is the pattern of contraction and release in which other characters have either a positive or negative interest in the Protagonist obtaining the goal.

The Protagonist's weaknesses are the main reason they haven't yet attained their goal. Their psychological needs frequently prevent them from personally attacking their weaknesses, and their moral needs prevent them from recognising them. While the Protagonist can't recognise their weaknesses to attack them, other characters recognise them all too readily, and are quite happy to launch attacks.

The relationship between any one character and any other involved in the pursuit needs to be tested against the Protagonist's weakness — it is the Protagonist's weaknesses that must continually come under fire until they are prepared to recognise the impact they have on them and face up to them. Each attack should peel back a layer of the character until eventually their core is revealed so that even they can see it clearly.

However, even though the Protagonist faces the challenge from all other characters involved in the pursuit, there needs also to be conflict *between* each of the other characters, also driven by the Protagonist's weakness. According to John Truby in *The Anatomy of Story*, each opposition character should attack the Protagonist's weakness in a different way, *and* be in opposition with each other through different values based on their motivation, purpose, method or evaluation. Truby calls this 'four-cornered opposition' and the following diagram illustrates the relationships between the four 'driver' characters.

At the primary level there is direct opposition between Protagonist and Antagonist. The Antagonist attacks the Protagonist's major weakness in order to prevent the Protagonist reaching their goal. The Contagonist attacks it to deflect the Protagonist from their goal. And the Guardian attacks it to help the Protagonist reach their goal. The different motivations behind the attacks offer you ways to exploit different methodologies in those attacks, which of course, then promotes direct conflict between each of the other characters. This presents increasingly complex levels of opposition at all three layers of conflict.

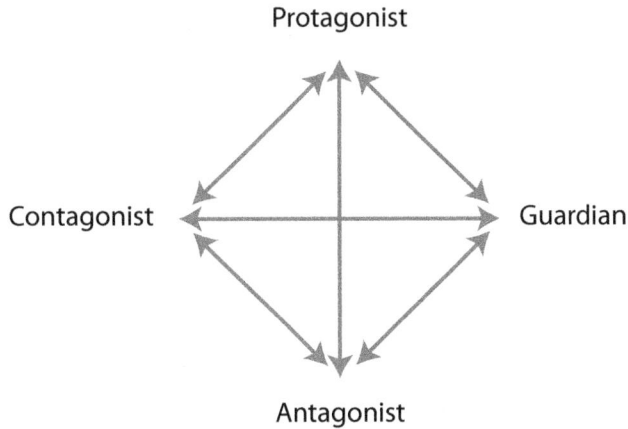

Conflict and the Story world

The story world is composed of the *circumstance* of the story plus the *circuitry of characters*. I.e., the *where, when and who else*. It impacts upon the Protagonist through situations and relationships, and the gadding that occurs between the circuitry of characters and the circumstances.

A Protagonist's direction or progress may be altered by the actions or decisions of another character (a prod), which can alter the circumstance in which the Protagonist finds them-self; or by the time constraints or physical limitations of the story world, which can influence the actions and decisions of other characters.

Story reflects life, but the creation of story is the reverse of real life. As we discussed earlier, in life we are born into an existing world; in story we find the characters to contest a central conflict and assemble a world around them. Therefore the arena of the story world must be an extension of the characters. The story world provides the physical limitations of the crucible.

The conflict of the story between the Protagonist and the Antagonist takes place in a limited space over a limited time. The conflict refuses to allow these characters to be separated from each other until it is resolved. The story world needs to reflect this conflict.

> *Joe and Sally's story takes place where their attachment occurs, if either were to remove themselves from that place, the conflict would simply dissolve and there would be no story — Joe would not learn what he needs to learn, and he would not overcome his weaknesses.*

Your story world must contain key visual oppositions based on the characters and their values: a physical expression of who the Protagonist is and how the character develops. Their story world at the beginning of the story will change by the end; possibly going through a number of positive and negative changes as it progresses. At the beginning, the story world should reflect the constrictions that the character is enduring — highlighting, embodying and accentuating their weaknesses, drawing them out in its worst form. This makes the reader aware of their psychological and moral needs and causes reader frustration at the character's inability to see it clearly (a process towards identification).

> *Joe is unorganised, his place is unorganised, he is behind in his rent; his landlord, seeing Joe face down in a pool of blood, is facing a dilemma —whether to let him die and regain his property, or call an ambulance and save him.*
>
> *Joe sees Sally's world as one of neatness and order, which is attractive to him because he cannot provide it for himself. The gap between the two represents one of the major conflicts of the story.*

By the end, the story world should reflect the 'becoming whole' of the character: a visual representation of balancing the feminine with the masculine — feelings and understanding with strength and order.

> *Joe's hospitalisation in the early stages of the story represents imprisonment and the separation from Sally. It symbolises all that is lost, and its ability to repair him is limited. In contrast, his hospitalisation at the end of the story represents his freedom, in particular his freedom from cowardice, and its ability to repair him is complete, offering him psychological repair as well as physical.*

Conflicts Abound in the Design of the Story World

Natural settings have their own inbuilt oppositions. For example, the ocean has both an above and a below the surface; the mountain stands in stark contrast to the plain; deserts — both hot and sandy and ice and frozen — contrast with forests and jungles; rivers bisect, as do mountain ranges, gorges and impassable forests. The natural world has many conflicts with man-made spaces too, impacting upon food, security, disease, animal kingdoms and more. Technology is yet another story world element that impacts both the natural world and the man-made in the form of transport, medicine, communications, materials, intelligence … etc.

Time is applied to the story world not only as an aspect of story but as an aspect of character. Time has three conditions, each of which can give rise to conflicts:

- Standstill — not physically possible but symbolic of 'nothing happening'
- Cyclical time — seasons, days, years …
- Sequent time — ageing, evolution, decay …

The story world manifests in both the *world of the everyday*, and the *mythological woods*, comprising both interior and exterior worlds. Crossing from the world of the everyday into the mythological woods requires some form of symbolic gateway which indicates that a psychological need has been uncovered.

The crossing usually occurs when the Protagonist encounters either a Guardian character or Contagonist character. But the reverse — getting back from the mythological woods into the renewed world of the everyday, needs to be an act entirely under the control of the Protagonist in the resolution of the story's central conflict. The return is often part of the realised and reconciled (at least to some extent) psychological and moral needs.

Summary

Conflict is the dynamics of forces of opposition being brought to bear on the story's characters, hindering and impeding their progress towards the object of desire.

Conflict arises from the sum of the Protagonist *plus* Goal *plus* Forces of Antagonism.

Conflict = Protagonist + Goal + Antagniosm

A character always has to have a choice to do one thing or another when faced with an obstacle. What they decide depends on their character and the decision they make will either complicate the situation or ease it.

Conflict arises from obstacles that are found within the landscape of the story world, and include illnesses or injury. Obstacles and the decisions of how to deal with them, lead to further complications.

Characters need ambition, they need to be idealistic, have wounds, histories, opposing goals, dreams and contrasting personalities.

Inner conflicts result in dilemmas and arise when a character is required to take action or make a decision that may not accord with their beliefs or emotional capacity. Inner conflict is a useful device for exposing the nature of the character, and extending advantage to external opposition.

A story is always only ever as good as the forces of antagonism allow it to be. It needs to contain negative forces of such power that the positive side must gain surpassing quality — a story must move from the point of aggression through the contrary, the contradictory to the complete suppression of the negative power. When a character is forced to fight back from that position, the reader will feel that the struggle to be worthwhile.

Chapter 6
Plot and Structure

Elements of Structure

Genre

In *Tools for Cultural Study*, Tony Thwaites says, 'A genre is a grouping of texts which are similar in structure or content'. The word, *texts* is how theorists in the reading community identify writing. Genre is the categorisation of forms of writing (novels, plays, film, comic, games …) based on characteristics they have in common, and then sub-grouping them according to class, category or style of writing within those forms. The publishing industry uses genre to 'pigeon-hole' story types, particularly in popular fiction, to help booksellers and libraries range the works in ways readers can easily identify genres they are attracted to and those they reject. It is a kind of intangible package of ideas presented by writers, and opinions asserted by readers, both of which can be linked by a common social thread that allows the understanding the story offers to be shared.

Both a work's internal structural elements and the expectations of readers and viewers form the idea of genre through selection and usage of signs and thematic devices, mode of delivery, conventions of readings and interpretations, comparative features with other texts, and the cultural and social environment that conditions production and reception. The reception of a story looks to its social context and its relationship with other texts for meaning, both within its genre and parallel to it. We find that genre evolves with the development of social structures and as a consequence provides readers with a framework from which they can examine social meaning according to a given contemporary structure.

Because of the social context, reader identity is very closely tied to genre. Readers engage with story based on its meaning within the context of its genre — a reflection of the social and cultural conditions of the times. A key structural decision for you as writer is deciding what effect you want to cause in your reader. This is the taste that the reader will have in response to your story when they have read it. Having a sense of what this taste will be before you begin writing is called a *prelibation*.

Having a clear prelibation will guide you to a genre decision. Knowing how a reader will react, what they will 'take away' from the story, means knowing the basic genre form of the work. An important distinction to understand is that genre is fundamentally a *responsive* categorisation of work rather than a *creative* one. Nevertheless, it is important for you to keep in mind the expectations of your reader while you are creating your story, for failing to pay heed to certain conventions that different genres dictate, may put you at risk of alienating your reader. Don't tell a reader it's science fiction if it doesn't have any science, for example.

We can begin to look at genres based on who your ideal reader is. At one level, libraries and our education systems class books according to how old the intended reader is. So there is a basic classification of 'children's books', which run from picture books that are usually read by an adult to a very young child, through to chapter books especially for young readers who are not yet teenagers. Then there is 'teen fiction' which of course suggests reading for all teenagers, however this is a very broad age classification, so Teen Fiction, perhaps, is much more addressed to readers aged between 14 and 16. Older than that we have the category of 'young adult', which extends into mid to early 20s (and much of which these days is read by adults), and at a younger age (especially in the US) the category of 'middle grade readers', which is a general category for readers aged somewhere between 11 and 14.

It is important that you have an understanding of who your ideal reader might be: if it's someone of similar age and life experience to yourself, someone younger, or someone older. This decision should help guide both your research and your writing.

Another important distinction in terms of story is the type of story experience — novel, novella, short story, movie, TV drama, play, comic, graphic novel, radio play or multi-media (including gaming). While each of these types are written differently — they use words in different ways — I maintain that the creation and development of 'story' is the central component of all of these forms.

This book's particular focus, however, is on the short story.

The short story differs from the novel in several ways. A novel may have several 'stories' woven through the narrative. A short story, however, usually deals with a single story and a single character at the centre of it, and a single situation in which that character is embroiled. This, of course, doesn't mean the story does not involve other characters. And, as I say in the introduction of *Stories from the Born Storytellers* (2013) a short story still features dramatic conflict, dynamic characters and strong climaxes, and will often bring you to laughter or tears, scare the pants of you, and remind you of something important about human nature. Short stories are an important part of our literary culture and an important stepping stone for the author who wants to develop their writing into any of the other forms of literary practice.

The third aspect of genre is the decision about the type of story you want to write, which we will develop further in this chapter when we discuss the different types of plot. As we will come to discover, genre and plot are interlinked. However, when you are thinking about your story and developing your story idea, you cannot avoid the question of what 'type' of story you may want to write. Your initial ideas will be conditioned as to whether your story will fall into a fantasy, adventure, romance, science fiction, horror, coming-of-age, crime mystery or thriller.

> **Make sure you read widely in the genre within which you are interested in writing. Make a study of your preferred genre by close reading, paying attention to common structural elements and how they are dealt with in that particular genre in order to understand the conventions.**

Plot and Conflict

Plot defines the internally consistent, interrelated episodes that pass through time to shape the story. A classically designed plot has an active Protagonist struggling against forces of antagonism to pursue their desires. This struggle takes place through continuous time and within a consistent fictional reality to a closed ending of absolute, irreversible change. Variations on this classic design might include multiple Protagonists, an open ending, internal conflict, nonlinear time, passive Protagonist, and inconsistent realities. The purpose of plot is to provide the reader access to the the *structure* of the work and its problem-solving methods by following the progress of the Protagonist.

The structure presents a reader's 'story mind', balancing four internally consistent views of the story. These views place the reader in a position to make judgements about the problem-solving going on within the story. They are perspectives that provide shape and distance.

- *The overall storyline* — an objective view of the story, the way a football coach observes the competition on the field, where the characters are represented by their archetypal functions

- *The main character storyline* — a view from inside the story, placing concern with what is happening immediately around the Protagonist, as though a player in the immediate heat of the game

- *The impact character storyline* — an alternative approach to the story problem than that of the Protagonist's; as if another character appears out of the mists of confusion and presents a dilemma because the Protagonist does not know whether it is friend or foe

- *The subjective storyline* — the view of the passionate contest between the Protagonist and the impact character of the moment (which can be, any other character in opposition).

(Source: Adapted from Huntley and Phillips, *Dramatica: A new theory of story*)

> ***The overall storyline*** *for Joe and Sally sees Joe lose the love of his life and any hope of its retrieval dashed. Sally has taken up with a man who represents everything opposite to Joe. In order to redeem his lost love, Joe attempts to remake himself in the image of his nemesis, plunging so far as to attempt robbing a bank, during which he unmasks the real Larry and overcomes his cowardice.*
>
> ***The main character storyline*** *follows Joe's first close encounter with death, his subsequent psychological downfall, and then his miraculous turnaround and second encounter with death in the face of extreme danger.*

The impact character storyline *is that of Larry and describes his impact on Joe as Joe tries to recover what he is lost, and Larry maintain what he has gained. Larry surprises the reader when it is reveled that he is the serial bank robber.*

The subjective storyline *describes the relationship between Joe and Luigi as they come to terms with the fact that each needs the other in order to survive the ordeal and recover what each has lost.*

The plot of a story therefore follows a given structure in which the four storylines are pursued, each meeting with the others at given story points, which are episodes of critical conflicts that propel the story forward. At the beginning of a story, the Protagonist declares an intention and sets out towards it. Without obstacles in the way, they would simply obtain said object and disappear. Of course, there would be no story because there would be no struggle, no transformation.

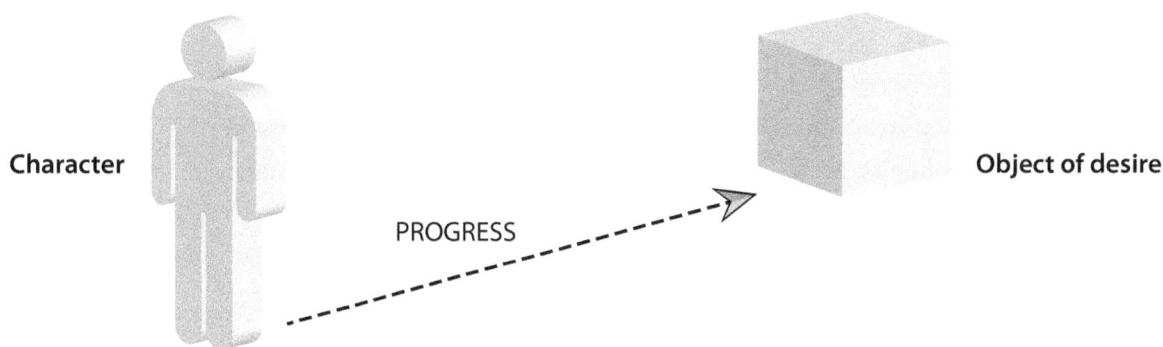

Plot: shaping story

A plot, however, encourages the writer to create, develop and impose obstacles to the character's progress that result in struggle. The structure of the plot follows the form of a series of constrictions and expansions — constrictions signal to the reader that the pathway has been complicated; expansions offer moments of respite after the character has successfully overcome an obstacle, negotiated a way around it or retreated in order to regroup and rearm.

As we have discussed earlier, the resistance to progress comes both from other characters impacting the main character, and the effects of the story world. However, these tend to follow pre-determined patterns, which can differ according to the genre of the story.

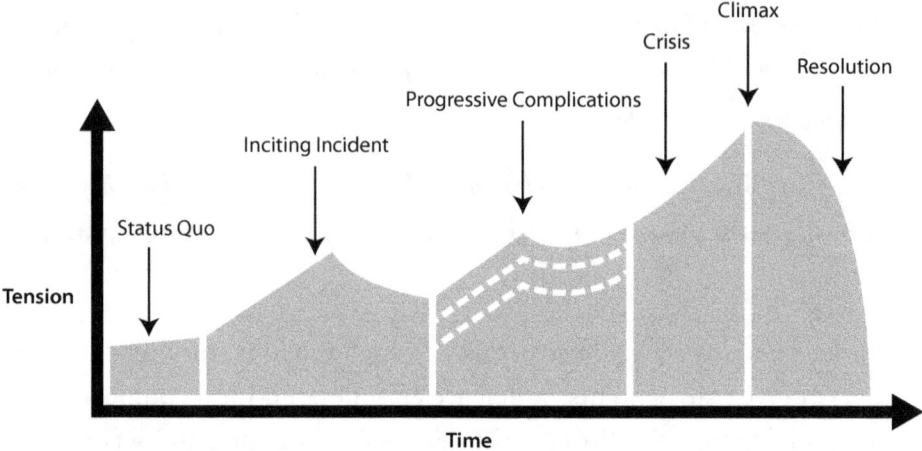

The overall shape of a story can be viewed as a type of graph that plots time against rising and falling tension. We can break the time down into five divisions, and one decisive turning point.

The status quo

The status quo is where you introduce the Protagonist in a moment of rising action in his world of the everyday. Use a moment of conflict to illustrate an important part of the character.

> *Joe declares his intention to marry Sally; makes a date and then faces a dilemma of whether he should go with Brian on a drinking binge or not.*

The Inciting Incident

This is a period where the Protagonist faces a conflict that alters the future. Quite often this is where the Protagonist receives a call to action, meets the Guardian or Contagonist, and is taken to a crisis point from which there is no turning back. At the end of the inciting incident, the Protagonist has been drawn into the special world of the story, known as the 'mythological woods'.

> *Joe's drinking binge causes him to injure himself and his landlord finds him in his house fighting for his life.*

Progressive Complications

This is a period of stages in the story with increasing contractions and expansions, in which the fortunes of the Protagonist change from positive to negative and negative to positive in increasingly desperate struggles.

Joe is dumped while in hospital; Joe learns about Larry; Joe confronts Sally; Joe drinks to excess; Joe's art goes sour; Joe buys a gun ...

Crisis

The crisis is the lead up to a critical point in the story where maximum pressure is on the Protagonist, and the Protagonist usually comes face-to-face with the Antagonist.

Joe enters the bank with the intention of robbing it.

Climax

The climax is the decisive turning point, which is the outcome of the final struggle on which the story turns. It is the trigger that brings about transformation. The Protagonist may experience an epiphany, claim the prize, solve the puzzle.

Joe tackles the masked bandit and gets shot.

Resolution

Following the climax is an essential wrap up, and dénouement (pronounced *day-no-mon* meaning unknotting) of the central conflict. It is where the realisation takes place that something fundamental has changed and the Hero has fulfilled their psychological and moral needs.

Joe is back in hospital where he is mended, and Sally and he are reunited.

In *The Poetics*, Aristotle introduced the idea of a 'standard' type of structure which has come to be known as the Three-act Structure. This is still widely used in scriptwriting for plays and screen, and can often be found in discussions on the novel and short story. Following the above model, Act One takes the story up to the conclusion of the inciting incident, Act Two covers the Progressive Complications, and Act Three takes the story from the beginning of the final Crisis through to its Resolution. There is no fixed duration for these dynamics, rather they fall where the story provides the appropriate turning point. After the inciting incident the Protagonist is committed to the crucible, there is no turning back: the only way out is through the duration of the story, come what may. Another turning point occurs at the beginning of the final Crisis when the Protagonist has been all but defeated and has to face their nemesis in order to live or die.

Seven Basic Plots

A plot is the essential scheme or plan of your story. It is the process by which your Protagonist moves from a situation that may be considered everyday through a series of consequential episodes of rising conflict, to arrive at a resolution that gives the reader satisfaction. This satisfaction comes from the character who has endured the process of the story becoming 'whole', that is, reaching a point of balance.

Christopher Booker, In *The Seven Basic Plots: Why we tell stories*, says:

> The plot of a story is that which leads its hero or heroine either to a 'catastrophe' or an 'unknotting'; either to frustration or to liberation; either to death or to a renewal of life. And it might be thought that there are almost as many ways of describing these downward and upward paths as there are individual stories in the world. Yet the more carefully we look at the vast range of stories thrown up by the human imagination through the ages, the more clearly we may discern that there are certain continually recurring general shapes to stories, dictating the nature of the road which the hero or heroine may take to their ultimate destination.

Booker's work attempts to settle an age-old argument about how many types of stories there are. And while the verity of it can be forever argued among the world's academics, his modelling of seven basic plots provides the writer with an excellent analysis of the different types of story, and the differences in those types. The following are summary sketches of Booker's seven different plots. Use them to help make a decision about the type of story you are writing, and to map out your basic story shape.

Overcoming the Monster and the Thrilling Escape from Death

> This shows the Hero being called to face and overcome a deadly personification of evil.
>
> The story begins in some anticipation stage — the status quo (1) where the hero is called to action. As the hero makes preparations they experience a dream stage (2) where they are remote from danger. This is followed by a frustration stage (3) when the hero is dwarfed by the menace of the monster. As the situation worsens, this turns to a nightmare stage (4) in which the hero battles against odds that are stacked against them in favour of the monster. But at the climax, (5) when all seems lost, there is a reversal of fortunes and the hero experiences a thrilling escape from death and the monster is slain.
>
> *Example: Jack and the beanstalk; Harry Potter(all books)*

Rags to Riches

This shows how some young unrecognised hero or heroine is eventually lifted out of obscurity, poverty and misery to a state of great splendour and happiness.

But the progress is laden with struggle. The status quo is a state of initial wretchedness (1). The most obvious reason for their misery is that in their status quo situation the Protagonist is overshadowed by some dark malevolent figure maltreating them in some way. Then something calls them out into the world (2). They have an initial taste of success, only to be 'brought back into line' by an act against their progress (3). The central crisis looms and suddenly everything goes wrong, separating the hero or heroine from the 'one' thing that has become more important to them than anything else in life, resulting in despair and the worst moment in their story. As they emerge from the crisis, (4) we see independence and the final ordeal ahead of them. Although unfulfilled, they are discovering a new independent strength that is put to an ultimate test in some battle against the malevolent force standing between them and their goal. This results in the climax of the story (5) and their reward for successfully overcoming the dark force is some final complete union with their 'Prince' or 'Princess'. They will reach some state of maturity, possibly represented by the ruling of their 'kingdom'.

Example: Cinderella, Aladdin

The Quest

This shows some pull on the hero or heroine driving them towards some distant, all-important goal.

The status quo is life in some 'state of decay or destruction' (1) and the hero is 'called' to action, recognising that they can only rectify matters by making a long and difficult journey, a recognition that has come through some supernatural or visionary direction. Thus, the hero sets out on the journey (2) usually with a small gathering of companions, battling against hostile terrain and encountering a series of life threatening ordeals. These may include monsters to overcome, temptations to be resisted and travelling between two deadly opposites, each ending with a thrilling escape. The hero may also encounter moments of respite and receive hospitality and helpful advice. The journey culminates (3) with an arrival and a new frustration, where the hero can see the goal but is prevented from reaching it due to new obstacles in the path. The hero then embarks on the final ordeals (4) undergoing a series of tests — often three in number — to prove their worthiness, culminating in a final and great battle (5), resulting in a last thrilling escape from death. The hero takes the prize to live happily ever after.

Example: Lord of the Ring; Raiders of the Lost Ark

Voyage and Return.

The hero's status quo shows them in a state in which their consciousness is somehow restricted (1) — bored, drowsy ... which makes them vulnerable to some shattering new experience. The world is interrupted suddenly by some inexplicable fall into a distant world. They arrive in an initial fascinated or dream state (2) and explore their new world enthusiastically, but it is not a place where they can feel at home. This leads to a frustration state (3) in which the mood changes to one of oppression and difficulty. Escape becomes the important issue as a dark shadow begins to encroach and leads to a nightmare stage (4) in which the dark shadow becomes a threat to the hero's life. Just as the threat is about to close in on the hero or heroine, they make a thrilling escape and return to their normal world (5). The real question posed by the adventure is: how much have they learnt or gained from their adventure? How much has changed?

Example: Alice in Wonderland, Narnia, Madagascar

Comedy

In a comedy, we see the hero in a world of confusion (1) where their true identity, and motivation, is not known, or is confused with the identity of another. This is a state of frustration as the two who belong together (hero and heroine) are shut off from each other by the forces of the confusion. The confusion gets worse (2) by a series of events that continue to move the hero and heroine in opposite directions and the dark pressure is at its greatest, in a nightmare state (4) in which everyone is in a tangled web. Finally an event alters the situation and sheds light on the confusion, bringing things not previously recognised into the light and perceptions change. The shadows are dispelled (5) and the situation is miraculously transformed and the little world is brought together in a state of joyful reunion.

Example: The Importance of Being Earnest; Shrek 2

Tragedy

The story begins in an anticipation stage where the hero is unfulfilled (1) and their thoughts are turned towards the object of some desire. This leads to the dream stage (2) where they become in some way committed to the course of action. For a while things go well and they appear to be winning the gratification once dreamed of. Then a frustration state (3) sets in and imperceptibly things begin to go wrong. The hero cannot find a point of rest and is compelled to further 'dark acts' which lock them even more irrevocably into their course of action. This leads to a nightmare stage (4) where things are seen to be seriously slipping out of the hero's control, and they are succumbing to a heightened sense of threat and despair, forces of opposition and fate are closing in. Finally a state of destruction or death-wish (5) arrives, either by the forces the hero has aroused against them, or by some final violent act which precipitates their own death.

Example: Romeo & Juliet, Othello

Rebirth.

A young hero or heroine falls under the shadow of a dark power. (1) For a while, things may seem to go reasonably well (2); the threat may even appear to recede, but eventually it approaches again (3) — this time much amplified until the hero or heroine appear to have been imprisoned in a state of living death. This state continues for a long time, and it seems the dark power has completely triumphed (4) but finally comes a miraculous redemption where a rescue (5) takes place and the hero or heroine is set free and united with their other half.

Example: Snow White

The Universal Plot in Three Acts

Beginning (Act One):

The beginning of almost any type of story shows us the hero or heroine in some undeveloped, frustrated or incomplete state. This establishing of their unhappy, immature or unfulfilled state sets up the tension that needs to be resolved, and this provides the essence of the story.

Middle (Act Two):

The middle of the story shows them sooner or later falling under the shadow of the dark power, the resulting conflict constitutes the story's main action. Through most of the story we see its little world divided into an 'upper' realm, in which the dark power holds sway and an 'inferior' realm, where the light forces remain in the shadows.

Ending (Act Three):

The end of the story provides its resolution. The action builds through a crisis to a climax, when the threatening and confusing forces reach their highest point of pressure on everyone involved, and this paves the way for the reversal or unknotting, the moment when the dark force is overthrown.

The nature of a story's ending then depends entirely on how its hero or heroine has aligned themselves to the dark power. If the central figure has remained or ended in opposition to the dark power we see that, in this final act of liberation, there is a prize of infinite value to be won. We see that the hero or heroine have ended up fulfilled or complete in a way which, through most of the story, would have seemed impossible. If, on the other hand, that opposition has not materialised we see the the hero or heroine slip into an unstoppable downward spiral.

From Plot to Plan

The plot should emerge from your initial statements:

- Your premise (the grand argument and what you truly believe in — see Chapter One)
- The snapshot statement (the summary statement of what the story is about — see Chapter One)

You should know a lot about your main character, (see Chapter Two) particularly their psychology and how they will react to changing circumstances because you are about to change their circumstances on them. And if you don't know them well enough, you will not be in a position to create the changes to the story that you need. If you haven't written character biographies, and done some journal writing or creative writing from their viewpoint, you need to do it now.

You then use the information you learn in the next step.

The Master Plan

Map out the overall structure using the six-stage model discussed earlier in this chapter. Follow the Protagonist's journey through to the end. This shape ignores subplots and focusses on the Protagonist's path only. In each stage you write a short description of what happens to the main character during that stage of the story.

What happens to the main character in …

1. the status quo (or world of the everyday)
2. the inciting incident
3. progressive complications — initial opposition after entering the 'mythological woods'; Hero's plan to win where the Hero is tested; retreat and regroup …
4. crisis and battle to the death and rebirth, or ordeal to leave the 'mythological woods' and return home
5. climax and turning point, the moment of the Protagonist's self-revelation
6. resolution — wrapping up the loose ends, resolving the character's moral needs

Doing this gives you a clear understanding of the overall story shape, a Master Plan, so to speak. Consider the specifics of the type plot you are working with, and the genre.

Joe and Sally is a comedy plot in a romance genre.

This first stage does a number of things:

- It gives you a broad Master Plan that shapes the whole story based on the journey of the main character
- It highlights where you might need other characters and what roles you need them for
- It shows up weaknesses in your knowledge of your Protagonist and their interaction with the story world
- It gets you to focus on some of the structural elements discussed earlier in the chapter, which ones are needed, where they might occur, how they might turn out
- It invites the introduction of subplots that are needed to enrich the drama.

A Hero should pass by a series of probable or necessary stages from misfortune to happiness or from happiness to misfortune. A character should grow from pole to pole. A coward becomes brave, a saint becomes a sinner, a policeman becomes a criminal, a lover becomes an enemy — or vice versa. These are the essential aspects discussed in Character Growth (Chapter Two).

Your story not only has a sequence of episodes, but it also has corresponding stages of character growth. Based on the six-stage model, this is how *The Lion King* might look according to its master structure:

1. *Simba is a wild and cocky youngster. He disobeys his father by going to a banned place and gets into trouble with the hyenas.(Status Quo)*

2. *Simba accepts the blame for his father's death because Scar, who is jealous of Simba's right to the throne, staged it. (Inciting Incident)*

3. *Simba runs away and nearly dies in the desert. He is saved by Pumbaa and Timon, but he has little will to continue living. He is introduce to the concept of Hakuna Matata — life without rules and responsibilities — in the jungle where he grows up, but realises he's missing something in his life. He saves Pumbaa's life when Nala, his childhood sweetheart, comes back into his life. Simba is challenged to take responsibility for who he is when Nala informs him that Scar has destroyed the Pridelands. Simba rejects Nala and is confronted by Rafiki, who appeals to Simba's spirit to accept his real identity as king. (Progressive Complications)*

4. Simba meets the ghost of his father who convinces him to return to the Pridelands.(Crisis from inner conflict)

5. Simba returns and faces Scar. He learns the truth about his father's death. The final conflict is resolved with Scar's death at the hands of the hyenas. (Climax and turning point)

6. Simba returns to the beginning of the story, but as an older and wiser lion, and a new life is just beginning. He has taken his place in the Circle of Life. (Resolution)

This Master Plan maps out the main incidents of the story out of which grow the main stages of Simba's growth; along with the conflicts arising from his story world, his inner self and then finally with his nemesis, Scar. It includes a number of minor conflicts (Simba and his guilt, Simba and his rescuers, Simba and Nala, Simba and who he really is) which are all resolved as the story comes to a close.

You can follow Simba's growth, from his youthful cockiness to his downfall. Then his acceptance of a carefree way of life, to asking questions about whom he is, his realisation and his final reconciliation with his family and the love of his life. It is Simba's growth that makes the story interesting to us, and that provides the overall story shape.

The evil plot is instigated by Scar motivated by his desire to ascend the throne and rid himself of the competition. He engages the hyenas in his plot, and enslaves the lionesses. Scar and Simba are bonded by their independent motivations: Scar's to steal the throne and Simba's to absolve his guilt. Neither can simply walk away, although much of the story is spent on Simba's attempt to escape facing up to the truth of who he is.

It's interesting to note that *The Lion King* engages features of three basic plots: *Overcoming the Monster*, the *Quest* and the *Rebirth*. This goes to demonstrate that, like the character archetypes of Chapter Three, nothing is firmly set in stone. A story like *The Lord of The Rings*, while it has all the hallmarks of a Quest, does feature the structural characteristics of five of the other plot types. Harry Potter can be located within four plot types: *Overcoming the Monster, Rags to Riches, Voyage and Return* and *The Quest*, although it is fundamentally about overcoming a monster.

This overall story map tells us what the main story events are while at the same time giving us an indication of how the characters will develop and grow as a result of those events. It helps keep the story in control.

Breaking Down the Master Plan into a Step Sheet — More Than a Simple Outline

Having now made crucial decisions about genre, plot, overall story shape and its structural elements, it's time to lay out the actual story events in sequence. By now you know how your main character progresses through the story, and what influences that progress, where the highs and lows are. It's now time to become involved in each step.

The crucial thing about the step sheet is that it focusses on the combination of *character and incident growing out of each other*. In other words in a sequence of A-B-C-D ..., D cannot happen if C didn't happen, C cannot happen if B didn't happen and so on. The step sheet is where you get involved with your characters and what is happening to them. What this means is that you are thinking about the 'how' of the story: how the story moves forward, how the character grows, how the conflict rises, how subplots grow out of character actions and decisions, and so on.

The step sheet is one of the most powerful planning tools. It is the tool you use to keep control of the story from beginning to end. You can use it to manage your writing production, to assess the writing you have done, to test your theories of a conflict.

Your step sheet needs to do more than simply 'outline' though. In your step sheet, you need to identify each scene in a cause-and-effect relationship, and describe the 'business' of the scene, which should including the characters who are in the scene, what they do, what happens, how tension is introduced, how the scene ends and moves forward. It also helps to include the story word details.

The step sheet is a creative act, and should be approached with a willingness for adventure, it is the time to try things out and experiment with the cause-and-effect in the events of the story.

Where Does the Story Begin?

When you wrote the premise of your story, you chose to establish that *character through conflict leads to conclusion*. Therefore you intend to establish a character and their role in the story. You will place a dilemma in front of that character which will lead to conflict with another character, nature or a situation, and through this conflict your Protagonist will grow and the reader will arrive at some conclusion, assisted by the change that has occurred in your character.

What are the things that have to happen?

- Your characters (Protagonist and Antagonist) have to be introduced
- Your Protagonist has to face a dilemma
- Your Protagonist has to overcome or succumb to, your Antagonist in the climax
- You have to deal with the remains.

Your characters have to be introduced before they are engrossed in conflict. Your reader, or audience, has to feel something about them — whether they are good or bad, capable or incapable. The dilemma you place in front of your Protagonist would be the 'normal' start of the story.

In Harry Potter, the dilemma is marked by Hagrid's entrance. Before that we are apprised of the situation Harry is in, his foster family, a touch of his capabilities with the snake. The story really begins with Hagrid.

In The Lion King, the story begins with the Elephant Graveyard, and Scar's intentions are revealed.

In Snow White and the Seven Dwarfs, the story begins with the Queen directing the huntsman to kill Snow White.

In each of these examples, one character is forcing change upon others and we are let into the private worlds of our Protagonists before they are faced with a dilemma. It lets us know something about them. It gives us an idea of their personalities.

You need to start your story just before it begins. We need to understand the character's situation before things change. This is the Status Quo. When things change, the core conflict of the story is introduced. However, you should always strive to put your character in terrible trouble as early as possible. The trouble of the status quo shouldn't necessarily be the core conflict in the story, but when the Protagonist assumes the trouble has been dealt with, things should get worse. The trouble at the beginning should portend the trouble to come, and show us something of the character's weakness.

Managing the Middle

A well-designed story structure leads you to maintain positive pressure on forward movement at all times through the story. Even allowing for the squash-and-stretch of rest after action, the Protagonist should be engaged in conflict, someone should be challenging their position at all times. Apart from the core conflict, there is the moral conflict, the conflict of rationality, and the conflict of trust. The Protagonist gets no rest from conflict until the closing moments, and even then, you might consider raising the spectre of something new.

This means that all action is action against an opposing force, whether it's internal or external. It can be physical, social or psychological (revisit Chapter Five). It means that all dialogue is in conflict. It means that the character at the centre of the scene wants something, and there is a force opposing their attainment of it; an opposition of wills.

As the story progresses, tension rises and dramatic action compresses, although it does so in waves, the waves become bigger and greater in number, and there is less distance between them. This is important because it represents the way a reader should be feeling as each event is triggered by its precursor. Your step sheet needs to follow that progression.

A desire line

Desire provides the impetus for the Protagonist's path through the story. It is the fundamental of the story's premise, what it is that the Protagonist wants in order to be where they need to be at the end of the story. It is the McGuffin.

Desire needs to be multi-dimensional. As the story progresses and the intensity of the opposition grows, so should the desire grow. The desire changes through the course of the story *only in intensity, not in nature*. In other words, it is not a new desire that emerges; it is an altered — new level — of desire. You should try to plot a 'desire line' that shows the levels of desire as the story progresses. This enables the stakes to be raised.

The first change in desire occurs at a revelation point that forces the Protagonist into a decision that changes their direction because they have gained some new information. In many stories this occurs in the middle of the middle, some call it the 'central pinch'. The Protagonist suddenly realises (a revelation) that they have passed the point of no return. At this moment the motivation to reach the goal notches up somewhat, which of course raises the stakes, increases the risks, and changes the level of desire — now the Protagonist wants it more than ever. It is the moment the tension gap produces an altered desire as a result of the new reality rather than simply recycling back to the original desire.

The second change in the desire line occurs when the Protagonist has reached the lowest point, usually after having resoundingly lost in some form of battle against the Antagonist. It is a moment of revelation coming off the back of an apparent defeat. Although the odds against winning are extreme, the Protagonist comes once again into possession of some new information which gives them some sliver of hope for success. The one driving force that might help them prevail is a changed level of desire for the goal.

Each change in the desire is a 'notch upward' in terms of motivation and drive. The object of desire itself has not changed, only the level of motivation, methodology, judgement and purpose … the story presence.

Story Questions

Story questions are important devices that keep the reader involved in the events of the story and, more importantly, anticipating what might be coming up. Story questions are not questions asked by the author or a character, they are devices that cause the reader to ask 'what's happening?...' There are two types of story question:

1. The short question or hook, designed to move the reader into the next scene. The question usually arises from an action or decision that has short term consequences, and answered within the next scene or two. It is almost a mini crisis that rises to a climax and is then resolved, giving the reader a moment of breathing space, and moving the drama to the next stage.

2. The long question, or sleeper, designed to ensure the central mystery is elevated and repeatedly tested by actions and decisions that characters take, suggesting there is hidden business. These questions are usually resolved at the resolution points throughout the rising action, but they may be resolved in such a way that a new question arises, taking the reader's interest in a new direction.

Story questions are important devices to use in the middle of the story. Make sure that you pique interest in choices and decisions a character makes that the reader can object to or sympathise with, giving them the desire to find out how that particular decision or action affects the character down the track. Make sure it's something the reader can care about.

Introducing a Subplot

A subplot is used to compare how the Protagonist and another character approach generally the same situation. Remember two key rules about subplot:

1. The subplot must affect the Protagonist's main plot, or it shouldn't be present at all. If the subplot doesn't serve the main plot, you have two simultaneous stories that may be clinically interesting to the audience, but they make the main plot seem too long. To connect the subplot to the main plot, make sure the two dovetail neatly, usually near the end.

2. The main character of the subplot is usually not the Sidekick or Guardian. The subplot character has a different function to the Sidekick and Guardian, both of whom help the Hero in the main plot. The subplot character drives a different but related plot that you compare to the main plot.

It improves the character, theme, and texture of your story. On the other hand, it slows the desire line — the narrative drive. So you have to decide what is most important to you. If you are going to use a subplot, you only have enough time to work through the six Master Plan steps. But be aware that if you can't cover all six, it won't be a complete story and will seem forced. Because of the limited time, you want to introduce your subplot as early in the story as is naturally appropriate.

Fuelling Danger

There are four techniques that can help you make the opposition in your story as dangerous as possible:

1. Create a hierarchy of opponents with a number of alliances. All of the opponents are related to one another; they are all working together to defeat the Hero. The main opponent sits at the top of this pyramid, with the other opponents below him in power.
2. Hide the hierarchy from the Protagonist and the audience, and hide each opponent's true agenda (or true desire).
3. Reveal all this information in pieces and at an increasing pace over the course of the story. This means you'll have more reveals near the end of the story. As we shall see, how you reveal information to the Protagonist and the reader is what makes or breaks your plot.
4. Consider having your Protagonist go up against an obvious opponent early in the story. As the conflict intensifies, have the Protagonist discover attacks from a stronger hidden opposition or attacks from that part of the opponent that has been hidden away.

Your characters have to be beset by complications, and these can only come from the energy of the events that precede them. It is a logical process. However the events of the story are organised, it's important to develop an internal logic: character and incident must grow out of each other.

Double Reversal

You may want to use the technique of the double reversal at the final climax. In this technique, you give a self-revelation to the opponent as well as to the Protagonist. Each learns from the other, and the audience sees two insights about how to act and live in the world instead of one.

Here's how you create a double reversal:

1. Give both the Protagonist and the Antagonist a weakness and a need.
2. Make the Antagonist human. That means, among other things, they must be capable of learning and changing.
3. During or just after the battle, give the Antagonist as well as the Protagonist a self-revelation.
4. Connect the two self-revelations. The Protagonist should learn something from the Antagonist, and the Antagonist should learn something from the Protagonist.
5. Your moral vision as the author is the best of what both characters learn.

Revelations

Revelations are a critical part of the plot. Two of them are tied to changes in desire. It's important to take some time to separate points of revelation from the rest of the plot and look at them as one unit, and allow them to 'thicken' as the story progresses. Tracking the revelations sequence is valuable storytelling technique, it can help you see if the sequence builds properly.

1. The sequence of revelations must be logical. They must occur in the order in which the Protagonist would most likely learn of them.
2. They must build in intensity. Ideally, each revelation should be stronger than the one that came before it. This is not always possible, especially in longer stories (for one thing, it defies logic). But you want a general build-up so that the drama increases.
3. The revelations must come at an increasing pace. This also heightens the drama because the reader gets hit with a greater density of surprise.

In addition to the first two revelations discussed in the section *A Desire Line* above:

- An audience revelation (usually following the second revelation) is one way of increasing excitement as your story approaches its climax. In this type of revelation the audience learns something that the Protagonist doesn't, allowing the reader to step back and increase their experience of the objective storyline view, from which they can assess the Protagonist's overall process of change.

- A decisive revelation is a third revelation of the Protagonist's in which they learn what they need to know in order to beat the Antagonist. (*Simba learns the truth of his father's death.*) This information emboldens and empowers the Protagonist and they become more driven because they can see with greater clarity what the stakes are.

- The self-revelation is the moment the Protagonist undergoes change learning for the first time who they really are, which either destroys them (tragedy) or makes them stronger. If the self-revelation is moral as well as psychological, the Protagonist also learns the proper way to act towards others. A great self-revelation is sudden, for better dramatic effect; shattering for the Protagonist, whether the self-revelation is positive or negative; and new — it must be something the Protagonist did not know about until that moment. Everything in the story leads to this point.

The most powerful of all revelations is known as a *reversal*. This is where the reader's understanding of everything in the story is turned on its head — suddenly every element of the plot is seen in a new light. All reality changes in an instant. The reversal is that twist in the tail that makes a reader go 'aha!'. They are common in detective stories and thrillers as well as romance.

What Makes a Climax?

The point of your story is its climax and resolution. At its most basic, it is where the *conflict* meets with the *conclusion*. But there are other things that readers need in order to be fully satisfied.

- *Surprise*. Not everything about the end should be predictable, there should be some sense of the unexpected, a sudden revelation, which may come as a surprise to both the character(s) and the reader. A comedy requires that there is a twist as an element of the revelation, but other story modes can also use a twist that takes the reader by surprise and shows the true purpose of the story. The twist can show up as either negative or positive, or as an ironic outcome that is both positive and negative.

- *Reward and punishment*. It helps, as James N Frey says, to 'issue a verdict in the court of poetic justice', in which the villain gets his just desserts, but by some means that is poetically related to his villainy. The same is true for rewards dished out for Protagonists and supporting characters, their justice should come organically out of the work they have carried out through the story, and the reward issued in a poetic act. The Protagonist should only get a reward they have worked for, not receive a gratuitously bestowed gift to simply recognise success — the success must beget appropriate reward tied to the sacrifice given. If a Protagonist fails to learn an important moral lesson they must attract penalty for that failure.

- *The McGuffin*. The prize of the story is what is brought back to the everyday world, it is what has been contested through the course of the story, and it has value to the Protagonist's world on their return. It's important to know what the value is so that it can be shown to be worth the journey, and used as evidence that the journey was undertaken by the Protagonist. The McGuffin can be literal or metaphoric, physical or virtual; or a personal drive causing people to go after something. The self-revelation should show the McGuffin's true worth, and the best of these are those that have a hidden value that is far greater than the surface value. Failure to return with the McGuffin, is a failure of the Protagonist's ultimate test.

Common McGuffins may be:

- Love. The Protagonist gets the love they deserve after the final sacrifice. Up to that point, they may be chasing shadows.

- Changed world. The wisdom the Protagonist brings back may be the McGuffin, new knowledge to right a terrible wrong, or lift the people out of despair into the light.

- Responsibility. Protagonists are sometimes required to take up a higher office on their return, because they bring back the qualities of leadership and vision on the sacrifice of their outlaw or loner status.

- Tragedy. The McGuffin of the tragedy is the correct moral behaviour, and through the downward spiral of a Protagonist's tragic decisions, show the consequences of errors.

- Richer, but not wiser. This is a McGuffin, albeit an elusive one. Wisdom in the end would raise the Protagonist from the pits of despair. But if, through the course of the story, the Protagonist takes positive steps, only to reach the end and repeat the errors of the circumstances the story originally found them in, that would push the McGuffin out of reach until the next attempt. This is an ideal ironic ending.

- Wiser, but not richer. Another ideal ironic ending, but the inverse of the former, where the Hero learns the lessons and ends up making morally sound decisions, but loses the prize because of misplaced trust, or the fact that life simply isn't fair.

Chapter 7
Dialogue & Scenes: Let's Talk About It

The Functions of Dialogue

According to Frank Thomas and Ollie Johnston in the Disney Animation book, *The Illusion of Life*, the easiest way to develop a story is to do it all with dialogue between the characters, explaining everything an audience wants to know. The hardest way is to do it all with pantomime. Why? Because the personality of a character rarely comes to life without their voice, and in particular the carefully selected lines that are given to that voice.

Walt Disney usually left out the dialogue until the sequence had been developed to the point where he could see just how little was really needed. Disney story men had to think visually first, and when they did write dialogue it had to tell something about the character and not be just exposition. But dialogue has to be more than emotional statement. There has to be action that supports the dialogue and demonstrates the emotions. Unless the reader can feel the emotions, any dialogue will seem flat and void.

Writing effective dialogue is an art in itself because effective dialogue has to perform specific functions, and should avoid functions that are best performed by narrative, action or other sounds. Yet writers frequently use dialogue to cover weaknesses in story development, exposition, action and character development. Dialogue is what pulls the reader into the characters' world. It helps create the illusion that a real person inhabits the pages. When it is poorly constructed, not producing movement in the story, flat and lifeless, it can also be what drives them away.

There are two parts to writing effective dialogue:
- knowing when to use dialogue, and
- knowing how to leverage its use for maximum story effect.

When to use Dialogue

Dialogue is an active component of a dramatic scene. When we consider the way a narrative works, we have writing that tells us what we need to know — that explains what the narrator is seeing and experiencing, and reporting it to us. Frey calls this 'dramatic narrative' because it dramatises the narrator's view. Writing of this type has little call for dialogue, although it could be argued that a dramatic narrative in the first-person voice is a kind of dialogue entirely. Dramatic narrative is essentially the 'telling' part of showing and telling. In a dramatic narrative, the narrator relates actions, shows character growth and exploits inner conflict, but does so in a summary fashion whereas, in a scene, the narrator describes actions as they are happening.

When two characters come together, however, there is often an exchange between them, frequently calling for words to pass between the characters. This is a scene and the exchange of words is called dialogue. It is where one character speaks (he said/she said/I said …) and another responds. In a dramatic scene, action is taking place and part of that action is the dialogue. The narrator suspends the reporting of events and shows the characters acting them out. The reader is experiencing the action as it happens.

Coming between these two is what Frey calls the half scene, which he describes as a 'dramatic narrative interrupted, blended with parts of a scene.' In the half scene, it is common to find dialogue in both reported and active modes. Reported dialogue (sometimes called indirect discourse) is when the narrator tells the reader what a character says as opposed to direct dialogue showing it.

Dramatic writing requires rising conflict, not only for the story as a whole, but for each dramatic episode (or scene), regardless of whether it is handled as a dramatic narrative, scene or half scene. Each episode in a story must come to a climax and resolution, even if the resolution of one climax leads to further conflict in the story. An episode has the same shape as a story: it begins at a low point of tension and rises to a point of climax, followed by a resolution.

> *Joe sat holding his phone. He felt alone: more alone than he'd ever felt. It's over, she'd said. Don't call me, don't come near me, don't even think about me. She finished by telling him she wouldn't answer her phone if it showed his number calling. The shattered memories of her words pierced his heart, their barbed edges sharper than fish hooks. He looked at Luigi looking expectantly back at him.*
>
> *'She's true to her word,' he said. 'She's always true to her word … what I love most about her.'*

This short half scene includes both reported dialogue (what Sally had said to Joe) and active dialogue (what he says to Luigi.) Using reported dialogue allows you to reflect on the dialogue through the filter of the character's mind. It places the reader in an intimate position with the character, creating a subjective point of view. The dialogue, while in the originating character's voice, is heard through the memory of the narrator, which filters it and adds a degree of pathos that isn't available from the active point of view.

Dialogue is often described as a conversation between characters. While this is true, it falls far short of what it means to have effective dialogue in a work. Effective dialogue must be more than a mere conversation. It must be an exchange of ideas, beliefs, knowledge, emotion and feelings that drive the story forward and add a unique voice to a character. It needs to be conversation in which the character lies, demurs, is clever, fresh, sarcastic, witty, argumentative, colourful … a conversation that is oblique rather than direct.

The principle functions of dialogue are:

- Positioning character
- Differentiating voices
- Advancing the plot
- Revealing a character's emotional state
- Demonstrating feelings
- Informing the reader of events that take place outside the narrator's viewpoint.

Positioning Character

Dialogue is not dialogue without character. But you need to give your characters more than simply words to put in their mouths. What characters say needs to support their actions; provide perspective for the reader. You use dialogue to establish, cement and further a character's position relative to other characters and to the circumstances.

We established in Chapter One that a story is a realisation that something fundamental has changed when we are told of what happens when someone does something to get what they want. Stories in which characters fail to change inwardly tend to be sentimental and unresolved. This usually occurs when the motivations are superficial and the dialogue between the characters is weak.

For a story to be worth getting involved in it must feature characters who are not only worthy and have human characteristics, but are also at odds with other characters. It must rely on archetypes of character whose motivations, methods, judgements and purposes put them in conflict with others over the story's main goal. These four dimensions must be grounded in physical, social or psychological realities as they apply to a character. Furthermore the story must allow the reader access to the main events of the story in an orderly and comprehensible way. It must lead to a resolution that is believable within the world of the characters.

Effective dialogue helps create, maintain and shift the position of characters relative to other characters and to where the overall story is heading. This 'positioning' is an odd thing that takes place inside the reader's mind. The reader makes decisions about the relative 'positions' of characters because of the sympathy, empathy and identification they have, deciding who's important, who's not, who stands on top of the ladder, who is beneath.

It is not something the writer does to the character, but rather what the writer does to the reader by giving characters the means of exposing their differences and morality through their dialogue. A reader is then able to see each character in relation to the story's plot and how it is fully explored and eventually resolved. It's the relative 'position' of characters that maintains competition over the story's main goal, giving the reader access to a mental hierarchy of the motivations and judgements of characters. If dialogue does not work to position characters, then the dialogue will appear flaccid, being used only to explain the relationships rather than exploit the differences.

Positioning one character against another is achieved through a combination of the language a character uses as opposed to the language of another, and how much of their inner thoughts are exposed to the reader. The choice of language will reflect a character's beliefs and attitudes in relation to the story's main goal. There is no point in simply having a difference of opinion with another character unless that difference is based on a *belief* that can be used to justify the character's position and actions. As a story advances towards the goal, the relative positions of the different characters become more defined, often more entrenched. Consequently, when a transformation occurs, it is clear. And the language of the dialogue will change accordingly.

A Protagonist emerging from a downtrodden existence in a rags-to-riches story to claim the keys to the kingdom will learn to include positive words in their language, evolving from the pain of overwhelming negative experience to that of more positive and successful experience. A tragic character on a downhill slide will become increasingly egocentric, and their dialogue will demonstrate this as the character progressively becomes more desperate and escape drifts further away. A character's language is what informs the reader that change is taking place.

From The Incredibles (Brad Bird 2004)

The following scene in the movie, *The Incredibles*, demonstrates how dialogue, when used effectively, positions the two characters in the scene.

Bob has been out secretly playing superhero.

> *Bob enters quietly through the kitchen, pausing in the kitchen long enough to nab the remaining hunk of chocolate cake. Humming pleasantly as he chews, he moves into the living room when a voice comes out of the dark—*
>
> HELEN'S VOICE: *You said you'd be back by eleven.*
>
> *Bob freezes, a light snaps on. A chair swivels round— it's Helen, wearing her robe and a peeved expression.*
>
> BOB: *I said I'd be back later.*
>
> HELEN: *I assumed you'd be back later — if you came back at all — you'd be … " back later." (uses*

her fingers to emphasise quotation)

BOB: *Well ... I'm back. Okay?*

Bob moves to go but Helen's left arm stretches and stops him, plucking a small, dusty fragment of concrete off his coat. She crosses to him, catching up with her hand.

HELEN: *Is this ... rubble?*

BOB (DEFENSIVE): *It's just a little workout. Just ... (stuffing the last crumbs of the cake into his mouth)...stay to loose—*

HELEN: *You know how I feel about that Bob! (She discards the piece of rubbish in an angry gesture). Darn you! We just got settled! We can't blow cover again!*

BOB: *—the building was coming down anyway—*

Bob turns away to leave the room. Helen stretches out her elastic arm and rounds on him.

HELEN: *Wha—? You knocked down a building?*

BOB: *It was on fire! Structurally unsound! It was coming down anyway!*

HELEN (exasperated): *Tell me it's not the police scanner again—*

BOB: *Look I performed a public service. You act like that's a bad thing!*

HELEN: *It is a bad thing, Bob! Uprooting our family <u>again</u> so you can relive the glory days is a very bad thing!*

BOB: *Reliving the glory days is better than acting like they didn't happen!*

HELEN: *Yes. They happened. But this, our family, is what's happening now, Bob. And you are missing <u>this</u>! I can't believe you don't want to go to your own son's graduation.*

BOB: *It's not a graduation! He's moving from the fourth grade to the fifth grade!*

HELEN: *It's a ceremony ...*

BOB: *It's psychotic! They keep creating new ways to celebrate mediocrity. But if someone is genuinely exceptional they shut him down because they don't want everyone else to feel bad!*

HELEN: *This is not about you, Bob! This is about Dash!*

BOB: *You wanna do something for Dash? Let him actually compete. Let him go out for sports!*

HELEN: *I will not be made the enemy here! You know why we can't do that!*

BOB (shouts): *Because he'd be great!*

> HELEN (shouts back): This is not ... about ... you!
>
> An abrupt breeze ripples the air, ruffling some loose papers on the coffee table.
>
> BOB (calmer): All right Dash. I know you're listening. Come on out.
>
> HELEN: Vi, you too young lady.
>
> Dash moves out from behind a door. Violet's head re-materialises from behind the couch, she stands up, embarrassed. Bob moves next to Helen, becoming parental.

A number of things are happening in this brief exchange. The most important thing is that Bob tells us precisely what this story is about ... There is no question what Bob's goal is, what his purpose is, although he doesn't say it directly, but when he says, 'Look I performed a public service. You act like that's a bad thing —' he is telling us precisely what his position is in regard to the government taking away the rights of the supers. Helen takes a very different position where it concerns their roles as former superheroes. She considers that her (and, by extension, his) core responsibilities are to their family. Bob considers that his responsibilities are to the community. These positions are evident, and pushed further into opposition through a dialogue that is one of the most gripping and important exchanges in the movie. Some of the key techniques that enable this include:

Deflection. While Bob doesn't outright lie about his activities, he deflects from it, suggesting he'd just had 'a little workout to stay loose'.

Demurral. Helen makes an objection to Bob's position regarding their circumstances, she objects to him 'reliving the glory days'. Bob makes an objection to the position of society 'creating new ways to celebrate mediocrity' and to preventing Dash from 'going out for sports'. While the objections are raised at the circumstances, they are directed to the position of the opposing character.

Changing the subject. Helen makes a very clever change of subject to regain the upper hand in the argument when she says, 'I don't believe you don't want to go to your own son's graduation.' This clever shift places Bob in an inferior position.

Obliqueness. While the argument is a direct opposition of wills, the dialogue is oblique, avoiding direct accusations in favour of suggestions 'You act like that's a bad thing' ... 'Tell me it's not the police scanner ...'. Such technique allows the reader to see into the deeper motivations of the character and form an opinion based on personal experience of personal conflict.

Sarcasm. One of the great tools of dialogue is sarcasm because it allows the reader to see beyond the moment into the history of the characters or the impossibility of the situation. Helen's sarcastic reproach of Bob's late hour, 'I assumed you'd be back later — if you came back at all — you'd be ... " back later."' tells far more than the words merely show.

Differentiating Voices

Differentiating voices is a similar function to positioning characters. In fact, it is directly related. The difference lies in the fact that positioning is what a writer does to the mind of the reader, whereas differentiation is what the writer does to the character.

Frank Thomas and Ollie Johnston in *The Illusion of Life* set out a number of rules for dialogue. Among them is this one: *The words and the thought behind them should be special to this one character.*

In real life, people converse with remarkable monotony in their choices of phrases and expressions. An argument between a real-life Bob and Helen would be far less entertaining and more direct. In real life, you will often hear one person adopting the language of another as words and phrases go through their trend cycles. In fiction, however, such dialogue is mundane and works against the positioning of a character. Therefore Homo Fictus need to have unique wording, colloquial phrases and colourful expressions that belong only to them.

Differentiating voice is how we demonstrate a character's attitude. Attitude is what a character puts on display for the reader. Attitude tells the reader whether the character will stand up to a tyrant, or fold under their power; whether they will be a sensitive lover, or a sexual predator; whether they exhibit leadership qualities or are destined to be a follower. To express attitude in dialogue we need to know a character's strengths and weaknesses, and avoid putting words into their mouths that would not be true to those strengths or weaknesses. If we have a character who is strong in social skills and graces, it wouldn't ring true to give that character uncouth expressions in inappropriate situations. Different characters can be visualised through voice, by choosing words carefully — words that distinguish a character's voice give the reader a clear picture of just what sort of person they are dealing with.

From Shrek (Ted Elliot and Terry Rossio 2001)

It's the end of the first day following the rescue of Princess Fiona. The princess has been safely ensconced in a cave for the night, while Donkey and Shrek are stargazing by the campfire.

> *They lie silent for a while, Donkey contemplating the stars and Shrek.*
>
> DONKEY *(sighs, looks at the stars)*: *Hey Shrek, what're we gonna do when we get our swamp anyway?*
>
> SHREK: *Our swamp?*
>
> DONKEY: *You know. When we're through rescuing the princess and all that stuff.*
>
> SHREK: *We? Donkey, there's no we. There's no our. There's just me and my swamp. And the first*

thing I'm going to do is build a ten-foot wall around my land.

DONKEY: You cut me deep, Shrek. You cut me real deep just now …

(Pauses, gathers himself) You know what I think? I think this whole 'wall' thing is just to keep somebody out.

SHREK: No! D'ya think?

DONKEY: Are you hiding something?

SHREK (warning): Never mind, Donkey.

DONKEY: Ohh. This is another one of those onion things isn't it?

SHREK: No. This is one of those "drop-it and leave-it alone" things!

DONKEY: Why don't you want to talk about it?

SHREK: Why do you <u>want</u> to talk about it?

DONKEY: Why are you blocking?

SHREK: I'm not blocking!

DONKEY: Oh, yes you are!

SHREK: Donkey! I'm warning you …

DONKEY: Who you trying to keep out? Just tell me that Shrek, who?

Shrek jumps to his feet and explodes.

SHREK: (explodes) Everyone! Okay?

Angle on silhouette of Fiona, seen peeking around the cave door, as she listens to Shrek.

DONKEY: Oh, now we're getting somewhere!

SHREK: Oh! For the love of Pete!

Shrek walks to the edge of the bluff, sitting staring out away from Donkey.

DONKEY: Hey, what's your problem Shrek? What you against the whole world anyway?

SHREK: Look. I'm not the one with the problem, okay? It's the world that seems to have a problem with me. People take one look at me and go, "Aah! Help! Run! A big stupid, ugly ogre!" (sighs) They judge me before they even know me. (beat) That's why I'm better off alone.

In the shade of the cave we make out Fiona's eyes listening. She seems sympathetic. At the campfire,

Shrek and Donkey see none of this. Donkey stares at Shrek silent for a moment. Donkey walks over to Shrek, the two of them silhouetted against the starry sky.

DONKEY: You know what? When we first met, I didn't think you was a big stupid, ugly ogre.

Shrek stares at him, then softens.

SHREK (almost a grunt): Yeah — I know.

DONKEY (off the stars): So… ah, are there any donkeys up there.

The differences between Shrek and Donkey's characters are highlighted through the choices of phrases and expressions. Donkey's language is grammatically less perfect than Shrek's. The minor imperfections seem to add weight to Donkey's wisdom, whereas Shrek's inability to recognise that he is lonely and in need of a friend is given greater credence by his dogmatic resistance to anyone getting close to his inner self.

Again, this passage tells us far more than merely the words show. It gives us a clear clue to what Shrek's real problem is. When Shrek says, 'Look. I'm not the one with the problem, okay? It's the world that seems to have a problem with me' he is telling us that he is scared and lonely, that he's the one who has been isolated. This is a key moment of audience sympathy, and Shrek's negativity is illustrated by Donkey's extraordinarily positive, 'Now we're getting somewhere!' Again deflection and demurral play a big part in the exchange. Even the central part of the argument which on the surface is direct 'Why are you blocking?' … 'I'm not blocking.' … 'Oh yes you are.' … is still oblique, because it is not directly on the subject. This piece of dialogue is an excellent example of how the innermost character is accessed through constant chipping away at the outer layers. The onion skin reference is an ironic illustration of this process.

Advancing the Plot

Alfred Hitchcock said: 'When we tell a story in cinema, we should resort to dialogue only when it's impossible to do otherwise … Dialogue should be a sound among other sounds, something that comes out of the mouths of people whose eyes tell the story in visual terms.'

Another function of dialogue is to advance the plot. Given that a story's plot is the framework around which the story is built, it stands to reason that dialogue which fails to advance the plot has no part to play in the story. In the previous example from *The Incredibles*, the exchange between Helen and Bob drives a momentary wedge between the two main characters. This is a defining moment in the story because it drives Bob further into secretive behaviour; when he takes on a secret mission as Mr Incredible and hides the truth from his family about being sacked from his day job.

The Incredibles is typical of an Overcoming the Monster plot. We see Bob, who cannot let go of his fundamental purpose, go into action to save the world, but as the story unfolds, in addition to the rise of Syndrome, there is an ego monster within that also has to be conquered. The argument in the example above exposes Bob's ego as a potential threat to the family and to the community at large.

But it is its very indirectness that allows us to move forward into the story. Although it is not said, it is very clear to us that this is not the first time that Helen and Bob have clashed over the use and containment of the family's super powers. We are given an inkling that son, Dash, has been a point of contention when it comes to exercising his abilities.

More importantly, this piece of dialogue gives us a clue as to where the core conflict of this story might lie. It suddenly grips us and pushes us into the field of battle. The reader is prompted here to take a position in the grand argument: should 'Supers' be allowed to perform public services, or not?

Advancing the plot through dialogue is achieved by maintaining a level of obliqueness. The reader begins to unravel the mystery because the talk between the characters involved is not straight, the reader begins asking questions of the character in order to dig deeper and find out what's really going on. Direct dialogue, on the other hand, limits the reader's capacity to imagine and form an opinion. This stops the plot cold.

From Point Blanc (Anthony Horowitz 2005)

Blunt was not alone. Mrs Jones, his senior officer, was with him, sitting on a leather chair, wearing a mud-brown jacket and dress, and — as usual — sucking a peppermint. She looked up at Alex with black bead-like eyes. She seemed to be more pleased to see him than her boss was. It was she who had spoken. Blunt had barely registered the fact that Alex had come into the room.

Then Blunt looked up. "I hadn't expected to see you again so soon," he said.

"That's what I was going to say," Alex replied. There was a single empty chair in the office. He sat down.

Blunt slid a piece of paper across his desk and examined it briefly. "What on earth were you thinking of?" he demanded. "This business with the crane? You've done an enormous amount of damage. You've practically destroyed a two million pound conference centre. It's a miracle nobody was killed."

"The two men in the boat will be in hospital for months," Mrs Jones added.

"You could have killed the home secretary!" Blunt continued. "That would have been the last straw. What were you doing?"

"They were drug dealers," Alex said.

"So we've discovered. But the normal procedure would have been to dial 999."

"I couldn't find a phone." Alex sighed. "They turned off the crane," he explained. "I was going to put the boat in the carpark."

Blunt blinked once and waved a hand as if dismissing everything that had happened. "It's just as well your special status came up on the police computer," he said. "They called us — and we've handled the rest."

"I didn't know I had special status," Alex said.

"Oh yes, Alex. You're nothing if not special." Blunt gazed at him for a moment. "That's why you're here."

"So you're not going to send me home?"

"No. The fact is, Alex, we were thinking of contacting you anyway. We need you again."

"You're probably the only person who can do what we have in mind," Mrs Jones added.

"Wait a minute!" Alex shook his head. "I'm far enough behind at school as it is. Suppose I'm not interested?"

Mrs Jones sighed. "We could of course return you to the police," she said. "As I understand it, they were very keen to interview you."

"And how is Miss Starbright?" Blunt asked.

Jack Starbright — the name was short for Jackie or Jaqueline, Alex wasn't sure which — was the housekeeper who had been looking after Alex since his uncle died. She was bright, a red-haired American girl who had come to London to study law but had never left. Blunt wasn't interested in her health, Alex knew that. The last time they'd met, he'd made his position clear. So long as Alex did as he was told, he could stay living in his uncle's house with Jack. Step out of line and she'd be deported to America and Alex would be taken into care. It was blackmail of course, pure and simple.

"She's fine," Alex said. There was quiet anger in his voice.

Mrs Jones took over. "Come on Alex," she said. "Why pretend you're an ordinary schoolboy any more?"

She was trying to sound more friendly, more like a mother. But even snakes have mothers, Alex thought.

"You've already proved yourself once," she went on. "We're just giving you a chance to do it again."

"It'll probably come to nothing," Blunt continued. "It's just something that needs looking into. What we call a search and report."

"Why can't Crawley do it?"

"We need a boy."

The plot of this story is Overcoming a Monster, in which Alex Rider is sent to a remote location in the French Alps to investigate a human cloning project. In this exchange, the head of MI6 (Blunt) is using Alex's recent misadventure, in which he dropped a barge containing a couple of drug dealers and their laboratory through a conference centre roof and interrupted a drug crime conference, to pressure him into undertaking a mission.

This brief exchange gives the reader a clue that Blunt is prepared to not play fair, leaving out the details and keeping his dialogue oblique, which means the mystery in the air deepens as the plot thickens. The scene is resolved with the defining point, "We need a boy" which rules out any other possible solution. Alex is committed to the job, whether he likes it or not. The dialogue tells the reader where the story is heading, and draws focus to the core conflict that is about to emerge.

Revealing an Emotional State

Throughout the course of a story, characters move from one emotional state to another. In a typical Quest story, for example, we may see our Hero move from a normal state in the beginning through an emotional state of courage to faith and freedom as the story opens out. Later in the story, as the 'nightmare' stage encroaches that faith may be shaken as the character becomes frustrated producing anger leading through apathy, conceit and despair to doubt, envy and fear. As the character plummets further into the grip of the dark power, new courage will bring him back towards positive emotions. By the end of the story, he may even experience the emotions of joy, love and respect. A character who has become whole by the end of a story will exhibit pride.

Much of a character's emotional balance and direction of movement can (and should) be revealed through his or her language and not left to the narrative. Using dialogue to reveal an emotional state — even inner dialogue — invites the reader to connect directly with the state of play between characters and their own personal demons or ambitions. If it is left to the narrative, readers are told what to think rather than be able to form their own opinions.

From Batman — Bruce Wayne Fugitive (Ed Brubaker)

Bruce Wayne has been arrested on suspicion of murdering his girlfriend and has escaped custody. Batman has decided that Bruce Wayne is just a mask, and therefore no longer exists. He has a fight with Nightwing over his decision to eliminate Bruce Wayne from his life and leaves Nightwing, Robin, Barbara Gordon and Batgirl behind, having refused to answer the question of whether he did or did not commit the crime. He is clearly frustrated by the turn of events and exhibits considerable anger and doubt. As he speeds away from the ugly situation with his loyal team in the batcar, he has the following conversation with himself.

Batman's face is grim behind the wheel of his car. He grips the steering wheel tightly.

CAPTION: I expected more from them.

The bat car speeds along a railway track.

CAPTION: No, I didn't.

CAPTION: Or I would have told them about my escape plan.

The car drives into the entry of a tunnel.

CAPTION: It doesn't matter. The only thing that matters now is my mission.

The car pulls off the track into a side tunnel.

CAPTION: Nothing will stand in my way anymore.

Batman gets out of the car and opens a steel door in the wall of the tunnel. He enters a hidden control room that looks a bit like the control room of a submarine.

CAPTION: Alfred did a good job preparing this temporary base of operations.

CAPTION: At least *he* hasn't turned against me.

Batman ascends a ladder through the ceiling of the control room.

CAPTION: He doesn't understand either, though.

CAPTION: I suppose none of them can.

Batman emerges onto the roof of a building.

CAPTION: They can't see that Bruce Wayne was always surrounded by pain…

Batman leaps feet first into the void between buildings with his batwings spread, fists clenched.

CAPTION: …but he could never react to it.

CAPTION: He was a protective shell that became a weakness rather than a layer of armour.

Batman sprints across the ramparts of a building's roof structure.

CAPTION: Bruce Wayne was a way inside…and there are no more of those.

Batman uses his Batrope to swing between buildings.

CAPTION: So I shouldn't expect them to understand the sense of relief I have now…

Batman swings onto a building's flagpole. Roosted bats scatter into the air.

> CAPTION: *Knowing that nothing stands between me and my work ... my mission.*
>
> *A car-jacking is taking place on a roadside below.*
>
> CAPTION: *No face on the front page. No-one to lock away in a cell.*
>
> CAPTION: *No-one forced to pretend the world is a better place.*
>
> *Batman swoops on the unsuspecting car-jackers below.*
>
> CAPTION: *And as the last remnants of this mask fade away ... I feel something I haven't felt in nearly all my life.*
>
> *Batman flattens the bad guys. The female victim is hysterical, scared.*
>
> CAPTION: *I feel free.*
>
> *Batman leaves the scene. The female victim is still in shock. Batman's retreating face is set grimly.*

This inner dialogue allows us to see into Batman's mind and understand a deeply complex and troubling emotional issue as he grapples with the turmoil of who he is. It appears that he has come to the conclusion that Bruce Wayne can never become whole, partly because of a fear of being discovered, and partly because of the hangover of witnessing the brutal murder of his parents. Bruce Wayne can never have a completely satisfying relationship with anyone. The stress of having to bury his real self behind a mask has become too much. But in an emotional twist, we are informed by Batman that Bruce Wayne is the mask that Batman has to wear (not the other way round). By removing Bruce Wayne from the picture, he believes he has set himself free.

Batman's emotional state appears to be highly egocentric. He is clearly angry with his team for seemingly 'turning' on him. He is envious of Bruce Wayne's false celebrity status. We see, in this dialogue, Batman move through the states of apathy, conceit, and despair to an ultimate state of doubt, where he exhibits distrust and suspicion, reflecting his own self-doubt. At this point, Batman maintains a completely selfish attitude, declaring that he is ultimately set free. The reader is left in no doubt as to Batman's emotional state, and it is not freedom, as he claims it to be. He is delusional.

Demonstrating Feelings

Akin to the previous section, dialogue is used to demonstrate how one character might feel about or towards another.

From The Secret Pilgrim (John LeCarre)

"So who or what is Stefanie, or do I get the usual loud silence," I asked him as I pulled open the glove compartment and looked in vain for traces of her.

For a while I got the loud silence.

"Stefanie is a light to the ungodly and a paragon to the virtuous," he replied gravely. And then, more deprecatingly: "Steff's from the Hun side of the family." He was from it himself, he liked to say in his more acerbic moods. Steff was from the Arno side, he was saying.

"Is she pretty?" I asked.

"Don't be vulgar."

"Beautiful?"

"Less vulgar, but still not there."

"What is she, then?"

"She is perfection. She is luminous. She is peerless."

"So beautiful, then?"

"No, you lout. Exquisite. Sans pareil. Intelligent beyond the dreams of Personnel."

"And otherwise—to you—what is she? Apart from being a Hun and the owner of this car?"

"She is my mother's eighteenth cousin dozens of times removed. After the war she came and lived with us in Shropshire and we grew up together."

"So she's your age, then?"

"If the eternal is to be measured, yes."

"Your proxy sister, as it were?"

"She was. For a few years. We ran wild together, picked mushrooms in the dawn, touched wee-wees. Then I went off to boarding school and she returned to Munich to resume being a Hun. End of childhood Idyll and back to Daddy and England."

I had never known him so forthcoming about any woman, nor about himself.

"And now?"

I feared he had switched off again, but finally he answered me.

"Now is less funny. She went to art school, took up with a mad painter and settled in a dower house in the Western Isles of Scotland."

"Why's it less funny? Doesn't her painter like you?"

"He doesn't like anyone. He shot himself. Reasons unknown. Left a note to the local council apologising for the mess. No note to Steff. They weren't married, which made it more of a muddle."

"And now?" I asked him again.

"She still lives there."

"On the island?"

"Yes."

"In the dower house?"

"Yes."

"Alone?"

"Most of the time."

"You mean you go and see her?"

"I see her, Yes. So I suppose I go too. Yes. I go and see her."

"Is it serious"

"Everything to do with Steff is massively serious."

"What does she do when you're not there?"

"Same as she does when I'm there, I should think. Paints. Talks to the dickie birds. Reads. Plays music. Reads. Plays music. Paints. Thinks. Reads. Lends me her car. Do you want to know any more of my business?"

For a while we remained strangers, until Ben once more relented. "Tell you what, Ned. Marry her."

"Stefanie?"

> *"Who else, you idiot? That's a bloody good idea, come to think if. I propose to bring the two of you together to discuss it. You shall marry Steff, Steff shall marry you, and I shall come and live with you both, and fish the loch."*
>
> *My question sprang from a monstrous, culpable innocence: "Why don't you marry her yourself?" I asked.*
>
> *Was it only now, standing in my flat and watching the slow dawn print itself on the walls, that I had the answer? Staring at the ruled-out pages of last June and remembering with a jolt his dreadful letter?*
>
> *Or was it given to me already in the car, by Ben's silence as we speed through the Scottish night? Did I know even then that Ben was telling me he would never marry any woman?*

The above exchange takes place between the narrator and a companion while they are driving through the night. The narrator is reflecting on the conversation and realises that Ben was telling him something important. While he is curious about Steff, the narrator is really fishing for information from Ben about himself. His closing comment is a show of doubt that he was listening correctly, and failed to hear and understand the messages that were being conveyed. A failure he believes leaves him culpable in some way in Ben's subsequent death.

Informing

Dialogue is used to inform the reader of past behaviours and future intentions of characters. However, this should not be confused with exposition — the explanation of behaviour or thoughts.

Dialogue is an effective way of filling in story information (relative to a particular character) about events that have taken place out of the reader's view.

For example, the Hero of a story is arrested on drugs charges. The reader is not present when the alleged offence took place, so the they have no way of knowing whether the suspect committed the crime or not. The proof of the allegation is the core conflict and the story is being told through the arresting officer's viewpoint. The reader gets to know the suspect's side of the story only through the opportunities that the suspect is given to tell his version of events, and to weigh the evidence as it is collected. Conflict in dialogue that takes place between the suspect and the arresting officer; the suspect and his legal representative; the suspect and any personal supporters can test the reader's belief in his innocence or otherwise. The writer can also use conversations that take place between the suspect and others to reveal information to the reader that is not available to the prosecuting team, such as a dark secret that would complicate the issue and make the proof of innocence more difficult.

Dialogue can also effectively be used to portray events that are planned for the future by one or another character.

From Mathew Flinders' Cat (Bryce Courtney)

This scene demonstrates the use of dialogue as a device to inform the reader of the events that are being planned. It enables the reader to see the action from the main character's point of view.

> *Billy turned up at Marcus Eisenstein's chambers on the appointed day. This time Ms Jebara met him with a smile. She was an attractive young woman, rather too thin and pale, and the conservative black business suit she wore didn't help her complexion. 'The chief justice is waiting for you, Mr O'Shannessy,' she said, leading him to the judge's chambers.*
>
> *'Hello, Billy, still on the straight and narrow, I hope,' Marcus Eisenstein said, tact not being among his major talents.*
>
> *'Hanging on like grim death,' Billy replied, laughing, although it was closer to the truth than even he dared to admit.*
>
> *'Billy I don't have to tell you that what I have to say can be shared with no-one, not even the boy,' he began.*
>
> *Billy nodded. 'Yes, of course,' though he thought it a bit patronising.*
>
> *'The new bloke took a little convincing, but finally agreed.'*
>
> *'What was he was worried about? Using women?'*
>
> *'No, as a matter of fact, he was delighted with the idea. But he's new in the job and already up against the establishment in the Force and in Parliament. An all-women police bust (pardon the pun) has never been done before in New South Wales.' Marcus laughed. 'We'll be making history.'*
>
> *Billy grinned. 'Only if it succeeds.'*
>
> *'That's what he said, it's great publicity if it succeeds, a disaster if it fails.'*
>
> *'Properly done, it has every chance. These people believe they're protected and if anything is going to happen they'll be warned in good time by the police in their pay. From my*

observation, they're not exactly paranoid,' Billy said.

'Well, let's hope you're right, but that's not the only concern.' Marcus Eisenstein scratched the tip of his nose. 'There isn't a charge for paedophilia, we'd have to get them on carnal knowledge and that's never easy. We're not dealing with the usual criminal here, they'll have the best silks in the business defending them. The German, by the way, is well gone, it's the word of an eleven-year-old boy against a powerful group of men.'

'What are you saying, Marcus? That the odds are against us?'

'Yes.'

'And you're reluctant to go ahead?'

'No, but we have to get it right first time. We don't know what we'll find at The Queen of Sheba or at the Flag Hotel. We could end up with egg on our faces.'

'But this is a covert operation. It could be made to look like a routine raid, nothing special, police got a tip-off that there's an illegitimate business being run in a pub and the other is simply a raid on a strip joint looking for drugs. Two separate operations.'

'Sure, with a history-making all-female squad in charge of both. The police, that is the male police, will be the first to call the media. All hell will break loose.'

'And you'll be in the eye of the storm?' Billy said.

'You're not wrong there, mate,' Marcus said. 'The premier wouldn't be too happy, I assure you.'

'So what are we going to do?'

'We're going ahead but it's tricky, according to Nora Watman, the assistant commissioner who's putting the team together. Ideally we need an insider with a video camera.'

Billy laughed. 'Do me a favour, Marcus. A video camera!'

'I know it sounds absurd, but evidently filming sex scenes with children is all part of the action. It's the trophy.'

'What? Well-known people, pillars of the establishment, collect videotapes of themselves in action?'

'Evidently.'

'With the greatest respect, Marcus, that's hard to believe.' But as he said it, Billy remembered something Ryan had said. 'Hey, wait a minute!'

> 'What is it?' the judge asked.
>
> 'Something Ryan said Monkey told him. I neglected to put it into my notes. Bloody careless. He said they'd have filmed the German raping him and it would be sent to him as a keepsake, a little thousand-dollar keepsake. Blackmail, I guess, or perhaps, as you say, paedophiles like to keep records of their conquests. If I recall correctly, Monkey said that he hated The Queenie.'
>
> 'Billy, I think you'd better see Nora Watman,' Marcus said. 'Monkey sounds promising.'
>
> 'I have his telephone number, he was confident enough to give it to Ryan.' Billy dug into his briefcase and after some time found the card Ryan had given him. 'I've never looked at it,' he said, opening it. He handed it to the judge.

The dialogue in this passage, while perhaps a little clunky and over-written, does provide the reader with a lot of important information that, if presented in narrative form, would be less adroit.

Apart from giving us Billy's opinion of the judge's tone of voice, it also informs us about planned action that is going to take place outside of the reader's view. We also learn that Billy has information that could progress the situation, and that it was information he'd neglected to include in an earlier episode. We learn through this conversation that the judge is going out on a limb with this plan, the outcome of which could place him in a difficult situation. But he has the courage to see it through.

Pacing the Narrative

Dialogue affects the pacing of the story and determines whether an episode is told as a dramatic narrative, a half scene or a full scene. A dramatic narrative has little dialogue, it is a summary account of what takes place, told from the point of view of the main character. Dramatic narrative is slower paced and holds the reader to the detail of events. A full scene on the other hand, engages the reader immediately in the action, and is the fastest paced, using dialogue and dramatic action to move the reader along.

Dropping in at a mid-point in an episode can speed up the read, as can leaving scenes to cut to the next one without reaching the climax. Sometimes a work that is too fast paced can appear disjointed and unsatisfying. And sometimes dialogue that goes too far in explaining the way it is delivered seems laboured and over-written (like the Bryce Courtney example above). Artfully pacing the scene so that the right balance can be brought to the story is key to writing great dialogue and takes a lot of practice.

From The Deceiver (Frederick Forsyth)

In Miami, Sabrina Tennant had checked into the Sonesta Beach Hotel as advised the previous evening and took a call just before eight on Saturday morning. The appointment was made for an office building in central Miami. It was not the headquarters of the CIA in Miami, but a safe building.

She was shown to an office and met a man who led her to a TV viewing-room where three of her video tapes were screened in front of two other men who sat in half-darkness, declined to introduce themselves and said nothing.

After the screening, Miss Tennant was led back to the first office, served coffee and left alone for a while. When the first officer rejoined her, he suggested she call him 'Bill' and asked for the still photographs taken at the dockside political rally of the previous day.

On the videos, the cameraman had not concentrated on the bodyguards of Horatio Livingstone, so they appeared only as peripheral figures. In the stills they were in full-face shot. Bill opened a series of files and showed her other pictures of the same men.

'This one,' he said, 'the one by the van. What was he calling himself?'

'Mr Brown,' she said. Bill laughed.

'Do you know the Spanish for "brown"?' he asked.

'No.'

'It's Moreno, in this case Hernan Moreno.'

'Television is a visual medium,' she said, 'pictures tell a better story than words. Can I have these photos of yours for comparison with my own?'

'I'll have copies made for you,' said Bill, 'and we'll keep copies of yours.'

Her cameraman had had to remain outside in the taxi. Covertly he took a few pictures of the office building. It did not matter. He thought he was photographing CIA headquarters. He was not.

When they got back to the Sonesta Beach, Sabrina Tennant spread the photos, hers and those unusually provided from secret CIA files, on a large table in the borrowed banqueting-room while the cameraman shot moving film of them all. Miss Tennant did a 'piece to Camera' with a backdrop of the banqueting-room wall and a picture of President Bush, borrowed from the manager. It would suffice to give the impression of an Inner CIA sanctum.

Later that morning the pair found a deserted cove down a lane off US Highway One and she did another address to the camera, backed by white sand, waving palms and a blue sea, a facsimile for a beach on Sunshine.

At midday she set up her satellite link with London and beamed all her material to the BSB in London. She, too, had a long talk with her news editor as the cutting room staff began to put the feature together. When they had finished it was a fifteen-minute news story that looked as if Sabrina Tennant had gone to the Caribbean with only one mission in mind—the exposure of Horatio Livingstone.

The editor rejigged the running order of the Sunday lunch-time edition of Countdown and called her back in Florida.

'It's a bloody cracker,' he said. 'Well done, love.'

McCready had been busy, too. He spent part of the morning on his portable telephone to London and part talking to Washington.

In London, he found the Director of the Special Air Service Regiment staying at the Duke of York's Barracks in King's Road, Chelsea. The leathery young general listened to McCready's request.

'As a matter of fact, I do,' he said. 'I've got two of them lecturing at Fort Bragg at the moment. I'll have to get clearance.'

'No time,' said McCready. 'Look, are they owed leave?'

'I suppose they are,' said the Director.

'Fine. Then I'm offering them both three days rest and recreation here in the sun. As my personal guests. What could be fairer than that?'

'Sam,' said the general, 'you are a devious old bugger. I'll see what I can do. But they're on leave, OK? Just sunbathing, nothing else.'

'Perish the thought,' said McCready.

The above passage demonstrates how dramatic narrative is effectively broken up by dialogue and turned into a half scene. The narrative takes us into the inner sanctum of a CIA building where Sabrina Tennant, a journalist working for the BBC was taken to compare photographs of known suspects in a crime against the state. We get a sense of the action as the dialogue unfolds, informing us (and Bill) of some of the details in her photographs. Later, the dialogue of her editor informs us that the news story is excellent, and this leads us into the next scene, where we find McCready (the Protagonist) setting up a new directive. We know from his tone of voice that the deal he is making with the general is false. What we don't know from this exchange, or from this narrative, is the relationship between McCready and Tennant.

A dramatic narrative is essentially the objective point of view. The story is being related to the reader by a form of 'omnipresent' being as narrator, and therefore can have little interactive dialogue. The drama of rising conflict is experienced when the reader accesses the main character or the obstacle character storyline. Scenes are almost always played out from one of these points of view. A half scene (as can be seen from the passage above) is almost always played out from the subjective storyline.

Dialogue is often used to break up long passages of narrative to prevent reader fatigue. A word of caution though: Where and when dialogue is used to break up the narrative is an issue that requires careful thought.

Where Most Failures Occur in Dialogue

There are some opinions that dialogue can and ought to be used for exposition. That is, feeding out story information through the dialogue. If you've ever sat through an episode of neighbours, you will have heard about 30 minutes of dialogue that fails to position characters, advance a plot, demonstrate genuine feelings, reveal an emotional state or inform the viewer of things that a character might know that the viewer hasn't been able to see. In this melodrama, characters are more inclined to tell the viewer that they are angry, than they are to actually *be* angry. They are more inclined to say where they are going, than to simply go.

Why is this?

Because, as Frank Thomas said, 'the easiest way to develop a story is to do it all with dialogue between the characters, explaining everything an audience wants to know. The hardest way is to do it all with pantomime.'

Using dialogue for story exposition is the easiest way to tell the story, but because it lacks space for a reader to have an imaginative relationship between the words that are spoken and the action that takes place, it results in dull exchanges that provide the reader with no deeper meaning or character values.

For a story to maintain its interest there has to be space between the action and the dialogue. The dialogue has to support the action, not explain it. The action has to lead the dialogue not follow it. For dialogue to be effective it must help create and maintain tension. And for it to do that, it has to be specific to the action.

Dialogue should give the reader information directly from the character that the reader does not already know. Such things as descriptions of people and places, greetings and departures, niceties and so on, should be summarised in narrative not given to characters. Good dialogue maintains brevity, keeping exchanges short and pointed.

How to Write Dialogue That is Specific to the Action

Readers demand action, whether they are reading a novel or a biography, watching a movie or a television show, a play or a reading a comic. They want to engage in the action of the drama. If you don't give it to them, they will leave the story unfinished.

Being specific means including details in the scene that are notable: details add texture, colour and sound, and give the reader access to the realities of the situation.

When a Hero is running, the details involve his muscular movements, the sweat soaking the armpits of his shirt, his hair flying in the wind, the position of the object against which he is running, the length of stride, the fall of foot, the pant of breath.

His dialogue before he takes off will be adrenalin soaked, pumped for action, it will come in incomplete fragments of sound, possibly even incoherent. He will speak about the object he is about to run against (the person, the clock, the impending disaster), he will say something to alleviate the pressure of the moment; he will issue a challenge against his competitor. He will *not* tell us he is about to run!

Dialogue following his run will be breathless and raspy. His words will be short and he will speak of what comes next, he might grimace at the pain of exertion, he might rouse himself for a loss, or say something that confirms self-congratulation. What he won't do is he won't tell us that he ran; he won't tell us what we've seen him do. He won't fill in the visual detail like a documentary — he will expect us to know these things from the narrative and he will expect us to assume certain aspects from the attitude of his talk. If he has won the race, he won't tell us he's won, but he will tell us how he feels about his victory.

Our Hero is always concerned with solving a problem, so he can't afford to waste breath on explaining actions to us. His words are reflections of his feelings about what is happening. They will be presented in a way that enriches his personality.

Keeping dialogue specific to action also means choosing the right number of words to support the business of the moment. A man in the middle of a fight is usually not very verbose. An exuberant young woman with her best friends in a coffee shop will probably be full of it. No-one can maintain strength in a long soliloquy unless some sort of oration is called for by the situation. So the young girl in the coffee shop must seem like she's talking a lot. Brevity of the dialogue should still be maintained, even with a verbose character. Excess verbosity should come from her actions rather than giving her strings and strings of words.

How to Write Dialogue That is Poetic

Readers are interested in things that are said in interesting ways. The last thing they want to read or hear is what they could hear on any street corner. Homo Fictus's dialogue is clever. It's peppered with phrases that readers and viewers wish they'd thought of. Often such phrases are taken from popular fiction and enter the real world. When popular phrases are taken from the real world and used in fiction they become cliché.

Giving characters poetic dialogue is what makes them memorable. In the movie *Madagascar* (Mark Burton and Billy Frolick) King Julian chants; "I like to shake it, shake it, shake it ..." His words support his actions. But because they are chanted, they have a poetic sense about them. They are highly memorable, and quickly found their way into popular culture.

Being a poet means using figures of speech to good effect, particularly metaphors, similes and personification. Rhyme and rhythm, hyperbole and alliterative phrases add colour to a character's personality as well as depth to the story. It's always refreshing to the ear to hear a character utter words that appear to be 'cleverer' than he or she might appear to be.

Dialogue needs to contain apt figures of speech and avoid clichés that have a stereotyping effect. Some guiding principles:

- Don't use 'oldies but goodies' (clichés)
- Don't string similes together
- Don't mix metaphors
- Use allusions readers understand
- Don't stretch comparisons to the unbelievable, or to ridiculous lengths
- Keep smart statements to a maximum minimum (use once, use well)
- Be careful not to use comparisons that resonate wrongly
- Make sure comparisons can be visualised easily
- Resist being extravagant
- Don't combine the figurative with the literal.

How to Write Dialogue That is Sensual

Sensual dialogue is dialogue that calls into play all of our senses. When a character speaks, we need to feel what he or she is feeling; we need to see what they can see. A discussion over a great meal, in a great place, with great company can also invoke the senses of hearing, taste and smell, as well psychic senses premonition, déjà vu and the sense of humour.

Writing dialogue requires that you work with characters. You need to understand their perceptions of their world, and you need to be able to step inside their heads to experience their own emotional responses to certain situations. Emotional responses must be sensual.

A Hero about to be dragged into a fight will feel his blood rise, his sense of smell will heighten, he will have a bad taste in his mouth. He will only hear what he wants to hear, his sight will focus on his objective. He will smell his opponent. His sense of humour may be the only thing that drives him on. Anything he says at this time must be conditioned by how he is responding to this situation.

From Gronups (Kevin Price)

In the following excerpt, Jerramunga and Lavender have only just met, having narrowly escaped injury from a nasty collision with each other, just inside the edge of a dense forest. A few minutes earlier, a puppy had stolen her ball and chased an injured joey that was under her care into the forest. Lavender chased the puppy in an attempt to recover both her ball and the injured joey.

> *As the boy swerved to avoid her, his sneakers found a bare patch of ground and he skidded, landing heavily, sprawled at her feet. When he righted himself he was breathless and red faced, sporting grazes on knees and palms, to which he gave only cursory inspections. Trickles of blood seeped into the wounds on his hands. He smeared them on his tee-shirt.*
>
> *'Spot the dog?' he asked, breathlessly.*
>
> *'Your dog?—' she asked.*
>
> *His smoky dark eyes regarded her. Then his brown features split into a wide boyish grin that she didn't appreciate.*
>
> *'Your dog stole my ball and chased my injured joey—and you should look where you're going … you could've killed me.'*
>
> *'You're standin' there like a bandicoot on a burnt ridge.'*
>
> *'A bandicoot? I'm no bandicoot … what are you talking about?'*

'Well ...' he began, struggling to explain himself, 'when there's been a fire, y'get bandicoots and.... Look it's something my grandmother used to say....'

She observed him coldly.

He towered a head above. His tee-shirt, black and loose fitting, sported the logo of a famous motorcycle brand and skirted baggy knee-length denim shorts. He wore his sneakers, scuffed and blackened, without socks. His eyes contained no frost as he studied her from beneath a strong brow, above which a wild shock of black hair exploded.

She pointed at the balga's drooping skirts with the bone.

'You've chased my joey into the bush,' she said.

He looked at the bush; then at her.

'I wasn't chasin' a joey.'

'It was sick, hurt—attacked by a pack of foxes. And now, your dog probably ...' She waved the bone in the direction of the balga bush, shrugged and turned away to avoid him seeing the tears welling in her eyes. She made to walk around the boy back towards home.

He stepped in front of her.

'Wait. How d'you know it's my dog?'

'Do you see anyone else here looking for a dog?'

'I didn't say I was looking for a dog—'

'But you are.' And she waved the bone at his chest.

'Hey. Watch where you're pointing that thing,' he said, turning towards the balga bush, leaning sideways as if it afforded him a better view. 'In there, eh? A joey and my dog?'

'Yeah I have to get him back. And my iPod too.'

'He took your iPod?'

'No, he took my ball and chased the joey. A magpie took my iPod. But I have to get all of them back.'

He shrugged.

'What's so special about your ball?'

'It's magic.'

He looked at her as if she'd just claimed to have landed from the moon.

'What kind?'

'It's just a yellow plastic cricket ball with all—'

'Not the ball. What kind of magic?'

'Air magic.'

He shook his head and grinned, and pushed his way past the prickles of the balga bush. 'That bone's likely to have more magic than your ball.'

'I think the magpie brought it.'

'The magpie?…' His brow furrowed as he looked at it. Then he flashed a grin and said, 'Well, come on then.'

Lavender shuffled and turned back in the direction of her home.

'I—don't know—I'm not supposed to be on this side of the fence.'

'Do you want to get your stuff back?'

And then he was gone.

In order to write dramatic dialogue, two conditions need to be in play. The first is that for any dialogue to be dramatic, it must be dialogue that is in conflict, and it must lead to some escalating action or a resolution, if even, perhaps, momentarily. In the example from Gronups above, Jerramunga and Lavender have just met and are sounding each other out. She lays the blame for all of her current troubles on him, even though the reader knows this isn't the case, the reader sympathises with Lavender's losses. Jerramunga doesn't accept such blame and this raises the conflict sharply.

The second condition is that the dialogue should be oblique: that is, it should not express directly what is on the character's mind. It should engage wit, subterfuge, demur and the like. This keeps the dialogue interesting and raises the stakes. Above, Jerramunga accuses Lavender of appearing like a 'bandicoot on a burnt ridge' and then fails to be able to explain his meaning; he objects to being accused of chasing a joey, and then claims not to have said he was looking for a dog; he challenges her claim to magic, alluding that he knows more about magic. Her responses jump from subject to subject in her attempt to blame him for her troubles. Each exchange raises the stakes and increases the pressure on the other: one driven by a confusion of loss, the need for protection and desire; the other by carefree adventurism and arrogance.

Dialogue that is too direct restricts the space the reader needs to create imaginary actions and body language that complete the conversation. No conversation can be complete without body language, and body language requires the speech to be oblique. A character at maximum capacity will use fresh, clever, indirect dialogue. What characters say and do in a story should seem spontaneous to the reader, their expressions grow out of the character and the situation. They appear like real people doing and saying clever things, have snappy comebacks, spontaneous wit and ooze charm. They are erudite, loquacious and full of panache.

They are this way because their writers have slaved over word choices that fit both the character's personality and the situation. They have maximised effect by not having them talk all the time; but when they do talk, they do so in such a way that the reader sits up and takes notice.

Dialogue Techniques

Modifiers and Speech Attribution Tags

When we speak, those listening to us hear our tone and take in other information that helps them understand us. As writers we strive to show rather than tell. To write effective dialogue we have to train ourselves not to slip into telling the reader what they are seeing, or what they should think by using descriptive modifiers that explain the meaning or tone, rather than develop the action that conveys that information. The addition of information about the speaker to dialogue is called the 'speech attribution tag' (often shortened to 'speech tag'). It is usually appended to the dialogue in some form of 'he said/she said …'.

Great dialogue writing lets readers feel the emotion without using descriptive language in speaker attributions, or speech tags. Many writers get sensitive to the overuse of 'said' as a speech tag. Many writers also often introduce modifiers that tell the reader what to think. As we have discussed in previous sections, we want to avoid describing the emotion our dialogue has to carry and get the reader to feel it from the language the speaker uses.

There is a current body of thought (especially in the USA) that dialogue should avoid tags other than 'said'. In many situations I support this. But I notice also that many of the world's great writers use different modifiers, and it's hard to notice that they 'distract' the reader from the dialogue. The key, in my opinion, is to use 'said' as the basic tag, and then vary the tags according to the appropriateness of the moment.

There are instances where the choice of tag is not appropriate. For example:

'What do you mean?' she hissed.

If a writer is going to tell the reader that a character has 'hissed,' the words given to the character should at least contain the sounds that are being suggested. There is no 's' sound in "What do you mean?" so how can it possibly be hissed? If you want it to be a hissed expression, then the dialogue needs to change.

'What's the meaning of this?' she hissed.

Modifiers are suggestions added to tags to let the reader know what emotion or attitude is being expressed. For example:

"What do you mean?" she demanded, huffily.

When the dialogue itself carries the emotion, descriptive modifiers actually incorporate a form of redundancy, the dangers of which include breaking the flow, distracting the reader and labouring the action. The other side of the coin is not to package explanations in the dialogue, unnatural conversations are signals to readers that the author has added information.

It is preferable to describe the action of the character that demonstrates the mood or attitude rather than tell the reader how the words were said. This is the use of an 'action tag' rather than a speech tag. An action tag, however cannot be connected to the dialogue with a comma.

To connect a tag to dialogue with a comma, the tag must show how the speaker issued the dialogue. You can combine an action statement with a speech tag, using a comma to connect the speech tag to the dialogue and a further comma to connect the action statement to the speech tag. If you use a tag to show the character's action alone, do not connect it to the dialogue with a comma. If you use an internal beat (that is, a speech tag in the middle of the sentence) connect both sections of the dialogue with a comma if it's a single compete sentence, or connect only one if it's more than one sentence.

Speech attribution tag usage

CORRECT USAGE:	
'Take me away from all this,' Eve pleaded. or Eve pleaded, 'Take me away from all this.'	A standard application of a speaker attribution tag.
Adam laughed. 'Sorry, babe, no can do.' or Adam laughed, saying, 'Sorry, babe, no can do.'	A standard application of an 'action' tag A combined speaker and action tag.
'You pig.'	Often a tag isn't needed and should be omitted whenever it is clear who the speaker is.
'Hey,' Adam said, 'we said no commitment, remember?'	An internal beat located in one sentence. The beat occurs at the first 'natural' break in the dialogue.
'You said it,' Eve protested. 'Not me.'	An internal beat separating two sentences.

INCORRECT USAGE:	
'Take me away from all this.' Eve pleaded.	The full stop implies these are two events, suggesting that Eve's pleading is not part of the dialogue.
Adam laughed, 'Sorry, babe, no can do.'	You can't laugh dialogue. Nor can you grunt it, snort it, chuckle it or smirk it. You can however, say things with such behaviours.
'You pig'.	With dialogue, place end punctuation marks inside quotes. When quoting a passage from another text, it is common to place the quotation mark inside the punctuation if the quotation does not end the sentence.
'Hey,' Adam said. 'We said no commitment, remember?'	This splits one sentence into a fragment and a full sentence. A fragment is an incomplete sentence, either missing a subject or a verb.
'You said it,' Eve protested, 'I didn't.'	This connects two full sentences with a comma. If you were to remove the dialogue attribution, it wouldn't work as a sentence.

Alternatives to 'Said'

There are many words that can describe a speech action, but care needs to be taken when choosing an alternative to 'said' that they are chosen correctly. 'Said' should remain the commonest choice. But limited variation can enliven the narrative to show changes in character development and mood.

- When a character asks a question: *asked, inquired, demanded, queried* (rare)
- When a character answers a question: *replied, answered, offered*
- When a character's volume/agitation goes up: *shouted, yelled, screamed, screeched*
- When a character's volume goes down: *murmured, whispered, peeped*
- When a character responds to another with attitude: *retorted, rejoined , snapped*
- When a character is surprised: *gasped, exclaimed, blurted*
- When a character is angered: *spit, snarled, rasped*
- When a character is subdued: *whined, bleated, snivelled*
- A character's particular style: *drawled, slurred*

The Order of 'He Said/She Said'

This is a contentious issue in many respects. The syntax (the ordering of words) of the English language has nouns preceding verbs; that is, when a character carries out an action, such as speaking, the character's identity (name or pronoun) precedes the verb describing the action. Joe ran; Joe jumped, Joe spat ... It's easy to see that Ran Joe; Jumped Joe, Spat Joe ... is illogical.

The same logic should apply to the speech tag. The character identifier should precede the verb that describes the speech action. Joe said, Joe shouted, Joe replied, Joe asked ... in preference to the inversion: said Joe, shouted Joe ... etc.

Fowler's Modern English Usage describes the inversion as something often resorted to as a stylistic variation and is *unobjectionable*, which means it is not actually 'wrong'. However, it should be used sparingly, when the rhythm of the language suits it, rather than be the common usage. The inversion should *never* be used to start a sentence or paragraph.

Descriptive Modifiers

It is quite common for writers to add an adverb or adverbial phrase to the speech tag in order to describe the tone of voice, mood or behaviour of the character. These kinds of modifiers should be kept to a minimum. Overuse of adverbial modifiers makes for pretty tiring reading.

Body Language

Descriptive modifiers can be avoided by showing action associated with the dialogue.

> *She pounded the table and thrust her face into his, the blast of her breath moistening his cheeks.*
> *"What the hell do you mean?"*

Actions infuse emotion into the dialogue and imply ownership of the speech. They are commonly referred to as 'beats'.

Internal Monologue

People frequently complain that movies generally don't measure up to books of the same title. Books give readers access to a character's thoughts, and therefore the character's point of view. Personal thoughts open the window to not only see the scene through the character's eyes but to connect readers on an emotional level with a clear understanding of the character's perception of available details.

In a story with a first-person point of view, internal monologue is usually published in italics. In a third-person story, they are usually just presented as part of the text. Quotation marks are not used with internal dialogue simply because they are not spoken.

> *Jane kicked the door hard. 'Get your slimy butt out here?' If he doesn't show up here by the time I count five, I'm gone. Outta here. For good.*

The beat shows that Jane is the one speaking. Her kick at the door shows that she is frustrated. Her internal monologue lets us feel that she's had enough. Internal monologue should be used sparingly.

Three or More Characters

Incorporating three or more characters in a scene necessitates the use of speech tags. A page of dialogue should not go by without a couple of 'he/she said' to indicate the speaker.

When in doubt, leave the 'said' out — add nothing.

In dialogue between two people, use 'he/she said' with one of the characters more than the other.

Dialogue for two characters is easy, three or more and you'll have to use a speech tag more frequently to identify the change of speaker. Take care to make sure any synonyms that are used for the word 'said' fit both the voice of the character and the moment of the story. The rhythm of the dialogue should dictate.

Jane kicked the door hard. 'Get your slimy butt out here?' If he doesn't show up her by the time I count five, I'm gone. Outta here. For good.

Jack emerged from the toilet and stared at the floor, shaking his head.

'What got into you?'

'I can't explain—'

'Mummy,' their four-year-old daughter pushed open the hallway door, crying, 'is daddy leaving?'

'No baby,' Jane said. 'Mummy and Daddy are just talking.'

'But you're crying.'

Jack lifted the girl and pulled her tight to his shoulder. 'Come on Grace, Daddy'll tuck you in. And don't worry, I'll still be waking you up in the morning.' He squeezed her tight and growled like an old grizzly bear.

Dialogue for each character starts a new paragraph, on a new line, signalling to the reader a clear understanding of who says what. Also note: When a character's dialogue continues beyond a paragraph end, the second paragraph opens with quotation marks, but the first is not closed with them. Closing quotation marks only occur when the character finishes, or the dialogue is interrupted by a speech tag, or other author intervention.

Dialect and Poor Grammar

Readers quickly tire of trying to 'interpret' speech that is represented phonetically, or with apostrophes everywhere to reflect dropped letters. Dialect is best portrayed by choosing one or two words or phrases that will give a taste of what the person is like to others. A little bit goes a long way.

***Correct**: "I'm telling you right now, there ain't no way you're going hunting this here weekend. Mama and Daddy's fixing to come for Sunday supper."*

***Overdone**: "Ah'm tellin' y' right now, there ain't no way yur goin' huntin' this here weekend. Mamma and Daddy's fixin' ta come fer Sunday supper."*

Punctuation

Single or Double Quote Marks?

For dialogue, British and Australian practice favours single quotation marks, while US practice favours double quotations marks. For quotations, such as quoting what someone else says within the dialogue, the inverse is used.

- 'Single quotation marks are favoured in British and Australian publishing,' the editor said, 'but I heard my publisher say, "Put my remarks in double quotation marks" yesterday.'
- "Well, it's double quotation marks that are used for dialogue in US publishing," the author said. "If you like, I can quote your comment, 'Singles are used in Australia' in my article."

As a general rule, Born Storytellers publications have followed the US model rather than the British and Australian model because in student handwriting, it is common practice for quotation marks to be double marks.

Punctuation Inside and Outside the Quotation Marks

For dialogue, the use of punctuation within quotation marks tends to be, but does not need to be, confusing. Punctuation leading up to the dialogue will either be a comma or a full colon when the preceding clause contains the speech tag verb, and a full stop if it contains an action verb before the quotation marks.

- Jane burst through the door, and yelled: 'Get down on the floor!'
- Jane burst through the door, yelling, 'Get down on the floor!'
- Jane burst through the door. 'Get down on the floor!'

Full stops and commas belonging to the dialogue go *inside* quotation marks.

- CORRECT: 'What do you mean?' Jane asked.
- INCORRECT: 'What do you mean'? Jane asked.

If a quotation is interrupted with a beat and continues in the same sentence, don't capitalise the first word in the second part of the dialogue. If the beat appears at the end of a sentence, but the dialogue continues as a new sentence, capitalise the first letter.

- CORRECT: 'Mummy,' their four-year-old daughter pushed open the hallway door, and asked, 'is daddy leaving?'
- INCORRECT: 'Mummy,' their four-year-old daughter pushed open the hallway door, and asked, 'Is daddy leaving?'
- CORRECT: 'Mummy, Daddy's leaving,' their four-year-old daughter announced. 'Why is he taking Spot?'
- INCORRECT: 'Mummy, Daddy's leaving,' their four-year-old daughter announced. 'why is he taking Spot?'

Only one punctuation mark at the end of the quote.

- INCORRECT: 'What do you mean?', Jane asked.
- INCORRECT: 'What do you mean!?'
- CORRECT: 'What do you mean?' Jane asked.
- CORRECT: 'That's what I mean!' Jane snapped.

Dashes

Use an em dash (— or --) to indicate a sudden break or change in thought, to set off a phrase or to show interruption. Dashes are commonly used in place of parentheses, colons, and semicolons in fiction. Also in fiction, spaces do not usually appear at either end of an em dash. (In non-fiction texts, such as this book, spaces are often used at either end of the em dash.)

- Sudden break: 'You can't—you wouldn't.'
- To set off a phrase: His tentacles—all ten of them—engulfed me.
- Interruption: 'I don't think I—' John was cut off before he could finish.

Ellipses

Use ellipses (…) An ellipses is three (not five, or nine, any other number!) consecutive full stops with a space before and a space after to show a pause, faltering speech, or speech that trails off and that there is something omitted from the quotation. Within a sentence, place a space both before and after the ellipses. If it indicates an unfinished bit of dialogue, place a space before and closing quotation marks without the trailing space. At the end of a sentence, that is if the thought is a complete one, place the full stop, question mark or exclamation mark before the ellipses.

- Pauses/faltering speech: 'I ... I don't know. Is it ... safe?'
- Trailing off, no end mark: 'I can't believe she ...'
- Trailing off, with end mark: 'That's true....' 'Is it, really?...' 'Oh, get out!...'

Checklist to Help Refresh a Dialogue That is Flat and Inactive

It pays to read your dialogue passages aloud and get a sense of the dynamics involved in each passage. You want the dynamics of the dialogue to match the character and the existing story moment. Improvements can be found by looking for the following:

- Is the dialogue in conflict? Does the conflict relate to the story's main goal?
- Does the dialogue further the character's position?
- Does the dialogue advance the plot?
- Is the dialogue fresh? Does it involve the senses?
- Is it colourful and clever?
- Is it indirect? Does it reveal the inner thoughts of the character? Dialogue reveals the inner thoughts of characters, shows their conscious intentions, propels action both by causing something to happen (a change of mind, a change or heart, an action undertaken or hindered) and by enriching the connections between the characters. Their language needs to reflect what the reader, in real life, would wish to say, not a real conversation.
- Does the dialogue pace the narrative appropriately? Don't ignore the emotional state of your character. If she's upset, don't let her think deep thoughts, or speak in long sentences. We're human. When upset, we speak in fragments. Clipped tones. To convert the emotion to the writing, use short, terse sentences and paragraphs.
  - Fuse forceful verbs
  - No frills
  - No fluff
  - Nothing to slow the reader down
  - This technique quickens the pacing. The reader reads faster, thus senses urgency
  - Conversely, to slow the pace during tender, poignant moments, do the opposite — allow your characters to think longer, more leisurely, unhurried thoughts, and let them speak in flowing, sensory-oriented sentences that slowly drift down the page

- Look for opportunities to use body language signals:
  - Angry? Fisted hands. Narrowed eyes. Stiff posture. Clenched jaw. Slashed mouth. Jerky movements. Rough handling of objects …
  - Happy? Smile. Wink. Twinkle in eyes …
  - Relaxed? Sprawl. Loose-limbed …
  - Crowded? Back up. Create physical distance between the characters …
  - Interested? Lean forward, draw closer to whoever is speaking
  - Questioning? Cock head. Widen eye. Elevate voice. Hands lifted, palm up. Hiked shoulders …
  - Nurturing? Clip a loose thread. Pat …
  - Tender? Stroke, touch, lips parted
  - Nervous? Pace, scratch, rub your arms …
  - Stunned? Wide-eyed. Stone still. Hand to chest, fingers spread. Gaping jaw …
  - Sad? Tears. Listless. Hand curled to chest. Shoulders slumped. Foetal position …
  - Trusting? Palm open …
  - Lying? Avoid eye contact. Dipped chin …
- Does the dialogue contain a subtext: Use dialogue to show what lies underneath — a flirtation? A secret? A deception? What's being concealed yet still revealed?
- Is it meaningful and provocative? Make each dialogue exchange count. Start conversations in a provocative way, like: 'Where the hell have you been?' or 'I should have known I'd find you here,' or 'Hey, it's you! I've been dreaming about you.'
- Does each character have a unique speech pattern, phrase or word?
- Is the dialogue mere exposition? If certain information has to be exposed through the dialogue, it should be written in such a way as to spur other characters into action. You can have characters argue over the information instead of presenting it straightforwardly. Use humour. Dream up interesting ways to deliver exposition, in terms of character reaction, word choice, etc.
- Is there an overuse of phonetic spelling? To represent geography and ethnicity, choose a few key words to spell phonetically and be consistent.
- Do the tags and modifiers feel natural? Are they being used to convey emotion?
- Are there long speeches? Fictional dialogue is a process of give and take sharpened by the fact that each character needs something, but those needs don't mesh.
- Punctuate to match the breathing that is appropriate to that dialogue moment.
- Does the action lead the dialogue? Does the dialogue support the action?

Writing Scenes

Stories are made up of scenes piled up next to each other, like stepping-stones from one side of the stream to the other. You have to step off one in order to reach the next. Scenes are the micro-business of the story. The atoms of the story matter. As discussed in the opening section of this chapter, dramatic writing consists of full scenes, half-scenes and dramatic narrative. Dramatic narrative is expository, filling in the details of the story from the narrative character in a narrative voice; a full scene involves the direct action and dialogue of the moment and the reader is being shown what is going on. The half scene (as you may have guessed) is some dramatic narrative and some action and dialogue.

Dialogue is an integral part of a scene, but a scene requires a great many more sensual details. The following principles will help you develop strong scenes.

A scene is a place where any action occurs

As we know a story is told in a series of episodes that shows something being contested and something fundamental undergoing change. The events of the episodes arise from action. And scenes are those 'pieces of business' that move the story forward, towards its climax and conclusion.

The essential elements of a scene include:

- A place
- A time frame
- A change that moves the story forward.

It's important at the outset of a scene that the reader is 'oriented' to the location. In other words, show the reader some of the details that place the reader's imagination on site. Such details might include atmosphere, buildings and surroundings, lighting, other characters and their relative locations.

The time frame of a scene is a combination of the calendar time (year, day, hour) — which can be shown symbolically using the sun and moon, and the light and shade that goes with them — and the duration of the scene. Given that one of the key aspects of a scene is moving the story forward, things happen in the space of time, the reader wants to know the scale of these dynamics.

A scene has a dramatic structure and purpose. It moves along in dynamic 'beats' — the fast/slow pacing and build and release of tension. Its purpose in advancing the story, may be a change of destination, a change in the direction of the action, or a change in a character's purpose. A scene may cause subsequent events. It may reveal subplot, or 'new business' concerning a character. It may be used to register or establish mood. It may be to convey action in the narrative, and expose one character's actions or involvement in another character's business.

The fundamental purpose of a scene is to illustrate change, decisions, influence, growth or manipulation. The important thing is to maintain forward momentum, making sure each scene has a cause-and-effect relationship with the preceding one and the one following, moving from scene to scene and resorting as little as possible to the history contained in the narrative. Ultimately, we are inviting the reader to become part of each scene, and take them on the journey of the story.

The sequences you laid out in your step sheet are constructed from scenes. Each sequence is the lining up of a number of scenes: places where action will occur that brings about change within a given time.

The Dramatic Scene

Dramatic writing requires conflict between the main character of the scene (which may or may not be the Protagonist of the story) and other characters or the circumstances they find themselves in. This conflict should unfold in a smoothly rising tension, it should not jump from 'nought to a hundred' in one leap, but should increase in pressure incrementally until it reaches a point of crisis/climax. Nor should it remain flat. Once it reaches the crisis/climax, it should resolve with a decision or action that takes the story into the next scene. The conflict within a scene doesn't have to be the same as the core conflict of the story. But it needs to be a conflict that is both related to the core conflict and helps take the story towards its natural conclusion.

> *For example: The core conflict of a story may be between a man and his wife; the opening scene may involve, say, a conflict between the man and his boss leading to him getting the sack from his job. This results in increased tension in the story's main conflict.*

A scene, therefore, has the same 'shape' as a story; it begins at a low point of tension and rises to a point of climax, followed by a resolution. A story is made up of a lot of scenes.

Staging

Staging is the presentation of any idea (or action) so that it is completely and unmistakably clear. An action is staged so that it is understood, a personality so that it is recognised, an expression so that it can be seen, a mood so that it will affect the reader or audience.

Each scene, as we have discussed, is relevant action containing conflict. The central question is: How will the action be staged so that the 'piece of business' has utmost clarity? Here you should consider what is being contested, how well it is lighted, where it is taking place, what sounds are associated with the place and action, what other obstacles are involved, what 'props' can be used in the business to further develop the action …

What is the story point being exploited in this scene? In other words, what *change* is occurring during the scene — change in character growth, change in character decision, change in location, change in time?…

Whose point of view is being used? (See the next chapter for a detailed discussion on the different points of view available.) How limited is that point of view? What can or cannot be seen as a consequence of that point of view?

What symbols are associated with the mood of the scene? How are they incorporated? If the mood is a 'spooky' feeling, what symbols can be used in the narrative to enhance the spookiness? What symbols can be used in the dialogue? You may want to incorporate an old creaking house, a dry leaf in a high wind, a ream of paper fluttering out of its pack and flying across the yard in single pieces, a lonesome dog howling on a hilltop…. Use powerful symbols to help readers become part of the scene.

When staging action, ensure that only one action is part of the scene at any one time. If one action leads into another action, strive for rise and fall in tension (known as 'beats'). Try to play action as 'close up' as possible. Play horror as darkly as possible. Play humour so that the payoff of the gag has all attention focussed on it. Leave space for surprise.

Action Scenes

Action needs to move quickly. Depending on what's going on, you may want to have things only partly seen by any particular character — this emphasises the chaotic nature of some forms of action scenes. Or a character may have thought everything out in advance. They may have a plan, and the tension of the action sequence arises out of whether or not the plan will work out.

If you're describing a fistfight, the way the characters bob and dodge, who hits whom, and where … is what excites the reader. How the person who's struck reacts. If your Hero hits bone, does it hurt their hand? If a bullet strikes a bad guy, is he thrown back, or does he jerk and slide down a wall? Even more frightening, does he look down at the wound and then back up at your Hero, only to advance another few, menacing steps?

Dialogue in action sequences is usually short and to the point. Most people in the middle of big action don't have time or breath to waste on conversation. Except perhaps, when two opponents are circling each other, looking for weaknesses in some form of hand to hand or non-projectile-weapon based combat.

Action allows you to show the unexpected resolve of characters who might usually be more intellectual than physical. The nerd who stops the runaway car from careening over the cliff, for example. Exploit the hidden talents your characters have; their inner strengths. Conversely, show what your big, strong, physical characters might have as hidden weaknesses that might come out in an action sequence. This is where the emotional aspects of action scenes can really be showcased.

Action sequences can play on a Hero's fears and emotional issues. And readers and audiences are hungry to share in these. Some of the emotional change that a character might undergo within a scene could include the following and their direct counterparts:

hate ⟶ love

fear ⟶ trust

anticipation ⟶ dread

belief ⟶ disbelief

joy ⟶ sorrow

anger ⟶ amusement

trust ⟶ distrust

courage ⟶ cowardice

understanding ⟶ bewilderment

freedom ⟶ imprisonment

gratitude ⟶ ungratefulness

respect ⟶ disdain

Chapter 8
Voice and Point of View

The Voice of the Work

At this point, you have decided on and considered in some detail the story you are telling, the characters driving the action, the conflict they are involved with, the world of the story, the type of story it will be and how it will essentially be structured.

Now it is time to consider whose story it is. That is, who is telling the story, and how they are to tell it.

This set of decisions is complex, even though on the surface it seems relatively simple. It goes to not just whether the narrative is presented in the first or third-person (and intrusions of second person), but the degree of subjectivity or objectivity that will best serve the narrative, the verb tense of the telling and the intimacy of the relationship between the narrative character telling the story and the author — the authorial voice.

A strong distinctive authoritative writing voice is relative to writing style, point of view and to some degree tense.

The development of style ideally arises in the service of the story — not applied to the story as an effect. It should vary according to the demand of a story and its circumstances. Style should not overshadow voice, nor be conscious in the reading of the work. Writing style should be integral to the characters and their circumstances; it should show no sign or effort; it cannot be obvious, rising above the content of the work.

But the voice must be distinctive: it must be yours. You find it when your writing states your meaning; is free of affectation, ambiguity and hyperbole; uses active and direct verbs; limits adjectives and adverbs for moments that call for colour. Your sentence structures will feature your own syntactical architecture if you allow your voice to be honest; if you attempt to copy others, it will not ring true. In *the Cambridge Introduction to Creative Writing*, David Morley says, 'Voice is a three-way metaphor: for writing as you speak; for writing as you speak at your best; and for writing with rigour, stripping away all the unnecessary apparatus from language that stop you from speaking clearly, that stop you being phoney.'

The author's voice is reflected in the characters, particularly the narrative character. According to Renni Browne and Dave King in *Self-Editing for Fiction Writers*, 'Character voice and authorial voice are intimately connected.' Which means you should try to write in your natural voice, as though you are embodying the character at that moment. Write as though you are acting.

The following is a comment on *The Casual Vacancy* (J.K. Rowling) by Juliette Marillier. It demonstrates the importance of these concepts.

I found The Casual Vacancy difficult to get through. The worthy message simply overwhelmed the storytelling. The novel is written in an omniscient voice, with rapid hopping from one character's thoughts to another's and a heavy overlay of the author's attitudes and opinions. There's a weight of telling rather than showing. The writing style sets a distance between the reader and the characters, most of whom did not come to life for me.

The teenage characters are drawn more effectively than the adults, and I did find myself caring about them and hoping they would overcome their various difficulties. The adult characters are often more like caricatures, but this is no village comedy. On the surface, The Casual Vacancy is a story about a local council election in a picture-perfect English community, brought about by the death, on page 2, of Barry Fairbrother, the only sympathetic adult in the book. The broad cultural and economic gulf between the leafy town of Pagford and the nearby council estate called The Fields is mirrored in the group of central characters. However, the deeper, more meaningful story develops from the way Barry Fairbrother's death alters the future for one marginalised teenager.

This is a novel with a message, and that message is worthwhile. However, Rowling would have got her point across more effectively with defter storytelling and a lighter touch – we didn't need the authorial sledgehammer. Humour and subtlety are great tools for conveying quite challenging subject matter; Terry Pratchett's later novels demonstrate this brilliantly.

Point of View

POV is a function of character: it is the character who becomes the teller of the tale. However, point of view is affected by the authorial voice. The authorial voice needs to have *status, contact* and *stance*.

Status — Positions the POV character in respect of others in the circuitry of characters. Consider the POV character's:

- Relationship to Protagonist
- Reliability and authenticity (Does this character know the facts? Can this character speak to the facts? How much of the facts does this character hide from view?)
- Dramatic engagement (dramatised or not)
- Political situation and privilege
- Inside view (how much of a psychological view does the character have?).

Contact — the level of access the character has to the reader along a scale from Subjective to Objective

Stance — the attitude, representation and agency of the character as one to speak for others; the level of self-consciousness

Successful verbal communication requires that the *status*, *contact* and *stance* of the speaker all be within the conventions of acceptability for a particular audience and a particular speech event. This means that the author needs to present the work in a way that positions the narrative character as someone who has the ability to deliver the story in a way that the reader finds acceptable in that form and in that time. Therefore *form* and *historical period* are considerations of the narrative voice. Consider Dr Watson's status, contact and stance in his telling of the Sherlock Holmes stories.

POV is the *textual* voice of the narrative — the fictional character narrating — which means it is both a character choice and function.

POV is central to constructing a picture of the world. A character's point of view will be filtered and coloured according to the ideology of the character's position within the narrative.

POV shapes and controls textual meaning and reader response. You can shape textual meaning and influence reader response through the choice of the POV character and the level of subjectivity that character brings to the action surrounding the goals of the central character.

Decisions:

- POV character and relationship to Protagonist
- POV character and involvement in acts of *Gadding* against the circumstances
- POV character and access to the details of a given situation.

There may be a difference between the POV character and the authorial voice:

Voice = the character who speaks

Vision = the character who sees

Is there a difference between the character who *speaks for* the narrative, and the one who *sees* it taking place?

POV devices that convey the presence and attitudes of a textual voice:

- *Commenting* — how the narrative character might comment about the main character, other characters or the circumstances governing character actions
- *Substituting narration* — how the narrative character might step into the shoes of another to provide information that would otherwise have to be delivered objectively

- *Juxtaposition of events and ideas* — how the narrative character might provide alternative points of view for given events or ideas contained within the story

- *Ordering of the plot* — how the narrative character lets out the details and sequence of the story's plot

- *Use of imagery* — how the narrative character might have particular turns of phrase, symbolic gestures or objects that become leitmotif or thematic strings through the story.

What ideological aspects of story are important can influence the choice of the point of view character, the point of view mode (the 'person') and the degree of subjectivity-objectivity of the narrative voice.

- The solving of crime
- Keeping political forces in check
- Demonising war
- Celebrating love
- Creating community
- Righting wrongs.

The Relationship of Character to Plot

It is the narrative character who provides the control of the plot — i.e., lets out the order of events or is ignorant of events until hindsight. When the character is a secondary character (say, Watson to Sherlock Holmes, Hastings to Poroit, or Nick to Gatsby) the Protagonist is the driver of the plot, the narrative character can only be a passenger who follows the Protagonist along in the action.

Point of View is essentially *perspective*. A shift in point of view has profound implications for the way the story can be told and how it affects the reader.

Perspective has a number of components — *elevation distance, horizon, vanishing point, angle, time, lens*. Consider how these concepts might affect the way a story is narrated, and how you can use the dimensions dynamically to focus scenes and sequences.

- *Elevation* — low to lofty. The way the POV character tells the story can be influenced on different aspects of elevation, which can be physical (observation point), sociological (position in the social order) or psychological (estimation of self-esteem).

- *Distance* — close to far. The POV character can bring the action close to the reader, or, using reflective language and hindsight, have it at a considerable distance.

- *Angle* — positive, negative, obtuse, oblique, reflex, adjacent … A range of different angles can be taken by the POV character, which too can be physical, sociological or psychological. Imagine, for example, how the character might view a piece of action from an acute angle (physical) and then report a negative view of that to another character (sociological) and maintain an internal belief that something completely different was going on (psychological).

- *Ground determining horizon* — although related to distance, it is not the same thing. The horizon (how far you can see) can be physical or temporal, and is affected by both the ground from which the horizon is observed, and the ground against which it is measured.

- *Lens* — field of view and magnification. A narrative character can retain close focus on a section of the action while leaving the remaining action in peripheral vision, or can magnify part of the action for closer examination, which shuts out all other action. While peripheral action can be either shut out or left out of focus it is still present though, and the dynamics of the POV character's lens can be a powerful technique in focussing reader attention.

- *Clarity* — obstructed to clear. A narrative perspective is affected by how clear the 'picture' is to the character. A POV character may have an obstructed view of the action that, when removed, is different from how it is perceived (crime fiction often has a narrator with an obstructed view and part of the chase is to remove the obstructions).

- *Time* — now/future/history. Time is also a verb tense component, you can tell the story in the present tense or the past tense. In either tense it can still be told in real time, or it can be relayed into historical time, or even possibly projected into the future..Consider the voice in terms of time distance from the action: is the voice reflective or insistent?

No two characters see the same thing: they each have a different perspective — see different details, interpret different realities and memories.

- Who is speaking: a narrator or a character?
- Whose eyes are seeing the events of the story unfold?
- Whose thoughts does the reader have access to?
- From what distance are the events being viewed?
- From what time are events telescoped?

Form

Does a fictional persona have a necessary connection to its historical creator's world view? In other words, is the narrative character in the story speaking on behalf of the author? Do the author's attitudes and opinions matter?

The form of fiction is an expression of the relationship between author and audience. Form is sociological as well as an aesthetic aspect of fiction. Form can also be viewed as a specific kind of 'content' as important to understanding the textual-cultural act as are story, theme and imagery. Thus the way the story is packaged, the way the plot unfolds, the genre and structure of the work contributes to the reader's understanding of it. Certain conventions are expected within certain 'forms' and the choice and handling of voice will contribute to the reader experience in different ways. A poor choice for one form could well be a good choice for another.

Language is the property of a social community impregnated with the values and thought-patterns of that community — personal expression is necessarily qualified by the social meanings which attach to the experience the author chooses. Consequently the language, the form and the structure will all play a role in the way the work is received according to the accepted norms of the community. Many stories leave out direct and specific details to be filled in by the reader because they can rely on the conventions of the society to reliably complete the picture. Knowing these conventions can affect the choice of narrative voice and the narrative character.

Levels of Objectivity

When we discussed Plot and Conflict (Chapter Five), we discussed the four storylines. These four storylines also serve to provide four points of view, of which one will dominate the experience at any given time, but the others must be present.

The range of dynamic forces that create and affect perspective are ultimately what create *meaning* in the story.

- *Objective viewpoint* — the broad (dispassionate) picture; a view from the distance observing the action as it plays out, pointing the reader to the *sequence of events* that constitute the story

- *Main character viewpoint* — a close (personal) view of the story from within the action, concerned with what is happening at the centre and *driving the immediate event* through to its conclusion

- *Obstacle character viewpoint* — an emerging (obstructed) view of the heart of the story opposing the path of the main character, creating an *alternative approach* to the goal but one which lacks clarity

- *Subjective viewpoint* — the narrow (passionate) view of the encounter between the main character and the obstacle character describing the course the encounter takes and its *progress* to the next event.

Ultimately, you are asking the reader to consider what it feels like to have the problems that your character experiences and to be part of their decisions to progress beyond that problem. The considerations include:

- Why does this problem exist here and now?
- What's the other (alternate) side of the issue?
- What's the big picture, or the grand scheme of things?
- Which perspective is the most appropriate for dealing with these issues?

The reader will follow the story from the narrative character's point of view, but will contribute by pitting reason against emotion and immediate advantage against experience through the course of the events. Therefore it is imperative that the narrative voice of the story expose all four points of view to the reader.

Who Provides the Objective Viewpoint?

The character who can best offer the overview of the story and is able to be involved in the full linearity of the narrative and observe the action from a distance — it can be the Protagonist, or any other character with similar access. Things to consider might include: How limited should the point of view be? How much can be left to the reader?

Who Provides the Main Character Viewpoint?

The character who can best provide access to the main character's motivations and goals — can be the Protagonist, but can also be a close observer. (Note earlier comments about Watson and Holmes.)

Who Provides the Obstacle Character Viewpoint?

The character who can see where the Protagonist wants to go (his purpose) and is also in a position to understand that there is an alternative path. This can be the Protagonist, but only in the most limited viewpoint. In many ways, the Protagonist needs to be discovering the motivations of the obstacle character. It is more likely to be the Antagonist but also could be the Contagonist or Guardian character at different times.

Who provides the Subjective Viewpoint?

The character who is providing opinions and inside information about the action that the Protagonist and the obstacle character are involved in — can be the Protagonist, or an obstacle character, or a third character involved in the confrontation, and subject to the outcome.

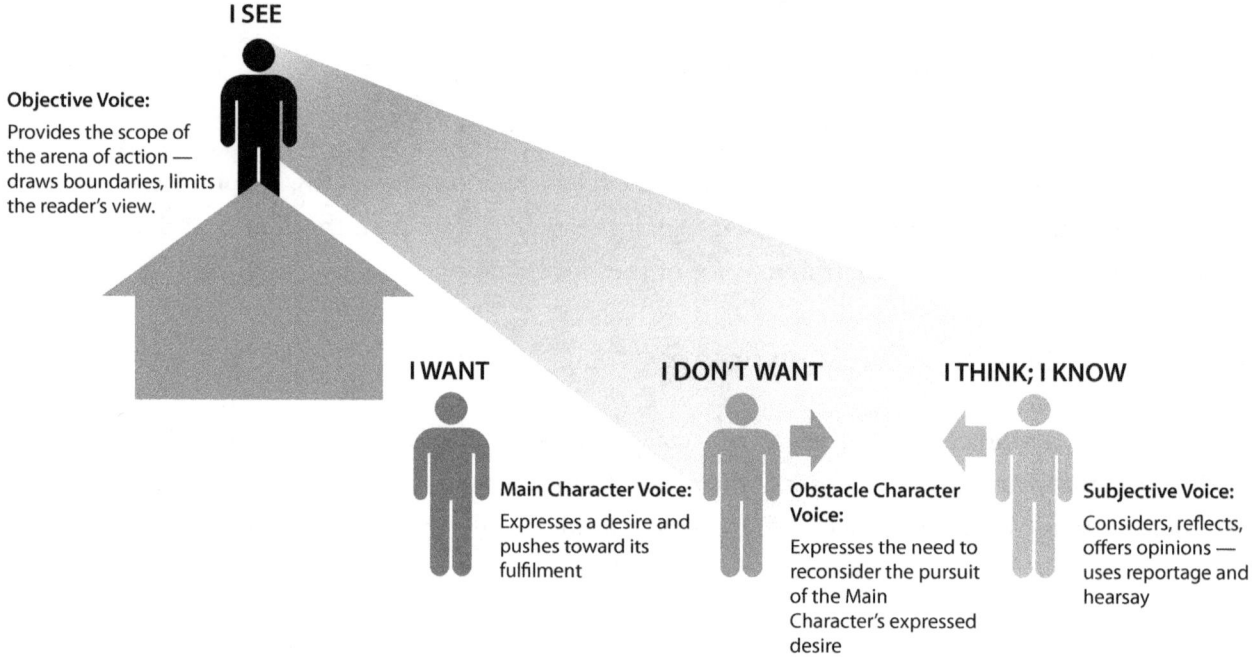

1. Ralph stood on the rooftop and watched (Objective)

2. I saw Ralph on the rooftop watching (Main character)

3. He was obscured from Ralph's view by the Commonwealth Building (Obstacle character)

4. Ralph told me what he saw from the rooftop (Subjective).

POV Decisions

The principle modes of Point Of View are:

- First Person (I/we)
- Third Person (He/She/Them/They)
- Second Person (You)

At first glance it appears that this is a simple division between subjective and objective, but in reality, it is a little more complex than that. The challenge is less about a choice of 'first' or 'third' person narrative than it is about subjective/objective viewpoints, and choices of how much story material is required to deliver the intended reader experience and what is the best way to handle that problem. In the end, it may require changing levels of subjectivity and objectivity, and changing the mode of the Point of View.

Editor, Pamela Hewitt says: 'Allowing multiple perspectives to emerge can reduce the need for an intrusive narrative voice. Alternatively, a fragmented perspective can work with a traditional structure. … Switching points of view can also work well but it takes skilled writing and editing to keep the text from becoming fragmented.'

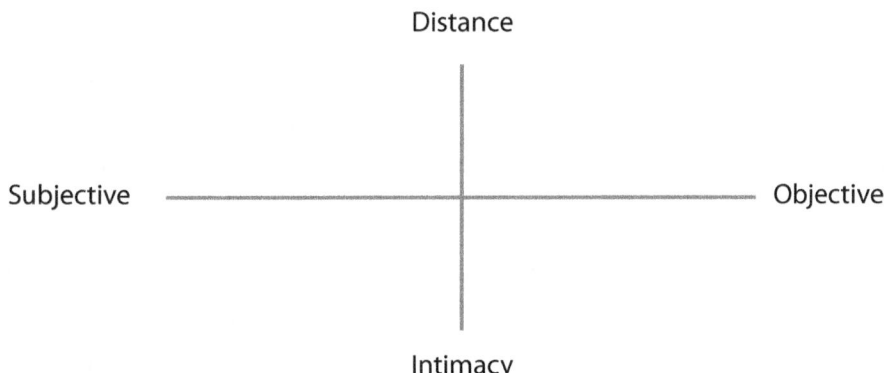

About Person

The notion of 'person' is only an arbitrary device that chooses whether the story is told by a character identifying as 'I' or another character relating and supplying comment on the actions taken by the characters in the story.

First Person

The first-person POV can be either subjective, where the narrator's thoughts, feelings and reactions to events are directly expressed to the reader. (I thought … I felt … I shouted…) or there is also scope for the first-person narrator to be objective too, in which the narrator tells the reader only what others said and did without offering any direct comment or opinion. (He told me he thought … He told me he felt …)

The challenge with offering the reader the objective viewpoint in this way is the risk of labouring the narrative with second-hand reportage and hearsay. Moreover, it is difficult to control proximity in this way.

First-person narrative can offer a range of narrator positions and character choices:

- the observer-narrator, outside the main story (examples: Mr Lockwood in Wuthering Heights, Nick Carraway in The Great Gatsby)
- detached autobiography (narrator looking back on long-past events)
- multiple narrators (first person accounts by several characters)
- interior monologue (narrator recounts the story as a memory; stream of consciousness is an extreme form of this narrative)
- dramatic monologue (narrator tells story out loud without major interruption)
- letters or diary (narrator writes down events as they happen).

The main advantage of first-person narration is intimacy. The writer can eliminate almost all distance between the reader and the story by placing the reader into the narrator's skin. Also, the narrator's voice can reveal a lot to the reader about the kind of person he is.

But the first-person POV does offer some challenges.

The writer is stuck in the narrator's skin, along with the reader. All you have to work with is that one character's observations and thoughts. You're not free to wander anywhere, physically or mentally, unless your narrator comes along. Which means providing the objective and obstacle character viewpoints can be especially challenging, and are often the causes of reader disengagement with the text.

You're also limited by the intelligence, wit and vocabulary of the character performing as first-person narrator.

One of the chief strengths of first-person multiple narrator POV is the reader's intellectual involvement in the story. It doesn't allow the reader to sit back and be told what to think and feel. The reader must piece things together (provide the objective viewpoint) for them-self, which can make for an interesting reading experience.

Although the first-person narrator is often the Protagonist, you may choose to have your first-person narrator be another character in the story. But there's a real challenge with this POV as the narrator must report on the Protagonist while stuck in the body of a bystander.

The unreliable narrator emphasises the philosophical view that there is no such thing as a single, static, knowable reality. Using an unreliable narrator forces the writer to create two versions of the truth, a steep challenge. But if the POV is handled well, the results can be quite intriguing.

Third Person

If the first-person narrative invites intimacy, the third-person offers a continuum, running from narrative intimacy to narrative distance. What determines where your writing falls on the continuum is perhaps word choice and syntax. The words we have at our disposal to describe the world arise out of our history, our education, our culture, even our weather, which is why the Irish have so many phrases for a rainy day. When you describe your settings and action using only words from your viewpoint character's vocabulary, you're not only telling your readers the facts, you're filtering those facts through your viewpoint character's history and sensibility.

But if the voice of your descriptions is more sophisticated, more verbose, perhaps more acutely observant than your viewpoint character can manage, you've put distance between the two.

How much the viewpoint character's emotions colour descriptions also affects narrative distance. A middle-aged man, who has cleared the leaves from the swimming pool every day in a scorching week and is already resting in the shade, might cause you to describe the heat as 'slowly and inexorably, smothering the landscape.' In the same situation, a little girl delighting in her first summer with a swimming pool, might have you describe the heat as how she sees the leaves 'floating gently down and making the yard fresh and new again.'

Broadly speaking, the more intimate the point of view, the better. Using the specific language of a character in descriptions conveys the sights and sounds around them as well as their history, education, and culture. When description also conveys a character's personality or mood, you can use it to vary your pace or add texture without interrupting the flow of the work and the description itself advances the story. Also, writing with narrative intimacy lets you convey a wide range of emotions, which can help keep the 'show, don't tell,' advice in balance.

If you want your readers to focus more on the action of a scene than on the personalities involved, you might want a more impersonal narrative voice. Or, if writing a scene from a minor character's POV, you want to limit the worldview, so that the reader doesn't assume the character is more important than they actually are. If you want to describe a situation or state of mind that is beyond your viewpoint character's vocabulary — because your character is uneducated or a child, for instance — then you might need to write with more narrative distance. If your viewpoint character is a psychotic killer, you may want to write their scenes using a more neutral, distant voice. After all, you want to engage your readers, not drive them to distraction.

The most important thing is to maintain control of the narrative distance and use it to deliver the best effect for a scene, which is why it's important to stick with a single viewpoint throughout a given scene — to decide which character you are using to tell that scene, get into that characters' head, and stay there until the scene is over. Even if you're writing with greater narrative distance, you would still describe only what your viewpoint character could see and hear.

Omniscience

Omniscient, a version of third-person POV that was universal in the nineteenth century but much less so now (although there is some evidence of it returning in recent literary writing), has two hallmarks. First, it goes into the mind of any character the author chooses, sometimes repeatedly and sometimes only once. Second, the author comments freely on the action, sometimes addressing the reader directly with comments and interpretations. Its unlimited flexibility would seem to make omniscient POV the easiest of all viewpoints for the writer. In fact, it is the most difficult but it is one among your options.

Second Person

Second Person is an unusual mode in fiction, where the author both addresses and involves the reader in the narrative. There is a lot of the use of 'you' in the vernacular sense used in first-person narratives, but they are passages that do not involve the reader in the course of the narrative, rather as devices to express common character expressions, *which you'd think was pretty normal.* Second-person narrative still assumes that the story is narrated by an 'I' character, not by a 'you' character. Second-person narrative can be quite useful in diary or biographical styles because you can engage the reader by directly addressing them (like I have done just now with you) as though they are part of the story and have a direct influence over its telling.

Conclusion

However you choose to tell your story will influence the overall narrative experience. I recommend you read both first-person and third-person narratives in your preferred genre and try writing a section in both POVs before finally deciding on which way you should eventually write the story. At the same time, you should give some thought to which characters are likely to have access to all the business of the story, and which are limited to either small amounts or none. By limiting such access, you can build considerable suspense in the telling.

Part Two
Your Project Workbook

A Story Planning Process

Use the following outline to guide you through the story planning process. Once you have established a story idea you will need to push and pull the idea to shape it and make it set imaginations on fire. This process is not necessarily linear: revisit it as you work through your story development to help keep you on track. Make sure you keep a separate notebook of 'notes and thoughts' to house 'arrivals' as they appear.

1. Develop a story idea. Mine for story ideas in the news, in your family and through observations. Develop an idea of what you want to write about, who is involved and what happens to them. Dream on it. Sketch brief and unconnected moments

2. Establish a premise for your story. The premise is: "*Character* through *conflict* leads to *conclusion*." (Substitute Character, Conflict and Conclusion for the specific elements of your story.) This guides you in exploring what you want to write about

3. Write a one or two sentence snapshot of the story. 'This story is about … [what someone did to get what they want]'

4. Develop the identities of the principal characters involved. (Develop at least the Protagonist and Antagonist)

   - Write profiles of them

     a. A paragraph describing their physicality

     b. A paragraph describing their Sociology

     c. A paragraph describing their Psychology

   - Be clear about their goals: what each of them wants; defined their talents and weaknesses

   - Describe the things that make them different from others; identify their hidden psychological needs

   - Interview them to get an understanding of their ruling passions

   - Write a journal entry from each main character's point of view

5. Map the relative archetypal positions and relationships of each character. Develop simple profiles of the minor characters; more complex profiles of the major characters.

6. Establish your story world; detail the locations and settings where your story will take place. Map out the settings so you know how the land lies, where you can build in obstacles and places your characters can call home. Identify the time of the story, detail the physical, social and technological elements; the natural and man-made aspects of the story world

7. Describe the central conflict of the story — what is being fought over? Define the ways the main characters will oppose each other over the central conflict

8. Know the ending of the story. Determine how it will end, what leads to the climax; what follows it?

9. Try to define the plot. Consider the seven basic plots and define the basic form of your story. Try to determine a genre for the story. Consider how a different genre might change it

10. Outline the story's sequences in a step sheet

    - Use a lined page and list the sequences (one thing leads to another), or

    - Write each sequence on a small card and lay them out in an order that works best — change the order around and see how it alters the story.

11. Test your story plan against our earlier definition of a story. Does it have a series of consequential episodes, involve worthy human characters, and is there a moment of transformation.

Tackling Your Project

The following pages sets out the project process outlined in brief above. Each step represents one stage in the story planning process, beginning with techniques for finding and developing a story idea.

This is challenging work and requires substantial commitment to work progressively and systematically at it. The process of story creation and story writing is a combination of creative and critical thinking, of imaginative and logical processing.

You need to spend time on both aspects, on dreaming and thinking, and on writing and note taking. It is often a very difficult task to think of a story to write.

Work a little bit on this every day. Twenty minutes spent every day is two hours and twenty minutes a week. It is far more effective to spend twenty minutes a day every day, than it is to spend a concentrated two hours once a week. The reasons are simple: it's easier to find a regular twenty minutes than a single block of two hours, the story is with you every day — you don't have to start from scratch to remember where you were, and you will be amazed at how much you can achieve in smaller blocks of time.

I have deliberately included additional and alternate exercises in most steps. This is because some exercises are more accessible than others, they can be easier to complete, and because sometimes you may want to go a little further with your ideas. I want this to be a flexible program, but at the end of the planning phase, you should have completed enough of the steps set out in the list above to be able to stand up and 'pitch' the story you are going to write as if you were pitching it to a publisher. In order to do that, you must 'know' your story.

Most importantly, I don't want you to feel overwhelmed by this process. However, there is a school of thought that 'writing stories is easy and it just comes to you.' This is not the case. The truth is that writing a great story is very difficult and you have to work at. All successful writers work at it every day. This project is to show you some of the things that you have to work at in order to be a writer. I don't expect that you will master all of these practices in the one project, or two. It is to give you an experience that I know will help you in all of your writing, both creative and critical.

Step 1: Find and Develop Your Ideas

This step has three parts and should be developed over a period of two weeks. First you need to develop a selection of ideas; then create a premise and a snapshot statement of the one you would like to turn into a story.

READINGS: CHAPTER ONE

1 Mining

This process for finding story ideas requires a few minutes each day for several days. You are going to be looking around you for story ideas — ideas that show promise for *intrigue*, a unique *twist*, colourful *character* and an unusual *item, object or moment*. There are three sources of ideas you need to explore. By the end of a week you should have a dozen ideas or more to choose from. Record your ideas on the following pages.

The News

Each day pay attention to the news (tv, radio, papers, internet). Find an article that you think has the potential for a story and write down the basic idea of the article.

The Family

Engage different family members in discussions about the past or other things members of the family did. Listen and dig for something that has potential for a story. Ask challenging questions about events in the past, where they were, who they met, what they did. Write down the basic idea of the story. Try to get at least three odd things in a week.

Observation

Be alert to your surroundings as you travel, when you go to the shopping centre, the pool, or are out with friends. Watch for something that you think is a bit strange and has potential for a story.

You should record one potential idea from each of these sources each day for 5 days. At the end of the week you will have at least 15 potential story ideas.

EXAMPLE:

> **DAY 1**:
> ***News Article***: *Four black swans are captured on video surfing on a Queensland Gold Coast beach.*
> ***Observation***: *Massive police manhunt operation involving helicopter and several patrol cars across Roe Highway.*
> ***Family***: *Mother's health deteriorates after hospital treatment.*

Day 1

Day 2

Day 3

Day 4

Day 5

2 Developing

Not every initial idea is going to pan out — many times ideas just don't seem to go anywhere. It doesn't matter. The more you do this exercise, the more you will become aware of ideas that have potential. And not only that, you never know when one idea you captured today will be useful while you are working on your story; when you are stuck, all you have to do is trawl through your idea bank for fresh inspiration.

This is when you get creative. Take each idea and ask 'What if …' of the idea, always looking for the answer to be what someone did to get what they wanted. Then add the question, 'and …' to extend the idea a little further. Be creative, be daring, be ridiculous! Yes, ridiculous! Test the ideas with absolutely absurd propositions. You can explore each idea with several *What if?… and …* scenarios. You can combine one or more, or splice one into parts. Try to work quickly, challenge yourself to stretch your imagination beyond the ordinary and mundane. Try changing the genders of the people involved, try shifting the ideas into different genres, try going back in time, going forwards in time … there are many ways you can explore each idea.

EXAMPLE:

What if the swans are really robots from a technology company and they are stealing data from mobile phones used to photograph them …

What if the guy the cops were chasing was innocent and the real criminal was wearing a police uniform …

What if the son investigates his mother's hospital treatment and discovers the doctor who prescribed the treatment is an alien life form masquerading as a human …

What if?... and ...

3 Refining

From the first two parts of this exercise, you should have somewhere around a dozen workable ideas. From your list, *choose 3* that appeal to you because they have the potential to fulfil what you want to write about. For each idea:

IDEA 1

What is intriguing about the idea?

What is unique twist could happen in the end?

Who is the colourful character?

What unusual item, object or moment is involved?

IDEA 2

What is intriguing about the idea?

....

....

What is unique twist could happen in the end?

....

....

Who is the colourful character?

....

....

What unusual item, object or moment is involved?

....

....

IDEA 3

What is intriguing about the idea?

....

....

What is unique twist could happen in the end?

....

....

Who is the colourful character?

....

....

What unusual item, object or moment is involved?

....

....

4 Further exploring (optional)

You can further explore each of these ideas by focussing on what it is you don't know about the situation. Focus your mind on an important question or concern within the situation that you do not fully grasp and write down your feelings as a means of digging around the issue. This will help you expose aspects of the story and characters that you may not yet have thought of. The following lead-in statements may help (you may think of others):

- What I don't understand about this story is …
- If I could see this from a different point of view, I would …
- I can see that (this character) is going to find …
- Why would this situation come about in the first place …
- What happened immediately before this situation was …
- What will happen immediately after this situation is …

5 Write a snapshot story statement

With the story idea(s) you feel strongest about, try to summarise the story idea as a story snapshot statement:

This story is about [*someone*] who [*had something happen*] and then [*did something*] to [*get what they wanted*]

-----

6 Create a premise (optional)

Take the story idea and decide what is important about the idea that you want to write about.
What does it mean to you personally?

What point would you like to make?

How does the character end up?

What human condition does the character go through?

Your premise: [*character through conflict leads to conclusion*]

Step 2: Create Your Main Character

This exercise involves a good deal of creative energy and writing. You need to spend 3-4 hours getting to know the main character in your story. And then you need to repeat the process getting to know your main character's nemesis.

READINGS: CHAPTER TWO

1 Your Protagonist

The Process

Study the list of character attributes in the following table and work through it, listing some of the details of your character. (Complete as many of the following details as you can. Remember, any decisions you make now can always be changed later.) You may also find you need to return to this list from time to time.

PHYSICAL	SOCIOLOGICAL	PSYCHOLOGICAL
Gender	Social class: Lower, Middle, Upper, Working, Monied, Management, Creative	Sexuality: Orientation, Engagement, Moral values
Age	Occupation (work or school): Type of work, Hours of work, Income, Conditions of work, Attitude towards work, Suitability for work…	Personal ambition
Ethnicity	Education: Level, Kinds of schools, Marks, Relationships with teachers/other students	Frustrations and chief disappointments
Height and weight	Home life: Family structure, Parentage, Character's Marital status	Temperament: Angry, Easygoing, Joyful, Pessimist, Optimist
Colours: Hair, Eyes, Skin, Clothing	Religion	Attitude towards life: Resigned, Militant, Defeatist
Posture: Walking style, Bearing	Race, Nationality	Complexes: Obsessions, Inhibitions, Superstitions, Phobias
Appearance: Attractiveness, Over/under weight, Cleanliness, Neatness	Place in community	Personality: Extrovert, Introvert, Ambivert, Intuitive, Judging, Idealist, Artist, Rationalist
Shapes: Head, Face, Ears, Limbs	Political affiliations	Abilities: Languages, Talents, Skills
Health	Amusement and leisure	Qualities: Imagination, Judgement, Taste, Poise
Defects: Deformities … Abnormalities … Birthmarks … Diseases (history as well as any current) …		IQ level
Language and speaking style …		Happiness

Character Attributes

List some of details that help identify your character.

Character Name ....

PHYSICAL	SOCIOLOGICAL	PSYCHOLOGICAL

Commentary and a Short Biography of Your Protagonist

Sometimes it helps to draw a picture of your character. (There is a blank page you can use on page 184.) However, if you draw your character, be sure to make notes on the drawing about specific details, such as colours (eyes, hair, skin), clothes (colours, shapes, styles), attitude (how the character stands and speaks) and so on …

From the details you have listed, write a short, structured biography of the character, covering the major stages of his/her life and the significant events that have caused changes. This biography should try to explore relationships with the character's parents, and others they grew up with that helped shape the character. In particular, you should try to map out the biography through the story, from before the story begins to after it finishes. Try to paint an interesting picture of the character. You can write the biography in either first or third-person point of view.

300 –500 words.

Interview your Protagonist

On paper, conduct an interview of your character, from *one* of the following perspectives. Either:

1. *Arrest report.* Imagine you are a detective investigating a crime that may or may not have anything to do with your character directly. Find out about your character's relationships, make judgements about his honesty and infallibility, try to establish the detective's impression of a character type, establish the character's recent history, attitude towards the crime. Your character might be hiding her drug habit while the police are investigating the murder of her next door neighbour. Be thorough.

2. *A job interview.* You are interested in hiring the character for a job. Find out about the character's work history and achievements, her attitudes towards social responsibility as it might apply to your workplace, her qualifications, marital status, ability to work beyond hours … be pretty demanding here. Remember, if you give her the job, you expect her to deliver, but you might also discover something darker and more interesting. Note: Expect your character to lie.

3. *A celebrity interview.* Your character has achieved something that is newsworthy and you are the journalist charged with interviewing her and reporting on the situation. As a journalist, you expect certain things from your interviewees; it may be easy or hard to get what you want. Be on guard for demurral and obfuscation — remember characters lie, cheat, demur, cloud the facts … yours could be doing all of them and more.

2 Your Antagonist

Developing your Antagonist is as important as developing your Protagonist — a story is only as good as the contest between the Protagonist and the Antagonist. Your Antagonist must be more than an equal to your Protganonist. Work through exactly the same process for your Antagonist as you did for your Protagnist.

The Process

Study the list of character attributes in the following table and work through it, listing some of the details of your character. (Complete as many of the following details as you can. Remember, any decisions you make now can always be changed later.) You may also find you need to return to this list from time to time.

PHYSICAL	SOCIOLOGICAL	PSYCHOLOGICAL
Gender	Social class: Lower, Middle, Upper, Working, Monied, Management, Creative	Sexuality: Orientation, Engagement, Moral values
Age	Occupation (work or school): Type of work, Hours of work, Income, Conditions of work, Attitude towards work, Suitability for work…	Personal ambition
Ethnicity	Education: Level, Kinds of schools, Marks, Relationships with teachers/other students	Frustrations and chief disappointments
Height and weight	Home life: Family structure, Parentage, Character's Marital status	Temperament: Angry, Easygoing, Joyful, Pessimist, Optimist
Colours: Hair, Eyes, Skin, Clothing	Religion	Attitude towards life: Resigned, Militant, Defeatist
Posture: Walking style, Bearing	Race, Nationality	Complexes: Obsessions, Inhibitions, Superstitions, Phobias
Appearance: Attractiveness, Over/under weight, Cleanliness, Neatness	Place in community	Personality: Extrovert, Introvert, Ambivert, Intuitive, Judging, Idealist, Artist, Rationalist
Shapes: Head, Face, Ears, Limbs	Political affiliations	Abilities: Languages, Talents, Skills
Health	Amusement and leisure	Qualities: Imagination, Judgement, Taste, Poise
Defects: Deformities … Abnormalities … Birthmarks … Diseases (history as well as any current) …		IQ level
Language and speaking style …		Happiness

Character Attributes

List some of details that help identify your character.

Character Name ....

PHYSICAL	SOCIOLOGICAL	PSYCHOLOGICAL

Commentary and a Short Biography of Your Antagonist

Sometimes it helps to draw a picture of your character. (There is a blank page you can use on page 194.) However, if you draw your character, be sure to make notes on the drawing about specific details, such as colours (eyes, hair, skin), clothes (colours, shapes, styles), attitude (how the character stands and speaks) and so on ...

From the details you have listed, write a short, structured biography of the character, covering the major stages of his/her life and the significant events that have caused changes. This biography should try to explore relationships with the character's parents, and others they grew up with that helped shape the character. In particular, you should try to map out the biography through the story, from before the story begins to after it finishes. Try to paint an interesting picture of the character. You can write the biography in either first or third-person point of view.

300 –500 words.

Interview your Antagonist

On paper, conduct an interview of your character, from *one* of the following perspectives. Either:

1. *Arrest report.* Imagine you are a detective investigating a crime that may or may not have anything to do with your character directly. Find out about your character's relationships, make judgements about his honesty and infallibility, try to establish the detective's impression of a character type, establish the character's recent history, attitude towards the crime. Your character might be hiding her drug habit while the police are investigating the murder of her next door neighbour. Be thorough.

2. *A job interview.* You are interested in hiring the character for a job. Find out about the character's work history and achievements, her attitudes towards social responsibility as it might apply to your workplace, her qualifications, marital status, ability to work beyond hours … be pretty demanding here. Remember, if you give her the job, you expect her to deliver, but you might also discover something darker and more interesting.

3. *A celebrity interview.* Your character has achieved something that is newsworthy and you are the journalist charged with interviewing her and reporting on the situation. As a journalist, you expect certain things from your interviewees; it may be easy or hard to get what you want. Be on guard for demurral and obfuscation — remember characters lie, cheat, demur, cloud the facts … yours could be doing all of them and more.

3 Discuss the differences

Review your biography of the Protagonist against the one of the Antagonist and make a list of the key differences, particularly those that will cause conflict, or make the conflict more intense.

Step 3: Populate Your Story

EXERCISE 3.1 List Others Involved

Draw up a list of the characters most directly related to your main character in your story and briefly describe their relationship with the main character and with each other. Try to identify the circumstances that connect them. Be creative about who is involved and why. Keep in mind all the while what the Protagonist wants; what the Antagonist wants to prevent the Protagonist from getting. One useful way of doing this is to draw a type of 'mind map'. Put your Protagonist in the centre and connect other characters, explaining their roles by what they do, and the relationship they have with the Protagonist. Draw a diagram. Use lots of notations.

List your characters

EXERCISE 3.2 Map Out Your Core Archetypes

From your list of other characters (above), use the following to identify your characters and place them in their relevant archetypal positions and discuss the ways in which they interact with the Protagonist. Use the following exercise to analyse your characters' relationships with your Protagonist and among themselves. Identify those who act within the realms of the core archetypes and discuss the kinds of influences they might have on the main character's progress through the story.

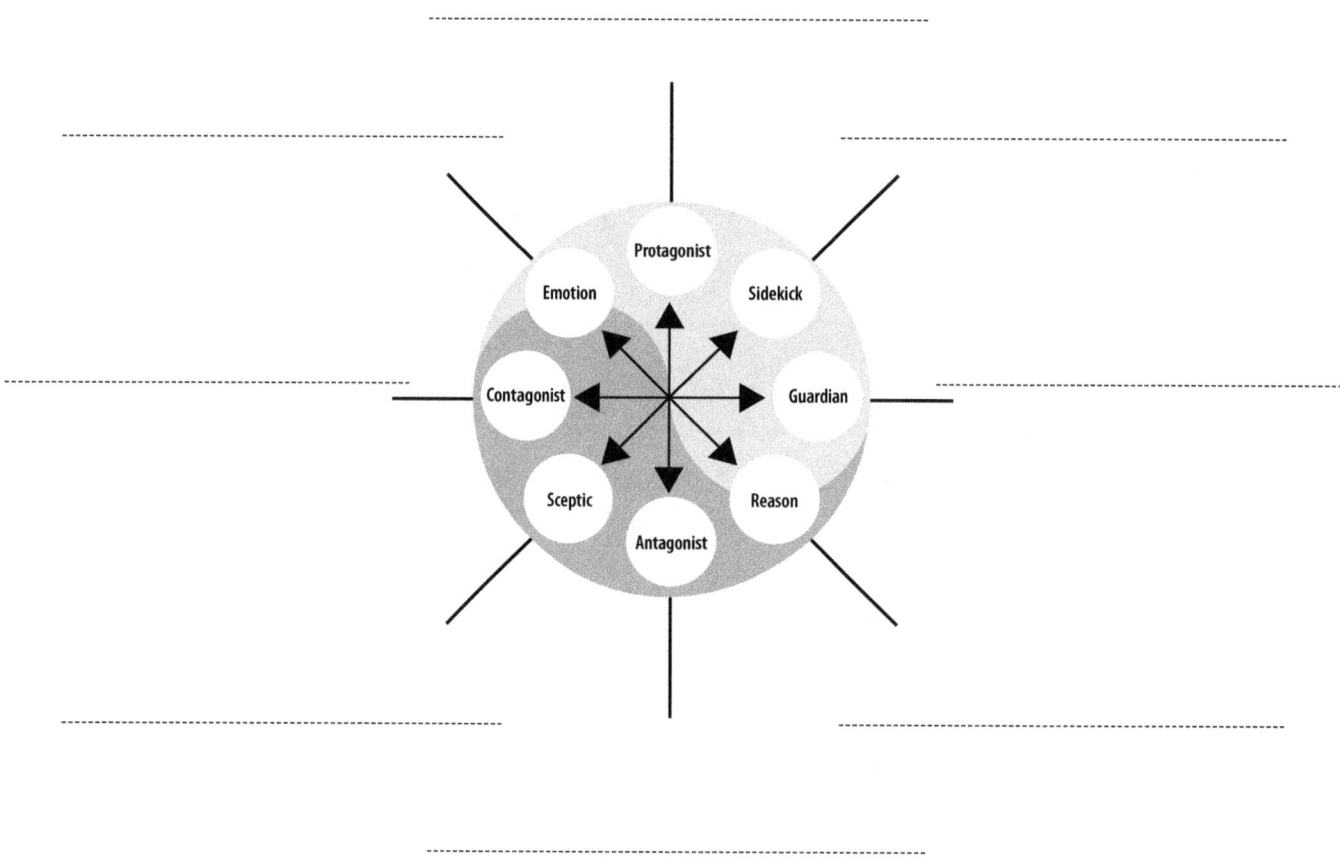

Protagonist:

Name ....

Brief description ....

Goal (What do they want?) ....

Weakness (Hidden need) ....

Special talent ....

Conflicts with other characters ....

Antagonist:

Name ....

Brief description ....

Conflict with Protagonist ....

Source of dark power ....

Weakness ....

Conflicts with other characters ....

Guardian:

Name ....

Brief description ....

Relationship to Protagonist ....

Moral value (challenge to Protagonist) ....

Special powers, knowledge etc. ....

How does this character function to provide help to Protagonist? ....

....

Weakness and conflicts with other characters ....

....

Contagonist:

Name ....

Brief description ....

Relationship to Protagonist or Antagonist Weakness ....

Conflicts with other characters ....

Personal agenda (What they want) and trickery ....

Conflict with Guardian (over what moral value) ....

How does the character function to deflect the Protagonist from the goal? ......

....

Conflicts with other characters ....

Sidekick:

Name ....

Brief description ....

How they came to have a relationship with Protagonist ....

....

Particular characteristic the Protagonist values

....

Specific annoyance or aspect of conflict with Protagonist ....

....

Conflicts with other characters ....

Sceptic:

Name ....

Brief description ....

How they will test belief in the Protagonist and their goal ....

Type of conflict with Sidekick ....

Relationship to Antagonist ....

Conflicts with other characters ....

Reason:

Name ....

Brief description ....

How they will challenge the logic of the Protagonist's actions ....

....

Particular strength the Protagonist needs from this character

....

Conflicts with other characters ....

Emotion:

Name ....

Brief description ....

How they will influence Protagonist's sentimentality ....

....

Particular weakness the Protagonist has towards this character ....

....

Conflicts with other characters ....

Additional notes about your characters.

Step 4: Create Your Story World

Read sections of Chapter Four for a deeper understanding of the story world.

EXERCISE 4.1 Make a Map

This exercise was adapted from Holly Lisle's Settings Workshop in *Mugging the Muse*.

NOTE: For this exercise, you will need a sheet of A3 sized paper, a pencil or pen or coloured (fine point) markers but no erasers!

If you are doing this as a class group, have the group leader announce the instructions and work along. If you are doing this alone, without someone to announce the instructions, I suggest you read the instructions through to #10 below before you start drawing, just so you know what you are going to do. It's fun to do as a group. This exercise leads you through mapping your story world, but you can use exactly the same process to map regions, towns, locales, even houses. Do not attempt to make this a work of art, in fact, make it chaotic and busy. If you make a mark and didn't intend it to be there, do not rub it out — we have uses for it later.

Take 15-20 minutes to make the initial map.

Okay, let's begin. Using a separate sheet of A3 (large) paper and some marking instrument …

1. Place a dot on the page. Now place another dot in a different location. Put in a third dot.
2. Draw some upside-down V's in a line. These are your mountain range so they should necessarily not be in a straight line, they can have some gaps to allow for passes. Name the range. You can have more than one. You can vary the height, or double up sections.
3. Draw some snaky lines from the mountain range outward in a couple of directions. These are waterways — rivers or creeks, give them names.
4. Draw some broken (- - - - - - -) lines separating at least two of the dots from each other. These are borders between states, councils, countries, tribes, groups … Name the areas on either side of each border.
5. You might care to sketch in a lake or a desert or fields.
6. If you give yourself a shoreline (another long, wavy, wobbly line) stick some islands offshore. Don't forget jetties, docks and reefs where ships come to grief.
7. Use cloud shapes to doodle in a forest, oblique lines for woodlands and clumps for grassland.

8. Name the dots you've already drawn – they're your major cities, make them bigger. You might want to include some roads and railways and other important infrastructure.

9. Draw a few more dots in interesting places, and name them, too — towns, settlements, mines …

10. Find a couple of out-of-the-way places in your drawing and plonk in a couple of squares. These are ruins from previous civilizations. Call them whatever you want.

Did you make mistakes?

11. Find the places where you wanted to erase — perhaps you drew a line someplace where it didn't belong, or you changed your mind later, like putting a mountain in the ocean. That's okay. That strange thing you added was designed by engineers. Really it was. It's an aqueduct, or a canal, or a tunnel or a missile silo … You have a road that goes nowhere? That's cool – somebody made it, and it used to go somewhere, and now all you have to do is figure out who made it, and where it used to go, and why it doesn't go there any more. Things do have to end sometimes, and sometimes that end is nowhere. It might have something scary there.

12. You have a ruin-box in what accidentally became a lake, or an ocean? No problem. Once upon a time that ruin was above ground. Or maybe it wasn't, and once upon a time there was a civilization that lived under the water.

This part of the exercise should take only 15-20 minutes.

Now put the art supplies away and answer the questions on the following eight pages. You can also notate your map, but if you do notate your map, make sure you transfer the notes to prose writing about your setting. You may also come up with other additions to your map as you write, keep working backwards and forwards, building the story world. Work quickly, writing ideas down as they come to you. This is about generating ideas, not about good grammar so do not spend time correcting mistakes or making sure it is neat (although make it neat enough to be read!).

Spend about five minutes on each question.

1. Why have people put in borders? A border always implies that conditions, people, philosophies, governments, or something else is different on each side. What are they protecting? From whom?

2. How are the people on different sides of borders different from each other? Religion, government, race, size, species ... go into detail, taking time working out what these differences are, and put some effort into figuring out why they were important enough to necessitate the creation of that border. Which side is your Protagonist's home side, which is your Antagonists?

3. What goes up and down the rivers? (People, contraband, products, boats, other things …) How does it get there? Who takes it? Are there dams and what are they used for?

4. What lives in the mountains? (Animals, people, big scary things, hermits, all of the above ...) Describe the mountain life, how those living there survive, any tensions between high living folk and those of the lowlands.

5. How does the climate and weather endanger the lives of the people who live in the different parts of your world? Along with weather think about stuff like tornadoes, droughts, hurricanes, snowstorms, avalanches, tsunami, sandstorms and so on — you can include things like areas where you'll have earthquakes and volcanoes. Don't be afraid to be generous in heaping out troubles. You'll find plenty of use for them.

6. What else endangers the people here? Plagues, barbarians, illnesses, invaders, people from the other side of the world, monsters from the oceans or beneath the earth …

7. Do a quick timeline in hundred-year increments, for maybe two thousand years. Write down one really big thing that happened in each of those hundred-year periods. It can be geological, political, religious, magical, whatever. But it needs to be big.

	-2,300 years
	-2,200 years
	-2,100 years
	-2,000 years
	-1,900 years
	-1,800 years
	-1,700 years
	-1,600 years
	-1,500 years
	-1,400 years
	-1,300 years
	-1,200 years
	-1,100 years
	-1,000 years
	-900 years
	-800 years
	-700 years
	-600 years
	-500 years
	-400 years
	-300 years
	-200 years
	-100 years
	Now

8. Write whatever else you can think of right now. Keep moving back and forth, from your map to your notes. Add stuff to the map as it occurs to you. Add stuff to the notes until something inside your brain goes "ding" and lets you know that you have a story world that you're genuinely excited about.

When you've finished, stick your map drawing into your notebook.

EXERCISE 4.2 Investigate Details

This exercise is to help you develop observation skills. *Spend 10-15 minutes on this exercise.*

1. Walk to a location outdoors and note down a list of things you see, smell and hear. Take particular note of the surroundings and note the details of the natural environment (the sky, trees, ground, weather, atmosphere, light, evidence of animals …) the man-made environment (buildings, gardens, domestic animals …) and the technological environment (power lines, solar panels, roads, cars …)
2. Move to another location and do the same.
3. Move indoors and do the same.

Be specific when you list what you see, hear and smell; describe these things in as much detail as you can taking care to avoid the use of adjectives that generalise your descriptions (words such as 'big' and 'small' are of little value). Work quickly, simply jotting down your observations; touch surfaces and describe the feeling — if something is smooth, in what way is it smooth? Consider how tasteful a particular object might appear to you and how it fits within the environment. The important thing here is to use all five senses in your descriptions of what you are observing and be specific (using nouns and verbs) about the details.

Now return to your desk and write a short narrative of one of your characters coming into contact with that environment for the very first time. This is a stranger's response to the setting. Try to use as many of the details you observed as you can, weaving them into the character's experience. *(10 – 15 minutes)*

Now, taking exactly the same details, write a short narrative of another of your characters leaving that environment for the last time — they will never return to it. Again, try to use as many of the details you observed as you can, weaving them into the character's experience. *(10 – 15 minutes)*

EXERCISE 4.3 Your Story's World

Using your experience from the two previous exercises, write a short description of the location where your story takes place. Consider that your story might move from a location of the 'world of the everyday' through some sort of 'portal' to a 'mythological woods' (such as how Harry Potter moves from the muggle world to Hogwarts). Focus on the special world of the story, providing details such as those you discovered in the observation exercise above. Describe what you see, hear and smell; how it feels what taste is present. Remember to be specific.

(300-500 words)

Step 5: the Conflict

Read sections of Chapter Five for a deeper understanding of Conflict. Note: The words 'central' and 'core' are interchangeable in discussions on the conflict at the heart of the story.

EXERCISE 5.1 Discuss the Following

What does your Protagonist want?

Why do they (he or she) not have it at the beginning of the story? (In other words what is preventing them from having the thing they most want right now? Is it an internal attitude, or an external obstacle?)

If your story has a McGuffin, what is it? — the object that everyone wants (e.g. buried treasure), or wants to keep away from (e.g. disease).

What does your Antagonist want?

The answers to the above questions will help you determine what central conflict you are trying to resolve by the events of your story. Write a simple short statement:

The central (core) conflict of my story is

EXERCISE 5.2 Hidden and Contradictory Attributes

Make a list of character attributes of your Protagonist that you will *keep hidden* until the last possible moment: (Note: Don't make this too exhaustive ... 2 or 3 for each will be more than ample.) Remember these are the kinds of things that will only be revealed under great pressure from the oppositions of other characters. Then make a second list of three or four character attributes that may be contradictions (in other words, the character may act one way, but think another).

HIDDEN ATTRIBUTES

Physical	Sociological	Psychological

CONTRADICTION

Physical	Sociological	Psychological

Comment on These

EXERCISE 5.3 Conflict and the Story World

What does the central conflict of the story tell you about where the story takes place and when?

Divide the story world into visual opposites based on how the characters oppose one another — (look at the oppositions of the main character archetypes ... what part of the story world 'belongs' to the Antagonist, what part 'belongs' to the Guardian and so on ... Use your story world map as a guide and find oppositions in the things you see, such as mountains/plains, under/above the sea, cities/villages, hi-tech/lo-tech, upstairs/downstairs ... and so on.)

Examine the three elements of your story world (natural, man-made, technology) in terms of how they impact on the central conflict of the story. What is the nature of the portal between the world of the everyday and the mythological woods? What obstacles are placed in front of it? What prevents immediate return?

....
....
....
....

What obstacles from Physical Space, Social Institutions and Influential Individuals of society impact upon the Protagonist's progress towards his goal?

Physical Spaces

....
....

Social Institutions

....
....

Influential Individuals

....
....

How Does Time Affect the Stages of the Protagonist's Progress?

....
....
....
....

Step 6: Develop Your Plot and Step Sheet

Read sections of Chapter Six for a deeper understanding of genre, plot and structure.

EXERCISE 6.1 Genre

What Genre are you writing in?

Explain two key concepts of this particular genre?

What books/stories have you recently read in this genre?

EXERCISE 6.2 The Plot: Devising the Master Plan

Which of the seven basic plots best suits your story?

....

Give a brief explanation of why

....
....
....
....
....

In your story, what happens to your Protagonist … (you should explore the conflicts and rising tension in each of the following stages of your story by following your Protagonist through the story)

In the status quo

....
....
....
....

In the inciting incident

....
....
....
....

In the progressive complications

In the crisis

In the climax

In the resolution

EXERCISE 6.2 Your Step Sheet: Breaking down the Master Plan

Taking each of the stages you have outlined in your plot, map out the scenes of the story. Provide enough detail to know who is in the scene, what happens to them, how the action of the scene rises and falls. There is no fixed number of steps, but you should step out the sequences of your story so that you can follow it through logically from the beginning to the end. Be prepared to work backwards and forwards, and leave plenty of working space to add in extras that you may discover.

Status Quo

Inciting Incident

Complication #1

Complication #2

Complication #3

Crisis

Climax

Resolution

Step 7: Moving Ahead

Pitching your Story

At this stage, you should be ready to begin writing your story. You should know your story well enough to be able to tell it in a three-minute pitch.

A 'pitch' is a verbal telling of the story so that a 'publisher' would be inclined to buy it. You need to stand in front of your group and pitch them your story. This is an important part of the process. Writing and delivering your pitch is not the writing of your story, it does not contain all the juicy action, snappy dialogue and gory battles, but it does tell the audience what they can expect when they read your story. It produces the pleasure they seek because it will lay out the structure in a way that helps them feel the suspense. More importantly it will test your own knowledge of your story.

The pitch will do a number of things:

- It will help you know your story
- It will help you develop confidence in your creative work
- It will highlight any 'plot holes' or weaknesses where the story doesn't hang together
- It will ensure the story ending works
- It will help you start in the right place.

Getting Prepared

1. Review the definition of story in Chapter One. Does your story tell of a change that takes place? Does it involve a worthy human character? (In other words is the character worth spending time with?) Does the story set out a series of episodes that tell of what the character does in order to get what they want? Do the episodes lead naturally from one to the other? (This should be the details of your step sheet.) Does the ending provide an experience of pleasure? (In other words, does the Hero get what they want? Does the Villain get their just desserts?)

2. Do you have a premise? Is there a point about the human condition that is important to you that your story sets out to argue? Can you say how a dramatic character goes through a dramatic struggle to reach a dramatic conclusion … in a simple, single sentence?

3. What is your snapshot statement? This story is about … Have you got a title? (*Most* important!)

4. Who are your principal characters (Protagonist, Antagonist)? Do you know them well? Do you know the other characters involved well? Do you know how they are connected to each other? Are they sufficiently different from each other? Do the differences between them serve the conflicts of the story?

5. Where and when does your story take place? Do you have a clear idea of the world of your story, its key features, how the characters fit into that world, how they move between the World of the Everyday and the Mythological Woods? Does the world of the story serve your premise naturally?

6. Do you have a clear understanding of the central or core conflict of your story? Is there a McGuffin? Have you created and placed sufficient obstacles in the path of the Protagonist towards their goal? Does your cast of characters contain sufficient conflict between them to carry the story through the middle?

7. Do you know what genre you are writing in? Have you considered any specific requirements of that genre decision? (Science fiction must have science; Fantasy must have magic; Horror must have supernatural; Romance must have attraction …) Have you figured out the plot type of your story? Have you mapped out the six steps of the plot Master Plan? Have you developed a step sheet? Do the scenes in your step sheet contain sufficient detail for you to know how you will write each one? Do the scenes lead logically from one to the next? Do you have a satisfactory ending?

Writing Your Pitch

Your pitch should take about three minutes to present, telling of the Hero's journey though the story from start to finish.

Put your premise at the top, followed by your story snapshot statement.

Then your title. (Note: this is the most important word or phrase in your story. It is the first impression anyone gets of what is to come. Spend time on it.)

Then in 200-300 words narrate the events of the Hero from the beginning to the end. Try to cover some small details of who the Hero is, what they set out to do, where and when the story takes place, who or what their opposition is, what obstacles they must overcome to draw closer to their goal, what setbacks they encounter and how they finally accomplish their goal. This is a summary version, it should not contain any dialogue, it is simply a 'telling' of the highlights of the narrative.

Presenting your Pitch

Introduce yourself — give your name as author, the title of your story, the premise and snapshot statement, and then tell the story.

If you can do it without reading all the better, but if you have to read it, do so slowly. Try to seek eye contact with your audience as you go in order to gauge reactions — if none have nodded off, then you can assume you're on the right track. When you reach the end of your pitch, thank your audience and ask if they have any questions or comments.

Listen carefully to the questions and comments, that's where you learn of any potential 'plot holes'.

Onward: Writing Your Story

By this stage you should know your story so well, you should be able to sit and write it fairly quickly. Before you begin your writing, review all of your notes, your pitch exercise, and any questions or feedback that arose from that.

Try to write something on your story every day — 15-20 minutes every day is far better than 2 hours every week. In your writing practice, spend a few minutes reading and correcting what you last wrote before moving on to write new material. This has the benefit of keeping the memory of your writing fresh, and helps you with your editing process later.

First Draft

Try to write the first draft of your story as quickly as possible. However, even though you are writing quickly, you should still try to write accurately — check your spelling, use correct punctuation, paragraph and sentence structures as you go. It is far more tedious and difficult to fix simple grammatical errors later.

In your first draft, follow your step sheet religiously. Write each scene you have described as it unfolds, and try not to get bogged down on parts where you may not know enough — leave notes to yourself to come back to it and move on. Sometimes it helps to write an ending early in the writing process and then go back to fill in earlier sections. This helps maintain focus on where you want the story to go.

Once you have completed the first draft, read it thoroughly without spending time making corrections. After reading, think about how well you think it answers the premise you started with. Look for sections where you may have got sidetracked from the step sheet — do these deviations add to the story or detract from it? If you have left sections of the story empty because you did not know enough, do the research that will help you write those parts.

Redrafting

You should be prepared to write three drafts. Your first is a draft to get your step sheet into its logical story and the scenes developed. You need to spend a little more time on your second draft refining your characters' interactions and the details of your story world, and completing scenes that may have been left unfinished in the first draft.

In the second draft, consider choosing a beginning a few paragraphs in from the one you used in the first — there's a good chance that your character will be better revealed and the action more interesting. Try to improve your language. This doesn't mean get a thesaurus out over every word, it's more about reducing unnecessary repetitions, using better sentence structures, varying sentence structures, finding harder sounding words for action sequences, softer sounding words for gentler sequences. In other words, put a little more concentration into the writing and less into the story itself.

When you've finished your second draft read your work carefully. Careful reading is looking closely at every word, every sentence, every paragraph. Make sure they are correctly spelled, the tenses are correct, and you've chosen the right words for what you want to say. Make corrections to these things.

Read your work out loud. This important step forces you to slow down and read everything on the page. If you find yourself skipping sections, it's a sure sign that something is wrong. Try to find out what it is. Make sure the story works. The ending should have a natural connection with the beginning. There should be rising tension through the middle — if there's not, you can be pretty certain that there is no conflict and nothing is happening.

Final Draft

A third draft (no this is not editing) should only be undertaken after you've spent time on the above steps. By this stage you will know your story well, and be aware of some of its weaknesses.

In your third draft, you should be considering things like the order of events, making sure that flashbacks and story questions are in the right places to propel the story forward, the growth of the main character — do they become whole? — is there poetry in the ending; does the beginning start with a promise?

In this draft you are refining the story structure more than the language (which you concentrated on in the second draft). When you've finished the third draft, you should be ready for a reader.

Some Mathematics

Wait! What's maths got to do with it? Well, a lot of people get confused over how long their story should be. What they do not take into consideration is the amount of time required to read the story, rewrite the story, read the story several more times, edit the story …. It is a long and tedious process, but the better you get at it, the better will be your command of critical and creative practice.

So, if you intend to finish with 2,000 words, you need to consider just how much writing you are going to do, and plan for it.

When your story is completely finished, you will have read it as much as nine times, and written it at least three. And that's before you start editing it. When we read carefully (that is, looking at each word, spending time on the sentence and paragraph), we read about 100 words per minute.

> **Therefore each reading per 2,000 words = 20 minutes (x 9 = 3 hours)**

Writing quickly (first draft) you should be able to produce at least 500 words per hour (that's 8.3 words per minute), which gives time for thinking about the sentence, finding the right word for the moment, punctuating … etc.

> **First draft: 2000 words @ 500 words per hour = 4 hours**

Your second draft will take just as long, but you will be concentrating on different aspects of your writing.

> **Second draft: 2000 words @ 500 words per hour = 4 hours**

Your third draft will quite possible take less time because you will know your story better and be more specific about what you want to address, so let's say we have a 50% 'productivity' improvement.

> **Third draft: 2000 words @ 750 words per hour = 3 hours (rounded)**

So, a quick summing up so far for a 2,000 word story:

> **Reading: 3 hours**
>
> **Writing: 11 hours**
>
> **Total: 14 hours (and this is before editing).**

Self-Editing

To effectively edit your work, you need to read it again at least three more times, in a process of finding strengths and weaknesses in the work and working on building on the strengths and reducing the weaknesses. You should consider that editing takes about another 50% of the time it took to write.

Note: Editing is not correcting grammar and spelling, that's *correcting*. Editing is learning how to read your work and developing a reader's response to it.

So all up, for your 2000 word story, you should be prepared to spend something like 20 hours to complete it. You can see how focussing on a shorter story will often produce a stronger one, because the writer has spent the time to strengthen it.

Part Three
Additional Discussions and Exercises

This section includes additional exercises that can be incorporated into group and class work or carried out individually. They are included to provide greater depth of practice and variety in the story development process.

1 Daily Writing Practices

Free Writing

Free writing is, as the name suggests, an exercise used to free up your writing mind. The idea is to write one word after another without lifting your pen from the page for a number of minutes. In this practice you do not think about what comes next, you let your pen do the work and simply place one word after another.

EXERCISE 1.1 the Raindrop

Imagine you are a raindrop, you have formed from water vapour and dust high in the atmosphere and fall to earth. Track the path of the raindrop, writing without stopping for five minutes. Capture the details of the raindrop's journey as it gathers sufficient gravity to fall, what it sees and hears on its journey, what interrupts its journey before striking the earth (a bird, trees, leaves, a window …) where it journeys to, how it tracks and runs before falling again, where and how it joins with other raindrops and becomes a rivulet, trickle, stream, river … what it observes as it passes on its journey, perhaps being soaked up in something spongy, how it escapes, and continues … when it reaches the ocean, evaporates into the clouds and becomes water vapour once again.

Write non-stop — as the raindrop — for 5 minutes.

EXERCISE 1.2 Who, Where What

This exercise requires you to do some visualisation and then some free writing.

Step One: Who — 2 Minutes

On the top of the page write a heading: 'Who'.

Close your eyes. (Yes! You! Close your eyes.) Imagine you are at the movies. The lights go down, the opening credits come on — the action begins. You see a character walk on to the screen.

Write down a quick description of the character you see (basic features that distinguish them, no more)

Do it again.

And again.

Visualise and describe as many characters walking on to the opening scene as you can in two minutes.

Step Two: Where — 2 Minutes

Draw a line under the list of 'whos' and write a heading: 'Where'.

Now close your eyes again. You are back at the movies. The lights go down, the opening scene comes on — This time you see a setting.

Write down a quick description of the setting before your eyes (basic features that describes where the action is about to take place)

Do it again.

And again.

Visualise and describe as many settings as you can in <u>two minutes</u>.

Step Three: What — 2 Minutes

Draw a line under the list of 'wheres' and write a heading: 'What'.

Disregarding the 'whos' and 'wheres' above, quickly write down as many one-line 'dramatic situations' as you can think of in two minutes. A dramatic situation simply describes some action going on. What is happening. Do this ignoring the characters and settings you have described above. They have nothing to do with dramatic situations: e.g., A man is pleading for his life … a girl is choosing which road to travel … two lovers have quarrel …

Write down as many you can think of in <u>two minutes</u>.

Step Four: Free Writing – 5 Minutes

Now choose a situation from your list of 'Whats' take a setting from your list of 'Wheres' and a character from your list of 'Whos' and develop the scene. Write for five minutes. About half way through, add another of your characters from your list of 'Whos'. Try to write a complete scene.

EXERCISE 1.3 Breaking In

A daily 5-10 minute practice.

This exercise is designed to help you get writing if you have trouble finding a way to put words on the page. It is best repeated every day for several days, but it can go on longer. It will develop your confidence in working with words, in expressing your own ideas and in understanding 'writing time'.

Choose a book from an author you really like, someone you have read and enjoyed reading. Choose a starting point (it doesn't have to be the beginning, but once you choose the starting point you must follow from there in subsequent days) and have a bookmark to mark your place.

Now, for ten minutes, copy the author's writing — copy everything word for word, comma for comma, full stop for full stop. Work as quickly as you can while being careful. When you reach the end of ten minutes, go through your copy and correct any spelling or grammar errors you have made. Write any words you Are unfamiliar with in your notebook and look up its meaning in a dictionary. Use Macquarie or Oxford dictionaries. Write the definition of the word down, study its pronunciation so you know how to say it, and write down whether it's a noun, verb, adjective , adverb or other type of speech.

Keep doing this every day for several days (a week is a good time). If you want to keep up the practice, choose another author you really like and do exactly the same thing.

You will find that after several days of doing this, your writing will take on its own form and your own ideas will begin to fall out onto the page when you go to write.

2 Discovering What to Write About

Supporting readings: Chapter One

EXERCISE 2.1 Understanding Story

The following exercise can be carried out as a group discussion or class exercise. It is to start you thinking about stories and their effects and what you might need in order to get started.

1. Think about a story you have recently encountered — you may have read it, watched it or heard it — and then complete the sentence below describing how the story affected you. You can't simply say, it made me feel *good*, or *bad*, or *indifferent*, you must describe how it affected you; that is, describe the *pleasure* you got from the story. If this is a group discussion, flesh it out a little and try to find experiences that might be different to those of others in the group.

    This story made me feel ... because ...

2. Now identify and say something about each of the following:

    Who is the character at the centre of the narrative and what do you know about them?...

    What change took place involving that character; in what way did they grow, what did they learn, how were they different at the end of the story from the beginning?...

    What did the character at the centre of the narrative want?...

    What did the character at the centre of the narrative do to get what they wanted?...

    What prevented the character from getting what they wanted?...

EXERCISE 2.2 What is Important to Me?

Do this exercise fairly quickly. I suggest 5-10 minutes.

1. Write the titles of three stories you have recently encountered (you may have read them, watched them or heard them) Titles only.

2. List two stories (not necessarily from the above list) which you believe are important — that is, they are important to *you* — and write a single sentence explaining why they are important. This is a little more complex, because you have to think about what is important to you, and recall stories that may have affected you in some way.

3. Now, complete the sentence below describing a story that you believe needs to be told. This is a personal statement. It may bet a story that does not necessarily exist yet, or a story that has remained hidden from view. Either way, it is something that you feel needs to be told; something that you, personally believe will make a good story. This will help you identify what might be important to you.

A story I believe needs to be told is …

EXERCISE 2.3 To Find your Premise

Begin thinking about the character involved in the story and the change in the character's *human condition* that you want to see take place. A change in a *human condition* is reflected in a change of internal characteristics such as beliefs, social position, levels of bravery etc. If your character grows older through the story, simply growing older does not constitute sufficient change of human condition — you need to consider the *internal character effects* of growing older, such as the getting of wisdom, learning compassion. Do you want your character to grow from a coward to a Hero, from loneliness to love, from a bully to a friend, from arrogance to humility, from a low social station to a high one, from powerlessness to power, from pauper to prince … or any of these in the reverse direction?… There are many different types of changes that can take place in life. Pick one that you can relate to; one you believe marks an interesting characteristic and you can see. Your decision determines what condition your character is in at the end of the story.

- *At the end of my story, my character is …* [state the newly attained human condition]

Now, from this position, work backwards with the question, *Why?*… and the answer, *Because* …

- Why does my character end up?… [the final human condition]
- Because they … [what action immediately before that cause that condition]
- Why did they … [take the action described above]
- Because they … [what action immediately before that cause that condition]
- Why did they … [take the action described above]
- Because they … [what action immediately before that cause that condition]
- Why did they … [take the action described above]
- …

Take this process as far back as you need in order to reach a point that provides a motivation for starting on this journey. Then combine the starting condition (the last one) with the ending condition, using 'leads to'. This is your premise.

3 Discovering Characters

Supported readings: Chapter Two

The following exercises can help you further develop your characters. They can be carried out as group or class exercises.

EXERCISE 3.1 A Naming Exercise

Try the following exercise to help you think creatively about naming your characters.

1. Starting with your own name, break it down into single letters and rearrange the letters into different words and anagrams. Do it with first name and surname. Choose a combination and write a brief statement on each of the following about this character name: What the character does (Deed), Where the character comes from or belongs (Place), What is said about this character and what they do (Word), How this character behaves and the cultural things they bring with them (Behaviour). Determine which of the four dominates the character's identity, and write a quick biography that sums up the central idea of the character. You can do also this with someone else's name.

2. Write down the letters of your own name in a vertical list on the left. In two columns next to each letter, write down something you like and something you don't like. Repeat the exercise with a character name you have just created. Discuss with others the clues as to who the characters might be.

EXERCISE 3.2 Walk with a Character

Do this exercise after you have completed some of the character creation work in Part Two. It helps to have gone through the list of character attributes before you do this, and possibly your character interviews. It helps to do this exercise prior to writing up your character's biography. You should know some basic things about your main character, particularly what it is they want, and what might be blocking their way to getting it.

NOTE: The following two exercises can be done as a group (class) exercise or individually. They require you to be highly imaginative. Do not be afraid to be ridiculous. You must enter your character's world completely, and let yourself be involved with the character. It is important that you do not engage with anyone else in your group while you carry out this exercise.

1. WALK 1.

   Consider what you have written about the character in Part Two (list of attributes, notes, interviews …) Now go for a private walk with that character and ask them questions about what it is they want, how they propose to go about getting it. Convince them that they can tell you, that their secrets are safe with you. During this walk, be mindful of how the character answers your questions; make a mental note of the mannerisms and speech used. Try to determine when the character is lying, obfuscating, demurring … breaching a trust, conniving. Walk in at least two directions (there and back) in this discussion. Try to ask questions that get information, not just yes and no answers.

   NOW WRITE.

   As soon as you've finished, sit immediately and write completely freely (free writing) about the experience of the conversation. You should write quickly trying to remember things your character told you, but more importantly, the way your character spoke. Did your character use interesting words, turns of phrase you were not familiar with, speak in an accent, swear, change subjects whenever you got close to the truth, forget things?…

   Do not engage with anyone else while you are doing this.

2. WALK 2.

   Close your eyes (YES! Close your eyes) and take a walk with your character by your side. Begin this walk by watching carefully the way your character moves as they are by your side. Is the character moving towards conflict or away from it? Note the tread of your character's walk, whether it is sure-footed or tentative; strident or light … As you walk, start to move in sympathy with your character's movement. Taking note of each body movement from the feet upwards, begin to adopt your character's walk, posture, attitude … first tread in the same way, match stride and gait, move your hips the same way, feel the way it affects your loins, position your back so that it matches your character's carry, swing your arms, hold your shoulders, neck, head as your character … adopt your character's inner character, find the centre of presence and project it through body poise — become the character and walk as the character now, with you by her/his side. You should walk with your eyes closed in two directions (there and back). Try to get a real feel of what it's like to be in your character's shoes.

   NOW WRITE.

   As soon as you've finished, sit immediately and write completely freely (free writing) about the experience of the walk. You should write quickly trying to remember things about the way your character walked, noting the gestures they may have used, the type of stride, length of stride, feeling of confidence or lack of confidence, changes of direction, reaction to bumping into others …

   Do not engage with anyone else while you are doing this.

EXERCISE 3.3 Further Character Development

By now you know quite a lot about your main character(s) … at least your Protagonist, and possibly your Antagonist.

You now need to establish the way in which your Protagonist will grow and develop, and change through the course of the story. Change and growth can occur in any dimension and in any direction. A character can grow outwardly physically, inwardly socially, remain steadfast psychologically. Growth should be pole-to-pole — that is, going from a negative to a positive position to a negative to a positive and so on, and it should be gradual, not jumping from nought to ten. Imagine dropping your character into a pond with crocodiles and watching how they get out of it. Growth and change should be organically structured, it should thoroughly test your character, and you should have some idea of what the character's end position will be (at least in terms of the story premise you have established). The following techniques will help develop a deeper understanding of your character and how the conflicts of the story are likely to affect her/him.

Trouble

Describe the core conflict of your story. Who is it between? What is the incident that triggers it? What is the moral position of the Protagonist? What psychological weakness in the character could cause the conflict to go away were the character aware of it? (This is the hidden need.) List all the possible avenues of escape for the character. How do you propose to block these off? (Create a crucible.)

Ambitions

Consider your central character and what ambitions they may have (What exactly is it that they want?). Projecting these ambitions, give some thought to what purpose the character's role in the story lends to the story idea. Is it the active functions of the character that dominate the story, or is it the character's relationship with the story's locations, or is it how the character informs others about their goals, or is it the way the character conducts them-self within the story's environment?

Sketch out a central idea of the character according to how each of the pillars of identity might relate to the others for that character; try to specify the character's driving force, what they stand for, believe in, intend to become, intend to leave behind … regardless of the story's outcome. Map out the core attributes that will keep the dominant feature consistent through the story. Try to identify symbols that can help keep this structure.

EXERCISE 3.4 Use a Timeline

A particularly useful tool is a timeline. (You might start by doing one of your own life before you do one for a character.) This is an excellent class exercise and particularly helpful prior to writing a biography.

1. Start the line at birth and mark off the present, leaving some space for the future. Mark out along the line key physical developments: weight, height, eyes, hair (colours, styles, loss), skin blemishes (freckles, pimples), puberty and how it was first noticed, weight gains/losses, body shapes, fitness, health (sicknesses, diseases, treatments, recoveries, afflictions, injuries, long term effects ...), growth spurts, suggestions for future employment made because of physical attributes. Mark out comparisons with parental (heredity) features, such as 'dad's nose', grandparent's eyes ... Mark out walking, running and posture, describe the walk, how and when it changes, capacity to run (speed, endurance, interest ...); mark out posture and changes, noting causes and effects.

2. Return to the beginning of the line and mark off social aspects including family composition at birth note the dates of new additions, deaths divorces; where the family lived (town, city, suburb, street, house), family's social position, note any changes to home and social class, 'fit' within the community; note the work parents did at birth and then track changes to that; note character's education path, religious connections (induction, orthodoxy, transgressions, changes, departure ...), political connections (parents' politics, family attitudes, voting history ...), hobbies and interests picking up all changes in direction of these and what might have caused the change.

3. Note character's romance, sexual and love life, including relationships, first sexual experience, separations, marriages, divorces, children, child-care, deaths, relocations; note character's employment record, type of work, employer (values), promotions, sackings, retrenchments and attitudes towards work. Mark out transportation methods, critical events in transport, and changes (cars, number of cars, first car, holidays, air travel ...) and other technology that affected life (phones, internet, imagined technology ...) Mark out food interests, how and what the character eats, how it changes, what effects changes in diet have had, successes and failures with diet.

4. Return to the beginning of the line and mark off psychological aspects, such as critical discussions on moral issues that have had a lasting effect, law-breaking (both that got away with, and that caught for), punishments (type, administration, reason, cause, effects, lasting reminders ...). Mark out any traumas such as accidents, beatings, losses that have had deep and lasting effects. Identify times where particular achievements and disappointments, frustrations and ambitions arose, note what they were. Consider attitudes to life and others and how they may have changed at particular points, and to what they changed; identify when certain phobias and complexes became apparent and how they manifested themselves. When did the character notice certain talents, what were they, how did they get put to use, how did the character respond to them? note any IQ tests or assessments, times where imagination either created or solved a problem, and cases of good and bad judgements that had ramifications for the future.

5. In particular, note any secrets that affect your character: secrets of their own they are keeping, secrets of others they have been entrusted with, secrets they have divulged.

Project your timeline into the future and take your character through to death, using all the same dimensions that were raised from the past. Once you've got a complete timeline, you can then mark out which part of the timeline your story takes place in. You can see how useful this can be, because you have a complete history to draw on for any given attitude or behaviour.

Then move straight on to the next exercise.

EXERCISE 3.5 Write a Journal Entry

Write a journal in the character's own voice. It's best to write several entries on different days. A journal should be a recount of activities that have affected the character's recent life, and their attitudes towards those events. Let your imagination run with this, you are not writing as you, the author, you are writing as your character and you are not going to pull any punches. You want to know exactly how it feels to be this character, and how to talk like them, act like them, how they perceive the effect she has on others around her.

You can create and keep a diary of your character, you can journal to report on the character's relationship with you the author; you can maintain a running record of some intense activity that lets you get into a deeper relationship with your character, even try a blog.

To write these journals you have to be prepared to inhabit your character's mind and live within for some time. You are hoping to discover a number of traits that may have been touched on in your biographical data, but not given a lot of depth. Here you will explore from the inside the character such things as courage (lack of it, discovery of it), resourcefulness and cleverness, special talent, 'outlaw' status determined by the character's own rules, ability to excel at what they do for a living (or in the case of a student, excel at particular subjects or sport …), what causes and action they are determined to take action in, what 'wound' they sustained in the past, how it occurred and how it affects them now, what ideals they are motivated by …

Suggest 500-1000 words.

4 Story World

EXERCISE 4.1 3D Modelling

In the same way we look at characters in three dimensions, so can we view settings. Except, with settings we can add the fourth dimension of time.

Physical Attributes

- **Geography and terrain** — Is the place mountainous, hilly, or flat? On what scale? Is it rural, urban, or suburban? Is it wilderness or farmland? Forested or desert? What is its relation to water — is it next to an ocean, a lake, a river? Is it landlocked and dry? What does a typical landscape look like? What are the geological features?

- **Weather and climate** — Hot, cold, dry, wet, sultry, windy or calm? Does the place experience storms? If so, what kind? What is the most extreme weather? What is the seasonal pattern? How does the weather differ from the norm (e.g., warm in the winter, cold and foggy in the summer)?

- **Flora and fauna** — What kinds of plants and animals are typical of this place? How do they affect it (e.g. spring wildflowers attract swarms of tourists; snakes in the backyards create a fear of danger)?

- **Built environment** — How have humans impacted the landscape? What are the architectural styles, housing types, other kinds of buildings? Streets, highways, roads—what are the traffic patterns? What other transport systems are in place? What is the nature of the built infrastructure? How is electricity or other energy distributed? How is it used?

Sociological Attributes

- **Types of people** — What kinds of people live in this place? What is the multicultural mix? How do they interact? Do they mingle or keep to their own kind?

- **Social and political climate** — Who runs things? What is the political structure? What are the general political leanings? What are the key local issues? What are the hot buttons — the topics everybody reacts to emotionally? How do people feel about their elected officials? How is the political landscape impacted by corporations?

- **Economic base and major industries** — How do people earn their livings? What is the socioeconomic structure — a blue-collar town, rich estates for the upper-crust polo set?

- **Education** — What level of education do people typically obtain? Do the locals value education or are they disdainful and suspicious of it? Are the local schools good or poor? What kinds of educational institutions are available?
- **Religion** — What religions are represented here? Are there many or does one predominate? How important a role does religion play in people's lives?
- **Local taste** — How do people dress? What is typical? What kinds of cars do people typically drive? What are the specialties of the local cuisine?
- **Holidays and celebrations** — What special occasions does the community celebrate, and how? Are there annual parades or festivals? What kinds of events bring people together?
- **Arts, culture, and entertainment** — What kinds of music, art, movies, TV, etc., are popular? What kinds of sports? How do people like to have fun? What sorts of facilities — theatres, museums, music organisations, playing fields, sports arenas — are available to people?
- **Crime patterns** — What kind of crimes predominate? What is the crime rate? Is this place dangerous or safe? What is the general attitude towards law enforcement? How do people respond to crime?
- **Image in the rest of the world** — What image does the place have in the eyes of outsiders? What is it famous for? Do outsiders come in droves or stay away? What would its tourist board tout as a lure for visitors?

Psychological Attributes

- **Prevailing viewpoints** — How do the people in this place think? What kind of attitudes do they have? Are they trendsetters or laggards? What are the conventional wisdoms? What local legends or folktales are told?
- **Normal behaviour** — What are the cultural mores? What is considered to be normal behaviour? How wide a range of behaviours is normal? What is considered to be deviant behaviour?
- **Attitude towards differences** — How do people respond to deviations from normal behaviour? Are they tolerant or intolerant? Are they welcoming of strangers? What happens to someone who is "different"?
- **Local legends, local heroes** — Whom do the people here admire, and why? Whom do they vilify and why?
- **Emotional impact** — What kind of emotional response does being in this place evoke in its inhabitants? In visitors?
- **Personality** — What key words would sum up the personality of this place?

Time Attributes

- **History**—When was this place founded? How has time affected it? Who was involved? What family dynasties have survived? How have the physical, sociological and psychological attributes changed?

- **Future**—How far into the future are you projecting? What physical, sociological and psychological attributes will not be present then that are present now? What will be present that are not present now?

- **Cycles and sequences**—What changes with the seasons? What changes from day to day? How is time measured? How is it valued?

- **Affect**—How does the passing of time affect the people? The landscape? The atmosphere?

- **Technology**—What technological developments are affected by time?

- **Records**—How are records kept? Who keeps them? How truthful are they?

When you've noted and listed a range of attributes about the location, write a brief article that describes the place — it could be a travel article, a historical reflection, a 'National Geographic' style of article ... Pick out the features that make the place interesting and write as though you are the outsider, seeing the place for the first time. Suggest: 500 - 1000 words.

5 Dialogue

The Dialogue Round Robin

Sit in groups of 12-16 people in a circle. Each person has a blank sheet of (A4) paper.

Read These Instructions Before Starting the Exercise:

1. Put your name at the top.
2. A scenario involving two people is given to the group (see below). The dialogue takes place between the two people. You only write the dialogue, you do not write any narrative ... everything must be done in dialogue.
3. You write the dialogue of the first person to speak.
4. Pass the paper to the person on your left as soon as you have written the dialogue.
5. Receive the paper from the person on your right as soon as they have written their dialogue.
6. You write the dialogue of the second person to speak, responding to the first.
7. Pass the paper to your left; receive the paper from your right.
8. Write the dialogue of the first person in response to the second person ... and so on.
9. When you receive your own page back, conclude the dialogue.
10. Pass the page to the group leader (teacher) who then, at random, reads all dialogues.

Rules:

- Write in script form.
  BOB: *Blah, blah ...*
  HELEN: *Blah, blah ...*
- Try to keep the dialogue out of the gutter
- Make sure all dialogue is in conflict, witty, clever, evasive, lies ...
- Respond only to the dialogue on the page in front of you, not to the version you started
- Find a way to conclude the dialogue that wraps up the scene
- Work quickly to avoid logjams.

A scenario:

Start with this scenario, but feel free to make up your own scenarios involving two people.

A man (boy) is waiting outside a house. A woman (girl) approaches. The dialogue begins.

As a group, give the characters names and decide which of them speaks first. Then write that character's dialogue and pass the paper. Write the other character's dialogue in response to the first character's on the paper you receive. Continue doing this until you get your own paper back. When you do, resolve the dialogue. Pass the completed dialogue to the group leader for reading out.

6 Developing a Scene

The following are two simple little exercises to help you experiment with scene development

EXERCISE 6.1 Dad in the Laundry

Dad has been instructed to get the laundry done. The problem is, he's never done it before. Write a scene in which he tries to do it but encounters obstacles. Show an emotional change in the scene. Involve aspects of the setting that impact on his choices. Consider time, place and change in character as well as light, sounds, smells and tactile elements.

EXERCISE 6.2 The Portrait

Study an interesting portrait for several minutes. Write a scene that describes the image and the details of place and time where that portrait was created. Try to capture an emotional change within the scene, exploring the events leading to the moment of the portrait, or leading away from it. Remember to invoke the elements of a scene in time, place and change in character, as well as staging and properties.

7 Exploring Voice and POV

EXERCISE 7.1 Trying Different Voices

Step 1 Consider the Following Facts of a Story:

- Raymond gets fired from his job early in the day …
- Raymond doesn't go home. Instead he wanders listlessly, unsure of what to do …
- He walks through a vacant block of land and stumbles on a handgun. The gun is loaded …
- He gets home at the usual time. He doesn't tell Jane, his wife, that he's been fired …
- He and Jane watch the television news. There is a story about a hold up at the local service station, and shots fired …
- The service station girl, Praakh, is interviewed about the event …
- A woman customer, Beth, called the police when she heard the shots …
- There were no details given of either the perpetrator or any victim of the shooting …
- The next morning Det Sgt Smith knocks on the door to ask Raymond to accompany him to the station …
- At the police station, Raymond is questioned about the hold up and shooting …

Step 2: Consider How the Different Possible Narrative Characters in This Might Write the Story

Write a scene drawn from the facts above, from each of the following three different character perspectives: (Note: this is three scenes, they can be of the same moment, or different moments, or consecutive.)

- Raymond's
- Jane's and
- Det Sgt Smith's.

Step 3: Same Scenes, Different Voices

Repeat the same scenes using a different character as the Point Of View character but retain both the tense (present or past) and the POV mode (first or third-person). Note how a different narrative character affects your authorial voice in the telling.

Try the same thing but change the POV mode (from first to third; or third to first-person).

References used in this book

Bachelard, Gaston. *The Poetics of Space*. USA: Beacon Press, 1994. Print.

Booker, Christopher. *The Seven Basic Plots*. New York: Continuum, 2004. Print.

Booth, Wayne C. *The Rhetoric of Fiction*. 2 ed. Chicago, USA: Univeristy of Chicago Press, 1983. Print.

Browne, Renni and Dave King. *Self-editing for Fiction Writers*. New York: Harper Collins, 2004. Print.

Burack, Sylvia K (ed). *The Writer's Handbook*. Writers Handbooks. Ed. Burack, Sylvia K (ed). New York: Writer, Inc., 1999. Print.

Cane, William. *Write Like the Masters*. First ed. Cincinnati, Ohio: Writers Digest Books, 2009. Print.

Egri, Lajos. *The Art of Dramatic Writing*. New York: Touchstone, 2004. Print.

Field, Syd. Screenplay: *The Foundations of Screenwriting*. Revised ed. New York: Bantam Dell, 2005. Print.

Frey, James N. *How to Write a Damn Good Mystery*. New York: St. Martin's Press, 2004. Print.

---. *How to Write a Damn Good Novel*. New York: St Martins Press, 1987. Print.

---. *How to Write a Damn Good Novel (Vol 2)*. Neew York: St Martins Prress, 1994. Print.

---. *The Key, How to Write Damn Good Fiction Using the Power of Myth*. New York: St Martins Press, 2000. Print.

Gardner, John *The Art of Fiction: Notes on Craft for Young Writers*. New York: Alfred A. Knopf Inc., 1983. Print.

Huntley, Chris; Philips, Melanie Anne. *Dramatica - a New Theory of Story*. 4 ed. Burbank, California, USA: Screenplay Systems Incorporated, 2001. Print.

Kempton, Gloria. *Dialogue - Write Great Fiction*. Cincinnati, Ohio: Writer's Digest Books, 2004. Print.

Koontz, Dean. *Writing popular fiction*. Cincinnatti, Ohio: Writer's Digest Books, 1972. Print.

Kress, Nancy. *Characters, Emotion and Viewpoint*. Ohio: Writers Digest Books, 2005. Print.

Lisle, Holly. *Mugging the Muse: Writing Fiction for Love and Money*. 2000.

Lodge, David. *The Art of Fiction; Illustrated from Classic and Modern Texts*. New York: Viking, 1992. Print.

Lucke, Margaret. *Schaum's Quick Guide to Writing Great Short Stories*. USA: McGraw-Hill, 1999. Print.

Maas, Donald. *The Fire in Fiction*. Cincinnati, Ohio: Writer's Digest Books, 2009. Print.

Macauley, Robie, and George Lanning. *Technique in Fiction*. 2nd ed. New York: St Martin's Press, 1987. Print.

Mayer, Bob. *Fiction Writers Toolkit*. 2001.

McCormack, Thomas. *The Fiction Editor, the Novel, and the Novelist*. New York: St Martin's Press, 1988. Print.

McKee, Robert. *Story*. New York, USA: Harper Collins, 1997. Print.

Melrose, Andrew. *Monsters under the Bed: Critically Investigating Early Years Writing*. 2012.

---. *Write for Children*. London: Routledge Falmer, 2002. Print.

Morley, David, and Philip Neilsen. *The Cambridge Companion to Creative Writing*. Cambridge ; New York: Cambridge University Press, 2012. Print.

Rozelle, Ron. *Description & Setting - Write Great Fiction*. Cincinnati, Ohio: Writer's Digest Books, 2005. Print.

Seger, Linda. *Creating Unforgettable Characters*. New York: Henry Holt and Company, 1990. Print.

Steele, Alexander (ed). *Gotham Writers Workshop, Writing Fiction*. New York: Bloomsbury, 2003. Print.

Truby, John. *The Anatomy of Story*. New York: Faber & Faber, 2008. Print.

Thomas, Frank, and Ollie Johnston. *Disney Animation: The illusion of life*. New York: Abbeville Press, 1981. Print.

Vogler, Christopher. *The Writer's Journey; Mythic Structure for Writers*. Studio City, USA: Michael Wiese Productions,

Wahlstron, Ralph L. *The Tao of Writing*. USA: Adams Media, 2006. Print.